Politics today

Series editor: Bill Jones

British politics today

Sixth edition

Bill Jones and Dennis Kavanagh

Manchester University Press

First edition 1979, reprinted 1980, 1981
Second edition 1983, reprinted 1984, 1985
Third edition 1987, reprinted 1989, 1990
Fourth edition 1991, reprinted 1991, 1992
Fifth edition 1994, reprinted 1995

This edition published by
Manchester University Press
Oxford Road, Manchester M13 9NR, UK

British Library Cataloguing-in-Publication Data
A catalogue record for this book is available from the British Library

ISBN 0 7190 5407 9 *hardback*
     0 7190 5408 7 *paperback*

This edition first published 1998

05 04 03 02 01 00 99 98   10 9 8 7 6 5 4 3 2 1

Typeset in Photina
by Northern Phototypesetting Co. Ltd, Bolton
Printed in Great Britain
by Clays Ltd, St Ives Plc

Contents

Boxes, figures and tables

Boxes

Figures

Tables

Introduction

Cynically witty judgements about politicians abound. 'Politics ruin the character' (Bismarck); 'Men who have greatness within them don't go in for politics' (Camus); 'Politics are ... nothing more than a means of rising in the world' (Dr Johnson). And there is no shortage of politicians to cite as evidence of venality, avarice and lechery. Yet these imperfections merely mirror those present within the general population; if we were all saints we would have no need for the profession of politics. It is because we are imperfect, and need regulation and protection from each other that we need politicians. It follows that we have to accept that those tasked with creating civilisation out of chaos might not be perfect; as Alexander Herzen said: 'We are not the doctors, we are the disease.'

Having said this, those asked to lead our societies have not all been thieves and liars. The British political system in particular has been much praised and imitated throughout the world as democratic and fair; it has provided for a relatively peaceful and successful political culture.

Whatever its shortcomings, government is still genuinely answerable, once every five years, to the popular will. This contrasts markedly with systems where political leaders capitalise on their power and seek to perpetuate it at the expense of general civic freedoms. The best guarantee against this has always been an educated and alert citizenry. The Politics Association, established in 1969, champions the notion of political literacy, especially among young people. It organises conferences and seminars to assist the political education process, often focusing on pupils preparing for public examinations in government and politics. It is this which explains the provenance of this short book. In the mid-1970s it became apparent to the organiser of conferences (BJ) and to one of their principal speakers (DK) that there was a need for concise, accessible and stimulating analyses of British politics. The first attempt to provide such a publication was a desk-top publishing effort, in extended note form, by the northwest branch of the Politics Association. We printed just under a thousand and they sold out before production was even completed. The aim then, as now, was not to produce a heavyweight textbook but a complement and a lead-in to more serious reading. Manchester University Press then became interested and brought out the first slim volume in 1979. Since then it has run through five editions and over 80,000 copies, helping to educate a generation of politics students. We have retained throughout the note-form style, with the emphasis on analysis rather than description and facts. This is no mere examination 'crammer'.

This sixth edition is as up-to-date as possible given the deadlines of authors and publishers, and takes account of events up to the spring of 1998. All chapters have been completely revised and updated, with a new one added on opinion polling, and 'boxes' added to chapters to focus on topics only touched upon in the main text.

We hope that teachers and students alike will continue to find the book stimulating, easy to read and useful for examination preparation.

BJ, DK
Manchester

1

Britain since 1945

A knowledge and an understanding of a country's history are essential for a student who wishes to understand its politics. Many of a State's political institutions, values and patterns of behaviour are traditional, handed down from the past (e.g. universal suffrage, the Cabinet system, the constitutional monarchy). Even where radical changes are introduced, the past is important because it helps us understand why such changes came about.

This chapter briefly reviews some of the more important themes in British politics since 1945. Of course, many of the more significant developments and influences occurred long before this date. However, 1945 is a reasonable starting point because:

(a) It saw the election of the first majority Labour government, which therefore had the opportunity to carry through its legislative programme. For the next decade or so Britain was regarded as the best example of social democratic planning.
(b) It saw the creation of what is often called the post-war political consensus (see below).
(c) Britain's international prestige was high: it was one of the victorious powers; indeed, the only independent country to be on the winning side from the outset of the Second World War in 1939.
(d) The party system was at its simplest; two-party domination by Labour and Conservative.
(e) Immigration from the Caribbean began, especially into inner-city areas – to be followed later by immigrants from the 'New Commonwealth', e.g. Pakistan and India.

The main developments since 1945

1. **International decline.** There has been a marked loss of international pres-

tige since 1945 when Britain was one of the 'big three' victorious powers, along with the USA and the USSR. But, of course, Britain was much the weakest of the three in terms of military and economic strength. With the onset of the Cold War in the late 1940s and the growth of East–West tensions between the American, and USSR-dominated blocs, Britain was clearly part of the Western Alliance and a junior partner of the United States. The loss of prestige has been hastened by relative economic decline. To a large extent the loss is really a readjustment. Britain, as a medium-sized State, could not hope to compete with the superpowers. The loss of influence was clearly illustrated in 1956, when the occupation of the Suez Canal had to be abandoned in the face of American disapproval. Since then Britain has retreated further from international responsibilities (see Box 1.1 and Chapter 17).

2. The Commonwealth. The post-war process of abandoning the British Empire began with the Labour government's granting of full independence to Burma, India and Pakistan in 1947. The main opponents of this process were right-wing Conservatives. But the retreat from empire was continued by Conservative governments in the 1950s and 1960s. Today, more than thirty ex-colonies are members of the Commonwealth, an association of independent States which look to the Queen as their head. The more affluent Western members are the predominantly white States of Britain, Australia, New Zealand and Canada. But the Commonwealth is dominated in terms of membership and concerns by countries from the Third World (Africa and Asia), which are more interested in the problems of poverty, aid to the underdeveloped countries and trade. The Commonwealth's economic importance to Britain has declined, there are few issues on which it can speak with one voice and its diplomatic influence has declined.

3. Europe. After 1945, moves to the greater economic and political integration of Western European States were encouraged by the wish to promote peace and Franco-German co-operation; the belief that economies of scale would lead to an economically more powerful Western Europe; and the expectation that a unified Western Europe would have greater international influence than separate medium-sized States.

Britain, though strenuously courted by other States, determinedly stood aside from the early stages of integration. It refused to join in:

1951   the European Coal and Steel Community (France, Italy, West Germany, the Netherlands, Belgium and Luxemburg.
1957   Euratom (for atomic energy), and the European Economic Community (EC) of the above six States established by the Treaty of Rome.

Britain was already a member of other groups, such as NATO for defence and the Organisation for Economic Co-operation and Development (OECD) for economic co-operation. Why did Britain stand aside from the EC?

Box 1.1 Britain in decline

Measured against the much faster growth being made elsewhere, the country seemed to be suffering from what the Germans unkindly called the 'English Disease' – a combination of militant trade unionism, poor management, 'stop–go' policies by government, and negative cultural attitudes towards hard work and entrepreneurship ...

The economic statistics offer a measure of 'the acceleration of the industrial decline of Great Britain'. Its share of world manufacturing production slipped from 8.6 per cent in 1953 to 4 per cent in 1980. Its share of world trade also fell away swiftly from 19.8 per cent (1957) to 8.7 per cent (1976). Its Gross National Product, third largest in the world in 1945, was overtaken by West Germany's, then by Japan's, then by France's ... By the early 1980s the decline seemed to be levelling off, leaving Britain still with the world's sixth largest economy and with very substantial armed forces. By comparison with Lloyd George's time, or even with Clement Attlee's in 1945, however, it was now just another ordinary, moderately large power, not a Great Power.

Source: P. Kennedy, *The Rise and Fall of the Great Powers*, HarperCollins, 1989, pp. 548–9.

(a) *A sense of superiority and national pride*, resulting from defiance of Hitler in 1940 and victory in war. This contrasted with the different experiences of the other six member countries, which were either defeated or occupied in the war.
(b) *Britain's international status* and links with the USA, the Commonwealth and Europe: the so-called 'three circles'. Why choose to be merely a Western European influence?
(c) *A sense of difference*. Britain has had a more secure experience of nationhood and stable democracy. Another difference was that most of the original Six had frequently experimented with coalitions and with proportional representation, and had written constitutions and multi-party systems. In France and Italy, the largest left-wing parties were communist and the centre-right parties were Christian Democrat in outlook. One may also add the sense of difference stemming from Britain's insular separation from its neighbours.

But British political leaders in the late 1950s and 1960s became aware of the faster economic growth of the EC States, as well as of the weakening of the Commonwealth ties and the 'special relationship' with the USA. As part of the search for a new role:

1961 Macmillan opened negotiations for British entry – which failed.
1967 Wilson repeated the bid – which also failed.
1971 British entry was achieved, and the terms were approved by Parliament. But Labour opposed until the:

1975 Referendum – which approved membership by a two-to-one 'yes' vote.

The impact of the EC on Britain has been seen in three ways:

(a) *Political and constitutional matters*. It has involved the introduction of the device of the referendum, the relaxation of collective Cabinet responsibility (in the 1975 referendum and in 1977 on the form of electoral system for the direct elections), and the introduction of a large element of a written constitution – with a consequently greater role for the courts and a limit to parliamentary sovereignty.
(b) The debate, and Britain's decision to enter, reflect an acknowledgement of Britain's reduced standing in the world, and the failure of 'special relationships' with the USA or the Commonwealth to provide sufficiently useful roles on their own. (See also Chapter 19 on Britain and Europe.)
(c) It has proved the most persistent internally divisive issue in party politics, for Labour in the 1970s, for the Conservatives in the 1990s, as the EC has developed into a more integrated European Union (EU).

4. Economic decline. Britain's economic prowess in the nineteenth century stemmed from being the world's first industrial nation. But since the end of the century, Britain's economic strength has declined in relation to many other countries as these have had their own versions of Britain's Industrial Revolution. For decades there have been complaints about British slowness to innovate, reluctance to invest, and unwillingness to abandon traditional industries and work practices. As recently as 1960, Britain was the most prosperous country in Europe. But for much of the period since, it has had higher rates of inflation than the average of OECD States, unemployment has risen faster and output per head in manufactures has grown more slowly than in any of the twenty-four OECD States. By virtually every indicator of economic performance, post-war Britain has performed badly in relation to its industrial competitors. The growing sense, and evidence, that Britain was falling behind in the 1960s encouraged politicians of all parties to compete in promising to make the economy grow faster. Invariably their hopes were disappointed and to an extent both big parties were discredited in government.

After high inflation in the 1970s the economy plummeted into recession in the early 1980s but recovered strongly under conditions of low inflation and high productivity. Many of these gains were wasted at the end of the decade, when low interest rates encouraged excessive borrowing and an inflationary spending spree by consumers. High interest rates brought inflation back under control but only at the cost of a deep recession lasting well into the early 1990s (see also Chapter 17). Since 1993 the economy has steadily recovered.

5. Social change. Yet for all the social dissatisfaction Britain is a more affluent country than in the 1950s and 1960s, and living standards have
improved. The spread of television, cars and home ownership is quite impressive. Home ownership spread from 29 to 65 per cent of the population
between 1950 and 1987. The biggest change since the war has been the
return of mass unemployment. The mid-1980s figure of 3.5 million reduced
to 1.6 million in 1989 but climbed again to over 3.0 million in 1993 and
then to below 2 million in 1997 (see Chapter 2).

6. The changing political agenda: the decline of consensus. The closing stages
of the wartime coalition gave birth to the *post-war political consensus*. This
term refers to the main features of public policy which prevailed until the
mid-1970s, regardless of whether Labour or Conservative were in office. It
was during the wartime coalition that the Keynesian White Paper on unemployment was produced, the Butler Education Act was passed and Beveridge's proposals for the reform of social security were made. The 1945
Labour government took three main measures:

(a) Taking the major industries of coal, gas, electricity, railways, steel and
    road transport into public ownership. This transformed the balance
    between the public and private sectors, established a mixed economy and
    gave the government more control over the economy.
(b) In 1947 it established a National Health Service, under which treatment
    was free to all citizens.
(c) In line with the Beveridge recommendations, it produced many other
    measures to consolidate the Welfare State.

The Conservative Party won the next three elections in the 1950s but
accepted much of the 1945 government's legacy. The first serious attempt to
undo some of its work, notably in reducing State intervention in the economy, was made by the Heath Conservative government of 1970. But by
1972 such policies had been reversed.

The post-war consensus involved a change in the relationship between citizens and the State. During and after the war the view gained ground that
economic and social conditions should be improved and that the State could,
and indeed had a duty to, do something about them. The policy of managing economic demand so as to sustain full employment involved a greater
role for the government. The heavy expenditure on the National Health Service, welfare services and education meant much higher levels of taxation.
Government became more active in the social and economic field than it had
been before the war.

This consensus between the two main parties gradually broke down in the
mid-1970s. Governments, both Labour and Conservative, engaged in bitter
conflict with trade unions when the former tried to control rises in wages
which outpaced growth in productivity. Slow economic growth gradually

sapped the support for the old policies and encouraged people to look for new ones.

The following section briefly chronicles the decline of the consensus after the election defeat of Labour in 1951 (see also Figure 4.1).

The decline of consensus since 1951

1. Conservatives in government, 1951–64: consensus reinforced. The governments of Churchill, Eden and Macmillan did little to undo their predecessors' achievements but chose to preside over them. The Keynesian policies of the Chancellor, R. A. Butler, were so similar to those of his Labour predecessor, Hugh Gaitskell, that the term 'Butskellism' was jocularly coined to describe them. Macmillan gently nudged his party down the 'middle way', strengthening economic planning with the creation of the National Economic Development Council. Labour, during this period, divided into a left wing, which called for more nationalisation, and a right-wing 'revisionist' leadership that wished to leave the mixed economy as it stood (see Chapter 4).

2. Labour in government, 1964–70: consensus sustained. During the 1950s Harold Wilson had been associated with the left, but in government he proved a cautious revisionist, strengthening the emphasis on economic planning and developing the social services. However, Britain's relative economic decline became a major political issue in the late 1960s; in reacting to it, parties tended to move away from consensus towards the fundamentals of their faith.

3. Conservatives in government, 1970–74: consensus fractured. Heath began with free-market economic measures to reduce government intervention in the economy, but when they raised problems he embarked on a celebrated series of U-turns which swung policy back to full-blooded Keynesianism in an attempt to stimulate economic growth by government borrowing and spending. Labour in opposition shifted sharply to the left under the impact of radicalised trade unions, and in 1973 produced a programme calling for withdrawal from the EC and nationalisation of the twenty-five largest companies.

4. Labour in government, 1974–79: increasing polarity. Back in power, Labour's leaders sidestepped the 1973 programme and pinned their hopes of beating runaway inflation upon the 'social contract', a deal with the unions whereby they agreed to limit pay demands. But this only alienated an embittered left wing, which elaborated an alternative strategy and used it to attack their colleagues in government. Fissures also opened up in the Conservative Party. Following Heath's second election defeat in 1974, he was replaced in

February 1975 by Margaret Thatcher, whose associates repudiated consensus Keynesianism and developed an approach based upon tight monetary control, an anti-inflation policy which eschewed prices-and-incomes measures but entailed (initially at least) unemployment and cuts in public spending (see Chapter 17). The Labour Chancellor's partial acceptance of strict monetary control after 1976 further infuriated the left. In the 1978–79 'winter of discontent', the 'social contract' finally collapsed amid a welter of high wage demands, strikes and industrial unrest. Margaret Thatcher's confident assertions caught the mood of a depressed and disillusioned electorate, and she was returned to power in the May 1979 election.

5. The Conservatives in government after 1979. The consensus on the mixed economy and the Welfare State virtually disintegrated and was followed by a polarisation of the centres of control in both parties and by much intra-party dissension. Margaret Thatcher's uncompromising right-wing policies caused bankruptcies, economic contraction, greatly increased unemployment and, initially, continuing inflation. The relevance of Labour's left-wing solutions consequently seemed to increase, and within the party the left made political advances, winning sweeping policy victories at the 1980 and 1981 Conferences and changing Labour's constitution to make MPs more accountable to left-wing party activists. The beleaguered right wing kept quiet or joined the breakaway Social Democratic Party (SDP) in March 1981 in an attempt to rebuild the centre ground in association with the Liberals. Initially this venture met with great success; it seemed that, among the public at least, the post-war consensus still had much support. However, Margaret Thatcher's coolness of nerve during the 1982 Falklands campaign and an economy at last emerging from recession paid the dividend of a crushing election victory in June 1983. But it was the (SDP–Liberal) Alliance, splitting the non-Conservative vote, which delivered Margaret Thatcher her huge majority. Her second ministry was characterised by bitter fights, such as that over trade union representation at General Communications Headquarters, and the 1984 miners' strike, as well as by well-publicised internal disagreements, e.g. over the Westland helicopter company in 1986. But economic growth leapt forward. Chancellor Nigel Lawson eased controls in public expenditure, slashed taxes and prepared the vote-winning package which helped secure the 1987 Conservative election victory.

Margaret Thatcher's third administration, however, was dogged by more resignations, internal disagreements – especially over Europe and the disastrous poll tax – and an economy which slipped back into deep recession. During this period Labour sustained its shift into the centre ground on such issues as the free enterprise economy, public spending, unilateral nuclear disarmament and Europe. It became clear that by 1992 a new consensus, further to the right than its post-war predecessor, had emerged. But when it came to election day on 9 April 1992 the voters returned John Major, confirming Henry Truman's adage that when voters are faced with a choice between Conservatives and a party trying to appear Conservative, 'they will always choose the real thing'.

John Major's government started out with a majority of twenty-one, which proved insufficient because of by-election losses, defections and internal dissent, particularly over Europe. The government was placed on the defensive at an early stage by its forced exit from the Exchange Rate Mechanism on 16 September 1992. Entry to the ERM and pegging the value of sterling to the German mark at £2.95 was seen as the key to taming inflation. But the economy was not strong enough to sustain the rate and when Britain was forced out, the government's economic strategy was in ruins. Yet the economy recovered in spite of all forecasts to the contrary, although the government gained little credit. Europe proved a constant source of difficulty, because such problems as fishing rights, action to tackle BSE, or 'mad cow' disease, and proposals for a single European currency and more integration divided the party. John Major's attempts to balance the pro- and anti-factions in his party satisfied neither. It also attracted the ridicule of the traditionally Conservative-supporting press which became increasingly Eurosceptical.

There was no 'Majorism' to compare with Thatcherism. But apart from repealing the poll tax he carried on with his predecessor's policies. He concentrated on curbing inflation, improving the delivery of public services and reforming the civil service.

6. Blair's Labour government: 1997. In the 1997 general election the Conservative Party was faced by a formidable and much reformed Labour Party. If in 1992 many voters felt that it was time for a change from the long period of Conservative rule, some could still not trust the Labour Party, not least to protect their living standards. Tony Blair's New Labour offered reassurance to such voters. In retrospect, it can be seen that the 1992 defeat of Labour was crucial in making the Labour Party accept more of the Thatcher reforms.

New Labour now accepted existing rates of income tax and levels of public spending – both of which as a share of national income were below most European States' levels – set tough targets for inflation and promised to reduce public borrowing. It also accepted most of the trade union reforms, the entire privatisation measures and a more selective approach to welfare – taking steps to get people back to work and making some services more dependent on private provision (e.g. ending free tuition in higher education). Labour not only abandoned public ownership but also appeared to abandon redistribution of income via the tax system. There was a good deal of convergence on many policies.

The new Labour government formed in May 1997 lost no time in delivering its radical agenda. In the first six months it held successful devolution referendums in Scotland and Wales. These are presented as the first steps in Blair's plans to modernise the constitution (see Chapter 6). The government also signed up to British membership of the EU's social chapter and promised to incorporate into British law the European Convention on Human Rights. The first budget raised £5 billion tax on the profits of the privatised utilities to provide funds for schools and health.

Further reading

D. Childs, *Britain since 1945: A Political History*, Ernest Benn, 1994.
P. Hennessy, *Never Again*, Jonathan Cape, 1992.
P. Hennessy and A. Seldon (eds), *Ruling Performance*, Basil Blackwell, 1987.
D. Kavanagh and P. Morris, *Consensus Politics from Attlee to Thatcher*, 2nd edn, Basil Blackwell, 1994.
K. O. Morgan, *Labour in Power 1945–51*, Oxford University Press, 1985.

Questions

1 Identify the factors which have made for stability and instability in British politics since 1945.
2 Assess the achievements of two post-war Prime Ministers.
3 Would it be fair to say that a new post-Thatcher consensus had emerged by the early 1990s?

2

The social and economic
context of politics

Political processes and decision-making are substantially about conflicts of interest between different groups in society, so it helps to know something about the class structure and the distribution of resources within society. This chapter provides a brief introduction to this important contextual aspect of politics in Britain.

Class and the economy

The way in which social groups are formed is closely connected with the way in which goods and services are produced. The ancient Greeks and the early settlers in the Americas used slave labour: a large group of people became the legal property of a smaller, richer class. Until the middle of the eighteenth century the economy of Britain was basically agricultural. The wealth of the nobility and gentry was drawn from land tilled by peasants and serfs whose descendants had lived for centuries in feudal village communities. Underemployment in the countryside, combined with advances in industrial production, provided the conditions for the Industrial Revolution. Entrepreneurial factory owners – financed often by the nobility and the professional and merchant classes – employed large numbers of people living close to their place of work in what soon became huge new urban centres.

Writing in the mid-nineteenth century, Karl Marx saw two main antagonistic social classes: the small 'capitalist' property-owning class (to some extent usurping and to some extent collaborating with the traditional aristocracy) and the vast subordinate class of skilled and unskilled workers. Marx perceived that these new social groupings, based upon their economic relationship to the means of production, had created class allegiances which displaced in importance previous loyalties such as religion or locality.

At the turn of the century the social structure was more or less pyramidal. The richest 1 per cent of the population owned two-thirds of the wealth.

10

Those comprising the wealthy tip of the pyramid were connected by bonds of education (usually private school and Oxbridge), marriage, kinship and social contact. This degree of cohesion helped them to occupy key roles in government, business and the Empire. The middle classes – the professions, small businessmen and white-collar workers – were less wealthy but usually owned their own homes and were eligible by education for positions of responsibility. The broad base of the pyramid was made up of skilled and unskilled workers – for the most part with no property, little education and dependent on weekly wages.

Those lucky enough to be at the 'top of the heap' had excellent choices or 'life-chances' regarding career, health and leisure activities. They also enjoyed high prestige or social status and were able as a result to exercise political power and influence. Those at the bottom of the pyramid had poor life-chances, no social status and little or no political power. Bilton *et al.* suggest that this situation has not changed much. They argue that society is still basically pyramidal, as Figure 2.1 illustrates. The diagram is useful for focusing our ideas, but any judgements upon its validity will have to await consideration of important changes which have occurred since the early years of the nineteenth century.

Figure 2.1   *The structure of British society*

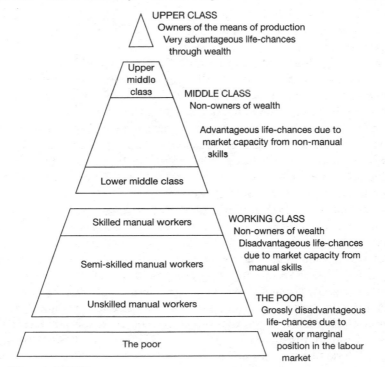

UPPER CLASS
Owners of the means of production
Very advantageous life-chances
through wealth

Upper middle class

MIDDLE CLASS
Non-owners of wealth

Advantageous life-chances due to
market capacity from non-manual
skills

Lower middle class

Skilled manual workers

WORKING CLASS
Non-owners of wealth
Disadvantageous life-chances
due to market capacity from
manual skills

Semi-skilled manual workers

Unskilled manual workers

THE POOR
Grossly disadvantageous
life-chances due to
weak or marginal
position in the labour
market

The poor

Source: Bilton *et al.* 1987.

1. The occupational structure has changed considerably, and this has had implications for the class structure. Traditional labour-intensive industries such as coal mining and shipbuilding have declined, to be replaced by highly automated light manufacturing and service industries such as tourism, leisure and information technology. Service industries employed 68.8 per cent of the workforce in 1988 and manufacturing a mere 23.1 per cent (slightly over 4 million in 1993). Another feature has been the growth of part-time low-paid workers: 34 per cent in 1985, the majority of them women.

There has also been a massive increase in the number of people employed by the State, from a few thousand at the turn of the century to 7.2 million in 1981. As a result of changes initiated by Thatcher administrations, this figure shrank to 6.1 million by 1989, while the private sector workforce increased from 17.1 million to 20.2 million.

The implications for class structure have been immense. In 1914 80 per cent of the workforce were working-class; now less than half can be so categorised. The professional and clerical classes have more than doubled, from under 20 per cent at the turn of the century to over 40 per cent now. The occupational pattern is more pear-shaped than pyramidal, with an expanded middle class and a smaller working class. For the first time in a century and a half the working class is out-numbered by members of other social groups. Various new white-collar groups have emerged, commanding a wide range of skills and being paid accordingly. As these new groupings have emerged from the old social structure, their attitudes are hard to characterise and in any case are in a state of flux.

The working classes now live and work under changing conditions, and their attitudes are changing too. At the turn of the century about 10 per cent of the population owned their home; now the figure is over 65 per cent and includes a large proportion of the skilled and unskilled working classes. Since 1979 over 1 million council houses have been sold to tenants under the Conservative government's Right to Buy scheme. The implications of this new property ownership for working-class political attitudes and behaviour are considerable. Working-class people are now less likely to live in a council house, to be engaged in a manufacturing job, to be a member of a trade union and live close to their workmates.

It is now much more difficult to generalise about classes in the old way, especially in relation to politics. Studies show that the traditionally crucial division between manual and non-manual workers is no longer so useful for explaining different social attitudes. Some political scientists have tried to reformulate social groupings to take account of all these changes. Dunleavy, for example, suggests that it may make more sense to distinguish between 'public-sector' employees, 'private-sector' big business, private-sector small business and groups dependent on State welfare support (see Moran, pp. 28–32). Marketing experts use a tried and tested objective scale running from A to E, as Table 2.1 illustrates.

Table 2.1   *Analysing class*

(a) The market researchers' view of class

Class	% of heads of household (1991)
A Upper middle class (e.g. professional, higher managerial, senior civil servants)	3
B Middle class (e.g. middle managers)	16
C1 Lower middle class (e.g. junior managers, routine white-collar or non-manual workers)	26
C2 Skilled working class (e.g. skilled manual workers)	26
D Semi-skilled and unskilled working class (e.g. manual workers)	17
E Residual (e.g. those dependent on long-term state benefits)	13

Source: *National Readership Survey*, NRS Ltd, July 1992–July 1993.

(b) The Goldthorpe seven-class schema (class classifications from British general election surveys, by respondent)

		1964 %	1992 %
I	Higher salariat	7.0	11.6
II	Lower salariat	12.3	16.3
III	Routine clerical	16.5	24.2
IV	Petty bourgeoisie	6.6	7.1
V	Foremen and technicians	7.6	4.8
VI	Skilled manual	17.8	10.9
VII	Unskilled manual	32.4	25.1

Source: Dr A. Heath, Nuffield College, Oxford. (From Adonis and Pollard, 1997.)

2. Wealth and income differentials have narrowed – but not by much. Income is what is regularly earned from work. In 1913–14 male higher profession-als earned three and a half times average male earnings, while unskilled manual workers earned 67 per cent of the same figure. Over seventy years later, real income had increased, of course, several times over, and the gap between the two groups had narrowed. Higher professionals earned 173 per cent of average earnings while unskilled manual workers earned 71 per cent (Moran, p. 17). During the 1980s the Thatcher government's tax reductions combined with benefit cuts caused a substantial increase in the differences between high and low earners. During the period 1979–95 the richest 10 per cent of earners (excluding self-employed and after housing costs) increased their share of post-tax income by 61 per cent while the poorest 10 per cent actually suffered a 4 per cent cut in real terms (see Box 2.1 and Table 2.2).

Box 2.1 The extent of the poverty problem

- One in three children lives in poverty.
- Divide between highest- and lowest-paid workers greatest since 1886.
- Almost four in ten adults earn less than the Council of Europe's 'decency threshold'.
- Women are still paid 20 per cent less than men.
- Benefits for lone parents fall short of their needs by £23 per week.
- Sixty-five per cent of disabled people live below the poverty line.
- Up to 30,000 young people experience homelessness each year.
- As many as 1.4 million homes are unfit and 2.3 million need renovation.
- More than 250,000 people a year suffer racial harassment.
- Numbers of children excluded from school have increased 300 per cent since 1992.

Source: 'Justice', *Guardian*, 17 November 1997.

Table 2.2   *Real income and total income after housing costs*

Shares of total income (after housing costs)

		1979	1993/94
Bottom	10%	4.1	2.5
	20%	9.8	6.8
	30%	16.0	12.0
Top	30%	47.0	54.0
	20%	35.0	41.0
	10%	20.0	26.0

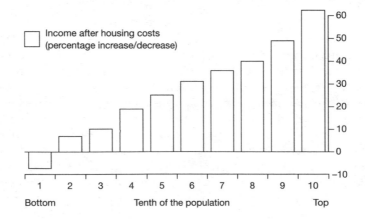

Change in real income, 1979–93/94
(excluding full-time self-employed)

Income after housing costs
(percentage increase/decrease)

Tenth of the population

But even the picture painted by Table 2.2 does not tell the whole inegalitarian story because it does not:

(a) indicate the very high salaries earned by top executives, ranging from a quarter of a milion pounds per year to well over a million;

(b) reveal the considerable additional benefits derived by high earners from expenses, company cars, sick pay and pension schemes, and other fringe benefits;

(c) reflect the advantageous position of management compared with workers regarding conditions of work: use of restricted facilities, time off for visits to the dentist, longer holidays and so forth;

(d) reveal the earning profiles of different occupations. The middle classes tend to double their twenties income by their late forties, but manual workers tend to increase their income from their twenties by some 15 per cent to a peak during their thirties. From this point it declines to a point below their twenties income before a poorly-provided-for retirement is reached;

(e) reveal that taxation has only a limited impact on the distribution of income: high earners can minimise their liability by employing skilled accountants;

(f) show the considerable differential which exists between the earnings of men and women. Female manual workers earn, on average, two-thirds of average male manual worker incomes and women non-manuals earn even less compared with male non-manuals;

(g) reveal that substantial differences exist between the low earners and the very poor, who are found among the old, the unemployed, immigrants and families with young children.

The distribution of wealth

In 1990 the Gross National Product (GNP) per head of population in the UK was $12,810. Compared with Japan's $21,020 Britain might not appear to be so rich but when the figures for Poland ($1,860), Egypt ($1,001) or Nigeria ($290) are considered it is clear that British citizens enjoy a favoured position. A substantial amount of wealth is owned by individuals in the form of bank deposits, savings accounts, property, and stocks and shares.

The pattern of distribution is much more unequal than that of income: the ownership of wealth is still highly concentrated (see Table 2.3). The situation has not changed much over the last two decades. The wealthiest 50 per cent of the population owned 97 per cent of marketable wealth in 1971 and 94 per cent in 1988. When the value of occupational and State pension rights are added, however, the degree of inequality is decreased.

Table 2.3   *Distribution of marketable wealth in Britain,
Inland Revenue estimates*

Marketable wealth – percentage of wealth owned by:	1976	1992
Most wealthy 1%	21	18
Most wealthy 5%	38	37
Most wealthy 10%	50	49
Most wealthy 25%	71	72
Most wealthy 50%	92	92
Marketable wealth less value of dwellings – percentage owned by:		
Most wealthy 1%	29	29
Most wealthy 5%	47	53
Most wealthy 10%	57	65
Most wealthy 25%	73	82
Most wealthy 50%	88	94

Source: Social Trends, 1996, p. 96.

Redistribution within the richest half of the nation is explained partly by the spread of private home ownership and the increase in property values: 22.1 per cent of all wealth in 1971 yet 33.4 per cent in 1987. Stocks and shares represented 21.7 per cent of all wealth in 1971, slumped to 7 per cent in 1981 but climbed to 10.5 per cent in 1987. Privatisation, however, has helped to spread share ownership from 7.5 per cent of the population in 1981 to 20 per cent in 1987.

Social mobility

Studies have revealed a fair degree of movement within the different social groupings in Britain. Lipset and Bendix observed that over a third of those from a blue-collar background moved into white-collar jobs – a higher rate than West Germany, Japan or France but less than Australia and Sweden. Social position, then, is not determined solely by birth: it is, after all, possible for a grocer's daughter to become Prime Minister. Goldthorpe, however, revealed an important feature. He distinguished between seven different social categories (see Table 2.1) and observed that the least socially mobile people in his sample were from class 1 and classes 6 and 7: the upper classes and the working classes. In fact nearly half the class 1 members and over half the class 6 and 7 members originated within their own class.

As for the really top decision-makers, they are more normally recruited from the upper levels of the social hierarchy. Boyd's study of entries in *Who's Who* revealed that in many cases those listed had parents who were also listed, e.g. 28.4 per cent of judges, 27 per cent of ambassadors and 45.4 per cent of bank directors. Heath estimates that children born to members of this elite of elites have a 1-in-5 chance of making the pages of *Who's Who*, children from class 1 parents a 1-in-200 chance, children from all white-collar worker classes a 1-in-500 chance, while those from working-class homes have only a 1-in-1,500 chance of winning some of life's glittering prizes.

Box 2.2   The super class

In their excellent study of class in Britain, Adonis and Pollard perceive what they call an emergent 'super class'. They argue that we have 'a new elite of top professionals and managers, at once meritocratic yet exclusive, very highly paid yet powerfully convinced of the justice of its rewards, and increasingly divorced from the rest of society by wealth, education, values, residence and lifestyle. It is a seminal development in modern Britain, as critical as the rise of organised labour a century ago and rivalled in contemporary significance only by the disintegration of the manual working class' (*Observer*, 19 October 1997). They argue that the well-publicised examples are not exceptions but examples of a new phenomenon: people such as Cedric Brown with his 75 per cent pay rise to nearly half a million pounds for running a monopoly utility. And Nick Leeson, who lost Barings Bank nearly £1 billion in a desperate pursuit of bonuses; most of his highflying colleagues still got their bonuses even after the ruined bank had been sold on for a nominal £1. The authors maintain that the new class was born of the financial services industry in the City which expanded hugely in the mid-1980s. A culture imported from Wall Street colonised the private sector of the country, raising expectations enormously and making astronomic salaries for chief executives and directors the rule. In addition such favoured people received fringe benefits in the form of regular bonuses, sometimes well in excess of their already large nominal salaries, and pensions which would seem like fortunes to ordinary wage earners. These rich pickings have served to transform the career ambitions of able graduates. Whereas in the 1970s the products of Oxbridge tended to look to public service, especially the administrative class of the civil service, they now look to the City and the law. In 1971 over 200 entered teaching; by 1994 there were only 91 recruits. In 1971 a total of 258 entered the worlds of commerce, chartered accountancy and solicitor's training; by 1994 the figure was 830. Moreover, many who opted for the public sector have since left it, seduced by the cricket score salaries of the private sector during the booming 1980s.

Education

Education has become a vital factor in determining social mobility. Clearly, people in well-rewarded, high-status occupations can give their children the best opportunities. Education is the means whereby skills are acquired that can determine occupation. Access to higher education, which provides the long training necessary for many elite jobs, is particularly important. The small percentage of children educated at fee-paying schools (about 7 per cent), notably those attending the prestigious Eton, Harrow, Westminster, Marlborough, Rugby and Charterhouse, have the best chances of entering higher education and going on to fill the top jobs. Over 80 per cent of senior judges in 1975 had been privately educated; over 60 per cent of civil servants above the rank of under-secretary; over 70 per cent of army generals; and over three-quarters of top company directors and Conservative MPs. Margaret Thatcher herself was an ex-grammar school girl, but six members of her first Cabinet were Old Etonians. Eton indeed provided 24 per cent of Conservative MPs in 1951, falling to a still significant 10 per cent in 1992. For Oxbridge the figures for these dates were 52 and 45 per cent, respectively. The lower one is down the social hierarchy, the less chance one has of entering higher education. The replacement of grammar schools by comprehensives has not changed much and has arguably made the situation worse. Anthony Crosland hoped he would be removing a layer of inequality but he merely substituted geography for wealth. Previously, middle-class children dominated grammar school entry but standards were high and three post-war Prime Ministers gave testimony to their efficacy.

Comprehensives, with no selection and no streaming, seemed to open up opportunities but in practice the 'good ones' soon became well known and property values rose in their catchment areas. In working-class areas schools were poor and attracted poor teachers, creating the vicious circle which reinforces class divisions. The leading educational theorist of the 1960s, A. H. Halsey, put it bluntly: 'The essential fact of twentieth century educational history is that egalitarian policies have failed.'

The vast increases in the numbers entering higher education – from 7.2 per cent of the young age group in 1963 to over 30 per cent in the mid-1990s – have greatly increased opportunity but inequality of life-chances remains. As Halsey comments, 'Measured in relative terms, the proportions of those entering higher education from manual working families have scarcely shifted by comparison with those from the professional and managerial classes . . . This is cold comfort for those who seek the "classless society".'

The North–South divide

When Disraeli spoke of the 'two nations' he meant the rich and the poor. Nowadays the term is often used to denote the differences between the North and the South, but the differences are chiefly economic: the growth of new industries in the South has kept income and employment high while decline of traditional manufacturing in the North led to falling incomes and unem-

ployment (Figure 2.2). In the 1980s the contrasts were stark, but in the early
1990s they diminished as recession hit the service industries of the South
East. In October 1997 *The Economist* perceived a reopening of the divide with
a new boom in southern service industries with growth rates of 5 per cent
and a failure to keep pace in the North, where growth barely touched 2 per
cent. Moreover, house prices were also taking off, with annual increases of
over 15 per cent in the South East compared with less than 2 per cent in the
North.

For most of the 1980s this divide was dramatically exposed in general elections, where vast majorities voted for Labour in the North and for Conservatives in the South. However, the revulsion against the latter party in 1997
was such that the Conservative lead over Labour in the South fell to 1.9 per
cent.

Britain, then, has a pattern of economic and social inequality which is
characteristic of Western industrialised countries. Private wealth is highly
concentrated, particularly the ownership of private-sector industry; income
reflects the earner's role in the economy; and while in theory elite occupations are open to all, in practice they tend to go to those higher up the social
scale. The pyramid devised by Bilton *et al.* makes a fundamental point about
the relation of position in the social hierarchy to life-chances, but it must be
borne in mind that:

Figure 2.2   *Regional variations in GDP and unemployment*

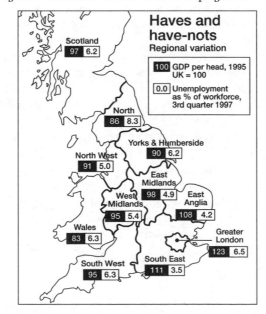

Source: The Economist.

(a) the working classes are no longer the most numerous occupational grouping;
(b) changes in occupational structure are heavily modifying and perhaps fragmenting traditional class-related attitudes;
(c) there is a fair degree of movement up and down the social hierarchy, despite an educational system which heavily favours the upper and middle classes.

The growth of an underclass

In recent years concern has been voiced at the growth of an 'underclass' in Britain comprising the long-term unemployed, single-parent families and pensioners living solely on State benefit.

Thatcher governments regularly adduced the trickle-down argument: that the increasing wealth of society as a whole will also benefit the poor. For a number of years studies seemed to support this contention but in the mid-1980s studies by Oppenheim, Dahrendorf and others suggested the reverse: that the very poor had been getting even poorer as the rich had been immensely more so. Just about the time that this had entered public awareness with the pathetic rows of homeless beggars in the cities, Cabinet minister John Moore declared poverty to be a product of the 'poverty lobby' who would 'find poverty in paradise'. As this mistake helped abort Moore's political career, poverty became worse. Roy Hattersley wrote: 'During 15 Tory years the number of people below the poverty line rose from five to 13.7 million and the number of children similarly deprived increased from 1.4 to 4.2 million' (*Guardian*, 4 August 1997).

Observers have noted that young men who have never worked are unlikely to be socialised into society and tend to adopt deviant lifestyles, often involving a rejection of family values and responsibilities, the use of drugs and a reliance on crime to make up income shortfalls. Small wonder, claim such commentators, that illegitimate births soared during the 1980s from 10 per cent to 25 per cent of the whole and that the crime rate increased from 2.5 million notifiable offences in 1979 to over 5.0 million in 1996. Certain inner-city areas – which exploded into riots in 1981–82 – are in a perpetual state of near-collapse, representing virtual no-go areas for the law-abiding majority and comprising contagious centres of anti-social values and behaviour. Professor Ralph Dahrendorf has called the problems caused by the underclass 'the greatest single challenge to civilised existence in Britain'.

Further reading

A. Adonis and S. Pollard, *A Class Act: The Myth of Britain's Classless Society*, Hamish Hamilton, 1997.

A. Bilton *et al.*, *Introductory Sociology*, Macmillan, 1987. (Diagram reproduced, by permission, from p. 55.)

D. Boyd, *Elites and their Education*, NFER, 1973.

R. Dahrendorf, 'The erosion of citizenship and the consequences for us all', *New Statesman*, 12 June 1987.

R. Dahrendorf *et al.*, *Report on Wealth Creation and Social Cohesion in a Free Society*, The Commission on Wealth and Social Cohesion, 1995.

F. Field, *Losing Out*, Basil Blackwell, 1989.

J. Goldthorpe, *Social Mobility and Class Structure in Modern Britain*, Clarendon Press, 1980.

A. H. Halsey, *Opening Wide the Doors of Higher Education*, National Commission on Education: Briefing No. 6, 1992.

A. Heath, *Social Mobility*, Fontana, 1981.

B. Jones and L. Robins, 'Political and cultural change in postwar Britain', in B. Jones and L. Robins (eds), *Half a Century in British Politics*, Manchester University Press, 1997, pp. 144–62.

S. M. Lipset and R. Bendix, *Social Mobility in Industrial Society*, University of California Press, 1959.

M. Moran, *Politics and Society in Britain: An Introduction*, 2nd edn, Macmillan, 1989.

C. Murray, *The Emerging British Underclass*, IEA Health and Welfare Unit, 1990.

C. Oppenheim and L. Parker, *Poverty: The Facts*, CPAG, 1996.

Social Trends, HMSO, 1997.

Questions

1　To what extent do you consider inequalities in society inevitable and desirable?
2　Do you think the removal of inequalities is best attempted via moderate or radical reform?
3　What problems for the governance of Britain are posed by the development of an 'underclass' of the disaffected poor?

3

Political culture

A stable democracy

This chapter looks at the main features of the political culture and recent changes. Britain's political culture has long interested students of history, society and politics. Because it was the first country to industrialise (for much of the nineteenth century, the foremost industrial power) and has long been regarded as a model stable democracy, students have tried to extract lessons from the British experience. Among the admired features are:

(a) The relative absence of force in resolving political differences (except for Ireland).
(b) The balance between effective government, on the one hand, and respect for the rights of opposition, an independent judiciary and basic civil liberties, on the other.
(c) The continuous and gradual process of change and adaptation which are important in building respect for traditions and support for the system. Compare this with the political systems of, say, the USSR, Italy, West Germany or France. Those countries have suffered ruptures in their modern political histories, e.g. the revolution in Russia in 1917; the collapse of the Fourth Republic in France in 1958; and the establishment of new post-war constitutions in Italy and West Germany (now part of a unified Germany); not to mention the anti-communist revolutions in the USSR and Eastern Europe in 1988–89.

Various explanations of political stability

1. Social and economic conditions, particularly affluence and industrialism. There is a high correlation between liberal democracy and levels of industrial development (i.e. virtually all stable democracies are highly industrialised and wealthy countries). But there are exceptions to this relationship (e.g. Nazi Germany and some Eastern European countries before 1989). So this can be only a partial explanation.

22

2. The special nature of British institutions, e.g. the two-party system (historically inaccurate – see Chapter 5), monarchy (almost certainly more a consequence of consensus and stability, rather than vice versa) and parliamentary institutions.

3. History. In contrast to many newly independent States, which simultaneously have had to confront the tasks of building a State (boundaries, institutions) and forming a sense of nation and identity, etc., Britain was able to meet these challenges sequentially. In the sixteenth century relations between Church and State were settled, following the break with Rome; in the seventeenth century the constitutional issue was decided in favour of a limited monarchy, and so on. Similarly, the suffrage was expanded gradually between 1832 and 1928 (1969 if we count votes at the age of eighteen). Except for the question of Ulster, issues involving religion and nationality were solved many years ago. This is not just a matter of the British State having a long history. France has been plagued by disputes about the form of the regime and Church–State relations from 1789 down to this century.

4. Social homogeneity. Class has predominated as the basis of politics because of the weakness of other cleavages. Only 5 per cent of the population are not white, only 5 per cent live in rural areas, two-thirds are members of the Church of England, and five-sixths live in England. Before 1922 Ireland's membership of the UK reinforced differences based on agriculture, nationality and religion. The removal of Ireland homogenised the composition and simplified the politics of the UK. For many years, therefore, there have been limited social differences to express in the political arena.

5. Political culture itself: the traditions and style in which politics is conducted. In their major study, *The Civic Culture*, Almond and Verba saw Britain as having the ideal civic culture, i.e. one that combined or balanced the values of citizen participation and self-confidence with a trust in the elites and a responsiveness to their laws. Such a culture, although a product of the above four features and the political system, can itself in turn affect the way people behave in politics. British politicians have generally been pragmatic, and the extremes of the ideological left and right have not gained much consistent support.

Change

Among the changes, it is worth noting:

1. The role of government. In the 1960s and 1970s – governments of both parties intervened in areas traditionally left to personal choice or the market, e.g. controls on prices and incomes, and outlawing discrimination on grounds of gender or race.

The Thatcher governments withdrew or reduced the role of government from many economic areas, e.g. prices and incomes, exchange controls, full employment policy and regional aid. On the other hand, they intervened in the health service, e.g. imposing contracts of service on doctors; and in education, imposing a national core curriculum, and a contract of service on teachers. New Labour has accepted many of the changes, including a determination to limit the range of activities which the government funds.

2. The growth of populism, which involves some diminution in the standing of Parliament. The notion of parliamentary sovereignty was associated with 'strong' government, self-confident leaders and a deferential electorate. The introduction of the referendum is one indicator of the willingness to 'let the people decide' instead of trusting to MPs. The Labour government used referendums in Scotland and Wales in 1997 and has promised to use them for other purposes.

The decline in the authority of Parliament was also seen in the willingness of groups to demonstrate against the poll tax in 1990.

3. Loss of pride in the political system. It is doubtful whether the famous satisfaction of the British with their political system is now so marked. Partly because of Britain's relative economic decline and the growth of 'sleaze' in the 1990s, the political institutions have also come under critical scrutiny. In the 1980s dissatisfaction with the political system and centralisation under Margaret Thatcher prompted calls for Britain to adopt, among other things, a written constitution (see Chapter 6), a Bill of Rights and a proportional representation voting system.

4. The decline of the post-war political consensus. Notwithstanding bouts of intense disagreement, e.g. over the House of Lords (1910–11), Ireland (pre-1922) and the economic crisis in 1931, foreign observers have been impressed by the extent of British agreement on:

(a) *Substance*. After 1950 the two main parties largely agreed on the mixed economy and the Welfare State. The main features of these policies had been established by the post-war Labour government, with its measures to nationalise basic industries and create the National Health Service. In 1970 the Heath government tried and failed to alter this consensus. It was pledged to more selectivity in welfare, less government intervention in industry and wage bargaining, and a reform of the unions. Margaret Thatcher's government set out with a similar agenda and was more successful in breaking the consensus (see Chapter 1).

(b) *Procedures*, or how politics is conducted. At the end of the century, constitutional 'rules of the game', e.g. UK boundaries, role of local government, powers of the House of Lords and a simple majority voting system, are about to be changed radically.

5. The decline of deference. 'Deference' has been used in two senses to describe British political culture and how it made Britain a relatively easy country to govern:

(a) *Political* deference, meaning respect for the government, the absence of a revolutionary tradition or militant working class and compliance with laws.

(b) *Social* deference, or the identification of leadership skills with high social status. This has been advanced as an explanation for the large working-class Tory vote and the continued presence in the elite of people with an upper-class and public-school background.

However, political deference has declined as people and groups have become more assertive about their 'rights', e.g. campaigns against planning decisions and anti-poll tax demonstrations.

Social deference has also declined. The leaderships of Ted Heath, Margaret Thatcher, John Major and William Hague have seen a more meritocratic grammar-school, middle- or lower-middle-class leadership take over from the 'magic circle' of Old Etonians who possessed landed estates. Not only are aristocratic origins becoming less advantageous electorally for the Tories but fewer aristocrats dominate the party. The exposure in the 1990s of cases of sleaze and corruption (cash for questions) and the rise in public cynicism about politicians also weakened deference.

6. Public disorder. The British have been noted for the avoidance of violence in politics and a general willingness to compromise. Northern Ireland is the outstanding exception. The riots in Bristol, Brixton, Southall and Toxteth in June 1981 and in Handsworth and Tottenham in 1985 illustrate a willingness to turn to violence among the young in socially deprived areas. It is widely believed that the inner-city riots owed more to deprivation than to race. But there is also growing concern about racial discrimination and alienation among young blacks. Some say that the emergence of an alienated underclass, hostile to the rest of society, poses a challenge to British political culture. It must be remembered, however, that in other areas threats to the polity have receded. Industrial action and related violence used to be a feature of the 1970s and early 1980s, but in the 1990s the number of days lost through strike action was the lowest for over a century.

Why the change?

This is difficult to say. Most so-called explanations merely re-describe the changes. They include:

1. Failures. Post-war Britain has experienced a sharp decline in international status and relative economic strength. In terms of Gross National Product per head, Britain has steadily fallen behind other Western European States (see Chapters 1 and 17). Apparent policy failures and consequent criticism have probably sapped the self-confidence of Britain's elites. All recent governments have started out promising to reverse Britain's relative economic decline.

2. Elite emphasis on the need for change in attitudes to boost economic growth, e.g. 'modernisation', more 'professional' government, entry to the EC, reforms in work practices, collective bargaining, local government, etc. The Thatcher governments tried to weaken many parts of the post-war consensus, which Margaret Thatcher thought was too 'soft' and made Britain uncompetitive. She sought with some success to promote a new 'culture' in the public sector, emphasising value for money and management in the civil service, local government and in the education and health services. She extended competition in the professions (such as law), extended the free market, e.g. share owning, home ownership and privatisation of State industries and services, and reformed the trade unions. Tony Blair's 'welfare to work' programme aims to reduce 'dependency' and promote self-reliance.

3. Changes in social class and the dissolution of old class loyalties (see Chapters 2 and 5), which placed many in different socio-economic relationships and changed attitudes accordingly.

4. New issues. Clearly, national identity in Scotland, religion and nationalism in Ulster, and race have weakened the validity of the old emphases on national unity and integration.

Did Margaret Thatcher change the culture?

An important part of Margaret Thatcher's agenda during her eleven years of power (1979–90) was changing the political culture, blamed by many critics for Britain's poor economic performance. It was alleged that the Welfare State undermined the work ethic and encouraged dependency; high taxes reduced work incentives; the State provided too much (e.g. guaranteeing full employment), and this sapped initiative. Margaret Thatcher wanted to restore what she called an 'enterprise culture' and create an environment in which people would be prepared to take risks, work harder and become more self-reliant. She therefore encouraged private home ownership, self-employment, the creation of small businesses and the extension of private share ownership. She saw herself as a crusader. In view of the long period which the Conservative government had in office, one might expect the widespread acceptance of Thatcherite values. But, according to Ivor Crewe, it appears that this was 'a crusade that failed'. By a margin of 5 to 1, voters say they prefer a society in which 'caring for others' is more highly rewarded than 'the creation of wealth'. The social and collective provision of welfare is preferred to the individual looking after himself or herself. People, by large majorities, seem to prefer increased social expenditure even if this means higher taxes. In 1979 there were equal numbers of tax cutters versus service expanders. By 1987 the latter out-numbered the former by 6 to 1.

However, these survey findings have to be interpreted with caution. What people say to interviewers is often what they feel they ought to believe rather than what they actually do. During the 1992 election campaign, opinion polls registered large majorities who made social and welfare issues their top priority and favoured Labour policies to deal with them. Yet on election day the Conservatives won the election by a margin of 7.6 per cent. Blair's New Labour believed that the culture changed during the 1980s and adapted accordingly.

Participation

The degree of popular participation in British politics is quite small – though probably no lower than levels found in other liberal democracies. This political model is predicated upon some degree of public involvement, though in practice apart from general elections most people declare scant interest in politics: only small percentages in surveys declare themselves 'politically active' in politics (see Figure 3.1).

Electoral turnout in Britain at 75–80 per cent of the electorate is lower than in the Scandinavian countries but higher than the mere 50 per cent mustered in US presidential elections (though their electoral registration system is more complex than in the UK). In 1997, however, it was only 71 per cent.

Party membership has plummeted since the war: Labour's 1 million individual (as opposed to affiliated trade union) members slumped to about 0.3 million in the 1970s and 1980s and recovered to over 0.4 million in 1997. Conservative membership has declined to a similar figure, but the number of committed activists is probably similar in both major parties. Between general elections it is doubtful if overall more than 2–3 per cent of the electorate can be described as genuinely active within political parties (see Chapter 5). In turn, this affects the ability of parties to raise funds from ordinary supporters and promote their causes.

Figure 3.1   *The level of popular participation in British politics*

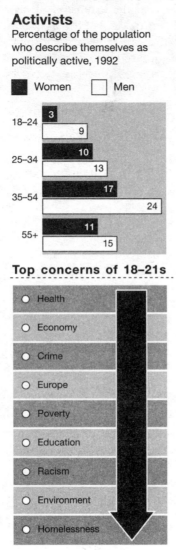

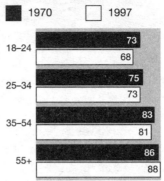

Activists
Percentage of the population
who describe themselves as
politically active, 1992

■ Women   □ Men

Age	Women	Men
18–24	3	9
25–34	10	13
35–54	17	24
55+	11	15

Voters
Percentage of the electorate who
used their vote at the general
elections of 1970 and1997

■ 1970   □ 1997

Age	1970	1997
18–24	73	68
25–34	75	73
35–54	83	81
55+	86	88

Top concerns of 18–21s

- Health
- Economy
- Crime
- Europe
- Poverty
- Education
- Racism
- Environment
- Homelessness

Voting and the 18–25s

● It is estimated that 31 per cent
of the 18–25s did not vote in
1987 and that 43 per cent did
not vote in 1992.

● At the time of the last census
(1991) nearly 20 per cent of
18–25s were not registered to
vote, compared with 2 per cent
of those aged 55 or over.

● A 1995 Mori poll revealed that
6 per cent of the 45–55s did
not intend to vote, compared
with 15 per cent of the 18–25s.
Exit polls after the May 1997
general election showed a rise
of between 6 and 14 per cent
of the under-25s compared
with 1992.

Source: *Guardian*, 29 January 1998.

Pressure-group activity registers a higher level of participation. As already
noted, British people – though mainly the middle classes – have become used
to the idea of organising themselves to press for or prevent certain things
happening. At the national level this has been noticeable quite dramatically
in groups associated with the environment, as Table 3.1 indicates. Other
pressure groups, however, suffered a fall in membership during the 1980s,

especially trade unions – from 12 million to around 8 million members in the 1990s (see Chapter 17).

Table 3.1   *Membership of environmental groups (000s)*

	1971	1988
Civic Trust	214	1,249
National Trust	278	1,634
Ramblers' Association	22	165
Royal Society for Nature Conservation	64	1,204
Royal Society for the Protection of Birds	98	1,540
Friends of the Earth	7	165

Finally, work by Jacobs and Worcester suggests that levels of participation in the conventional political system witnessed a slight decline over the Thatcher years. For example, in 1984 32 per cent of respondents 'urged someone outside my family to vote': by 1989 the figure had fallen to 10 per cent. Other activities reflected smaller reductions: from 17 per cent to 13 per cent for presenting 'views to a local councillor or MP'; from 16 per cent to 13 per cent for making a 'speech before an organised club'; from 16 per cent to 13 per cent for 'being elected an officer of an organisation or club'; and from 4 per cent to 3 per cent for taking an 'active part in a political campaign'. The decline in the role of local government in these years may have contributed. Parry *et al.* (1992) showed that the people are still prepared to protest; 15 per cent had attended at least one protest meeting and 63 per cent had signed a petition.

Further reading

G. Almond and S. Verba, *The Civic Culture*, Princeton University Press, 1963.

G. Almond and S. Verba, *The Civic Culture Revisited*, Little, Brown, 1981.

I. Crewe, 'Has the electorate become Thatcherite?', in R. Skidelsky (ed.), *Thatcherism*, Chatto & Windus, 1988.

W. Glinga, *Legacy of Empire*, Manchester University Press, 1986.

E. Jacobs and R. Worcester, *We British*, Weidenfeld & Nicolson, 1990.

D. Kavanagh, 'Political culture in Great Britain', in G. Almond and S. Verba (eds), *The Civic Culture Revisited*, Little, Brown, 1981.

G. Parry *et al.*, *Political Participation and Democracy in Britain*, Cambridge University Press, 1992.

Social Trends, HMSO, 1997.

Questions

1 What factors decide citizens' attitudes to the government?
2 Explain the relative lack of violence in Britain's post-war political history.
3 'One side effect of the Thatcher decade has been to reduce people's belief in the value of political activity' (Jacobs and Worcester). Discuss.

4

Changing political ideas

Ever since the ancient Greeks, philosophers have been fascinated by such questions as 'Which is the best form of government?', 'How much authority should a government have over its citizens?', 'Why should citizens obey their governments?' and 'How should wealth be distributed?' Over the centuries ideas about these perennial questions have been influenced by religious and revolutionary ideas, the emergence of new ruling elites and nation-states, and changes in the means of creating wealth and other technological advances. It comes as something of a shock, however, to realise that the ideas currently found in the political market-place are of relatively recent provenance. If we go back to the mid-seventeenth century we encounter a startlingly different set of dominant ideas, e.g. religious dogmatism, absolute monarchical power and the divine right of kings (the notion that hereditary succession to the throne is ordained by God).

The liberal philosophers

The transition into modern frames of thinking was affected substantially by the liberal philosophers of the eighteenth century, especially John Locke, who argued for:

(a) *Rationality*. Reliance upon supporting evidence for ideas rather than assertions based upon tradition.
(b) *Toleration*. The belief that religious and political beliefs are a matter of personal conscience rather than a concern of governments.
(c) *Liberty*. The belief that each citizen is entitled to certain liberties, such as freedom from arbitrary arrest and freedom to buy and sell.
(d) *Checks and balances*. The idea that the main government institutions should each have a degree of independence to prevent any dangerous concentration of power.

(e) *Rights*. The idea that people have rights which are personal and independent of the State and that citizens therefore have a contractual relationship with it. The revolutionary impact of this idea was that the
authority of government is dependent upon the consent of the governed.

In America and France these ideas were cited in support of violent revolutions. In Britain the conflict was largely non-violent but the results over
time were also revolutionary. In 1832 the notion of popular sovereignty was
endorsed by the Great Reform Act: elections, not monarchs, would hence-
forward determine the colour of government.

The classical liberals

The so-called classical liberals, some of whom went on to form the Liberal
Party in the mid-nineteenth century, further underpinned emergent democratic ideas by arguing for more individual freedom and representative
parliamentary government elected by a much wider proportion of the population. The classical liberals, however, were not just concerned with the
nature of government; they vigorously addressed the matter of what it
should and (especially) what it should not do. They argued for minimal government:

1. Socially. To inhibit intervention to support the poor – as Herbert Spencer
asserted, 'to protect people from the consequences of their folly is to people
the world with fools'.

2. Economically. To encourage a laissez-faire economic system. In accordance with the ideas of Adam Smith, this entailed freeing entrepreneurs from
legal restraints to:

(a) set up businesses to produce products at prices consumers were prepared
     to pay;
(b) employ workers, take a profit and invest in other enterprises.

In this way, argued the classical liberals, through the pursuit by each
person of their selfish interests, the whole of society benefits. People are
employed and wealth is created. The greater the wealth the higher the
wages, and the more profit available for reinvestment. Competition will
ensure profits are not too high and that the public will be offered the best
goods at the lowest price. The 'invisible hand' of the market will ensure efficiency is rewarded and inefficiency punished by failure. The vibrant growth
of the British economy in the nineteenth century appeared to support these
arguments.

Traditional conservatism

In the mid-nineteenth century classical liberalism was pitted against the ideas of the Tory, or Conservative, Party, as it became known after the 1830s. Conservatives allege that theirs is the open-minded rather than the ideological party, while their opponents claim they merely adopt whatever policies are necessary to gain power. Neither view is correct. Over the last century and a half, a number of core ideas can be identified:

1. Human nature. Conservatives believe that people are by nature selfish, weak, corruptible, even sinful. To think otherwise, they argue, is to delude oneself and risk disaster. Nor do Conservatives think that much can be done about this condition; attempts to change human nature – social engineering – are likely to make things worse rather than better.

2. The rule of law. Weak human beings must be protected from their own darker natures. Widespread acceptance of the rule of law is necessary to prevent anarchy. To be acceptable the law has to be impartial and to be effective it must be reinforced by penalties backed by the overwhelming force of the State.

3. Harmony and balance in society. Conservatives wish to resist whatever they see as extremist tendencies, such as the unbridled capitalism of the nineteenth century or the over-mighty socialism of Labour in the 1970s. Like Edmund Burke, they believe that 'all government is founded on compromise'. They oppose dogmatism and prefer pragmatism: finding the right policies to stay in power and preserve social harmony.

4. Social institutions and the nations. Informal relationships such as family and community, together with formal institutions such as schools, voluntary associations, Parliament and the Royal Family, play a vital role in binding society together. They provide continuity with the past: a sense of belonging. The idea of 'nation' – one's country – is a source of pride, a reason for laying down life itself in a time of war. In peace, Queen and country are vital unifying symbols: Conservatives claim theirs is the patriotic party. The foreign policy corollary of this view of the nation is a concern to defend national interests first and to be suspicious of internationalism – beyond generalised (and at times equivocal) support for the EU and the Commonwealth.

5. Liberty. Lord Acton described liberty as 'the highest political end'. Preserving it is the fundamental purpose of government and politics. People should be allowed to do as they please – provided they do not infringe the liberty of others. Legislators must show wisdom when deciding how far individual liberty has to be curtailed in the interests of liberty as a whole. Economic freedom is central to Conservative notions of liberty: the freedom to set up in business, employ people, make a profit, etc. Liberty must be preserved through the dispersal of power: centres of power in society will check or balance each other, creating a tension which is the guarantor of freedom. Government therefore should be limited.

6. Government. It follows that the executive power of government should be limited in what it seeks to do; strong enough to maintain law and order or to take steps which are necessary; and balanced or restrained by other constitutional powers, such as the legislature and the Crown, and by forces within society itself, especially the owners of property. Corruptible human beings should not be allowed too much power, for their own good or for that of society.

7. An acceptance of inequality. Conservatives believe in equality before the law and in career opportunities but are opposed to the idea of equal rewards because:

(a) people are born with unequal talents. Equal rewards would be unfair to the gifted, who might otherwise not bother to develop their talents. It might also encourage people to be lazy;

(b) people are motivated by personal gain. If talent is rewarded, as it should be, a hierarchy of wealth and status will inevitably emerge. But this is desirable so that poor people will be fired to 'better' themselves by working hard. Inequality is therefore an essential element in the motor which runs a capitalist economy.

Traditional Conservatives, however, do not wish inequalities to be too dramatic, otherwise the poor will become alienated from society and subversively hostile.

8. Political change. Conservatives seek to conserve; to avoid radical change; to let change occur naturally, as it will if people are free to pursue their own interests. Government's role will often be to formalise change after the event rather than to promote it. Traditionally, Conservatives have agreed with the Duke of Cambridge that 'the time for change is when it can no longer be resisted'.

The impact of Thatcherism

From her election as leader in 1975 Margaret Thatcher drove a battering ram through traditional Conservative ideas. She would not disagree over human nature being flawed, and the primacy of the rule of law and liberty,

but on most other issues her views were at once different and more emphatic.
She was:

(a) less interested in balance and harmony than in maximising her own
    ability to achieve her own clear political objectives. These included the
    obliteration rather than the mere containment of socialism. As a 'con-
    viction' politician she held compromise in contempt and sought to build
    a new consensus around her own ideas;
(b) much less concerned to limit inequalities resulting from the unfettered
    working of a market economy: on the contrary, she defended the right
    of people 'to be unequal';
(c) opposed to the 'dependency culture' which she believed the Welfare
    State creates; she vigorously advocated self-reliance;
(d) in favour of radical change, even describing herself as 'a revolutionary'.
    Her desire to promote an enterprise culture moreover smacked a little of
    the 'social engineering' which traditional Conservatives condemn as
    socialist fallacy;
(e) not keen on the Commonwealth (happy to flout its unanimity over
    South Africa) nor on Europe (hotly opposed to plans for political and eco-
    nomic union);
(f) monetarist on the economy: she wanted to control the money supply
    through high interest rates to keep inflation down; remove government
    controls over the economy; privatise State-run activities; and end the
    power of trade unions to distort market forces.

Woodrow Wyatt, a close friend and adviser, described her as a classical liberal. Following her departure from power in 1990 her views receded in
importance, but the influence of Thatcherism in the Conservative Party will
long survive its author.

John Major and conservatism

Many Conservative MPs voted for John Major in November 1990 because
they believed he would carry forward Margaret Thatcher's torch. To some
extent he did: proceeding with Thatcherite reforms of education and the
health service, pursuing a strict anti-inflationary policy and arguing for further cuts in taxation. But in other respects he betrayed those of his sympa-
thisers who supported traditional conservatism by declaring his support for
a 'classless society' (though see Chapter 2); introducing a Citizen's Charter
to improve public services; abolishing the poll tax; substantially increasing
spending on welfare; and conducting a more emollient, consultative style of
government. He also proved himself much more enthusiastic over Europe
than his predecessor, supporting the 1991 Maastricht agreement on further
economic and monetary union and defending Britain's 1990 membership of

the European Exchange Rate Mechanism, even after the catastrophic run on the pound forced Britain's withdrawal (see Chapter 19). Disputes over Europe were highly influential in the disaster which struck the party on 1 May 1997. Major resigned, complaining that all Conservative policy 'clothes' had been stolen by the slick New Labour. He was replaced by the more Eurosceptical Hague who, at the time of writing, is struggling to give his party a new identity.

Traditional socialism

Critique

Socialism begins a critique of the kind of economy classical liberals idealised. Socialists argued that capitalism creates:

1. Exploitation. The value of a product is the sum of the labour put into it. Under capitalism the factory-owner takes the lion's share while the worker receives a fraction. Labour is bought cheap and cast aside when no longer needed.

2. Inequality. Capitalists become fabulously and unjustifiably rich, often living off inherited wealth, while the mass of workers have to combat poverty.

3. Inefficiency. During its booms the capitalist economy cannot meet demand; during slumps millions languish unemployed, with the poorest suffering most.

4. Dominant values. Dominant groups have always used their power to inculcate values which underpin their own position. Conservative ideology, argue socialists, is merely a rationalisation of dominant-group interests: the notion that free enterprise benefits the working class does not stand up to examination – the number of workers who become rich is negligible by comparison with those who become rich via inherited wealth; the vicissitudes of the market can just as easily mean unemployment as higher wages. Moreover, these are the values which enthrone selfishness instead of fellowship, competition instead of co-operation, the urge for material goods instead of real happiness. Yet these are the values which workers themselves are induced to accept as 'common sense' in a capitalist society.

Principles

From this critique socialists adduce a number of principles:

1. Human nature is fundamentally good. It is the distorting impact of capitalism which creates the flaws. A benign socialist economic and social environment will allow man's innate goodness to develop fully.

2. Equality and freedom. Capitalist inequalities are not only morally unacceptable but prevent all but the rich minority from becoming genuinely free. For example, how can the daughter of an immigrant family in Bradford enjoy the same choices in life as the son of a wealthy aristocrat?

3. Collectivism. Individuals need to recognise their economic interdependence with, and moral obligation to, society as a whole. It follows that the means whereby wealth is created should be owned collectively rather than privately.

4. Efficiency and fairness. Planned economy would create wealth more efficiently and distribute it more fairly.

Post-war Labour programme

Labour's huge 1945 majority enabled it to make the transition from abstract to broad practical principles:

1. Keynesian economics – more compatible with socialism – had already replaced classical economics as the orthodoxy of the age. Keynes argued that various forms of control and intervention made it possible for a capitalist economy to be managed and guided towards a number of desirable goals such as full employment and buoyant production (see Chapter 17).

2. Centralised planning would iron out anarchic booms and slumps in the economy.

3. Nationalisation. Large areas of economic activity would be taken out of private hands and placed under national boards accountable to Parliament.

4. A mixed economy. While the public sector was to be dominant, a vigorous private sector was still thought desirable.

5. Universal social services. Following the recommendations of the Beveridge Report (1942), social services were to be overhauled – made uniform and universally applicable.

Revisionism in the 1950s

With the 1945 programme implemented, Labour politicians such as Anthony Crosland and Hugh Gaitskell began to re-examine the roots of socialism. In his 1956 book *The Future of Socialism*, Crosland argued that the wonders of Keynesian economic management now enabled socialists to win the fruits of revolution without the inconvenience of having one. Ownership of the economy was irrelevant when the development of the joint stock company had placed managers rather than owners in direct charge of big business. Nationalisation, moreover, should no longer be sacrosanct. If most of the economic battles had been won, it followed that all that was needed to achieve dignity and equality for all was a vigorous egalitarian social policy.

Left-wing revolt in the 1970s ... and failure in the 1980s

The Wilson government in the 1960s implicitly followed the revisionist line, but after the Conservative victory in 1970 a radicalised trade union movement combined with left-wing Labour MPs to mount alternative socialist policies: a reassertion of state control over the biggest companies, especially multinationals, plus a call for more workers' co-operatives; democratisation of British life, starting with the Labour Party and proceeding through Parliament to embrace economic activity as well; improved welfare services to remedy the failures highlighted by the 'poverty' researchers (e.g. Professors Titmuss and Townsend, who rediscovered poverty very much alive in the big cities); unilateral abandonment of nuclear weapons; and a withdrawal from the EC and a weakening of NATO ties.

A yawning chasm opened up between revisionist Labour Cabinets in the 1970s and an increasingly embittered left-wing and trade union movement. The conflict took a damagingly public form in the winter of 1978–79, when the lower-paid refused to accept Labour's incomes policy norm.

Margaret Thatcher's 1979 victory gave the left the chance it had been waiting for. The 1980 and 1981 Party Conferences were victories for left-wing ideas, many of them inspired by Tony Benn. Left-wing policies were put in place and Labour's constitution altered. But while left-wing activists were faithful to socialist principles, their debates during the 1970s had been rather closed intellectual affairs. Those who claimed that the British people would respond warmly to genuine left-wing socialism were brought sharply in touch with cold reality in 1983 when Labour's manifesto was resoundingly rejected by the electorate.

Kinnock's revolution

Neil Kinnock, the new Labour leader elected after the 1983 debacle, resolved
to move the party towards an electable programme. In practice this meant
abandoning left-wing ideas and moving into the centre ground. By painful
degrees he achieved a near-revolution in Labour policies by 1990. The
socialist rhetoric remained but the policies laid out in the party's May 1990
statement were unrecognisable from those of 1983.

1. Defence: unilateral abandonment of nuclear weapons was phased out –
a negotiated settlement with other nuclear powers (multilateralism) was
preferred.

2. Public ownership: no more nationalisation; some privatised companies to
be returned to public ownership, but fair market-price compensation to be
paid to shareholders.

3. Trade unions: no commitment to restore the pre-1979 position; substantial
amounts of Tory legislation to be retained; 'our framework for industrial law
will be even handed between employers and trade unions'.

4. Taxation: no return to super-tax but a banded system with 50 per cent
maximum.

5. Europe: reversal of withdrawal policy and closer co-operation: 'Britain
must play a positive role in shaping the future of Europe.'

6. Economy: no radical change; a 'partnership economy' envisaged, which
'welcomes and endorses the efficiencies and realism which markets can
provide'; no statutory incomes policy; 'we particularly welcome foreign
investment'.

7. Social services: restore spending and improve services, but all public
spending ultimately dependent upon economic growth. 'We have to meet the
bills of society out of improved performance. It cannot come out of an extra
slab of taxation. That would be folly' (Neil Kinnock, 15 May 1990).

8. The constitution: an elected upper chamber (possibly via proportional
representation); regional assemblies; a Scottish Parliament; plus fundamental
rights protected by statute.

The May 1990 document represented a total routing of Tony Benn's
socialist alternative, which had been virtually endorsed in the early 1980s.
He called the document 'a breathtaking revelation of the extent to which
revisionism has gone in the Party'. Left-wingers claimed that Labour's 1992

election manifesto – with the possible exception of its taxation proposals – marked an even further movement to the right: but all to no avail. Perhaps Neil Kinnock's policy reversals – heroic to the right, a betrayal to the left – were too much too soon for many voters fully to believe in and trust. His successor in 1992 (following his election defeat), John Smith, enjoyed the advantage of being a revisionist by conviction rather than conversion, but his tentative reforms of the trade union block vote and 'one member, one vote' were tragically cut short by his death in 1994.

Tony Blair

Blair took over and vigorously continued Smith's work, his outstanding initial achievement being the rescinding of the 1918 Clause Four in the party's constitution, committing the party to blanket collective ownership. After a national campaign he confounded doubters by winning a crushing victory – 75–25 per cent – over the Old Guard at a special conference on 25 April 1995.

Box 4.1 Blairism as marketing

'As marketing text books recommend, they (Blair and Mandelson) reformulated the product (old Clause IV ditched, old policies emasculated). This was accompanied by a small but momentous tweak to the old brand name. ("New", said the legendary adman David Ogilvy, "is one of the most powerful words in the advertising dictionary.") Market surveys – particularly focus discussions – were used constantly to check the acceptability of every policy, every message, every idea. The strengths and weaknesses of the competition were assiduously analysed. The target group was carefully selected: only middle of the road, wobbly Tories need apply. Then all communications were coordinated to maximise impact.'

Source: Winston Fletcher, advertising executive in the *Guardian*, 23 October 1997.

Blair's political ideas were formed quite early at school when he decided he 'wanted to make a difference'. By nature anti-establishment, he was attracted to the left rather than the Conservative Party his father dreamed of representing at Westminster and for which his public school and Oxford background would have suggested he was destined. At Oxford he developed a brand of Christian socialism, arguing that people had responsibilities as well as rights and found their identities through being part of their local and national communities. On to these foundations he built a package of ideas designed to attract the middle-class voters Labour needed in the wake of the shrinkage of the working classes. Essentially these represented compromises with the values and ideas introduced by the Thatcher revolution: acceptance of market economy and of privatisation as a *fait acompli* plus a desirable approach to certain kinds of welfare reform; tough on crime; severe restrictions on tax and public spending; and agnostic on the desirability of joining the single European currency. Helped by the brilliant (though much criticised – see Box 4.1) political marketing of Peter Mandelson and Alastair Campbell, 'New Labour' swept to power in 1997 with a majority of 179, committed to little except low tax, low spending and constitutional reform (see Box 5.1).

Figure 4.1 illustrates some of the ideological fluctuations which have taken place in the Lab our and Conservative Parties since the war.

Figure 4.1   *Ideological fluctuations, 1940–97*

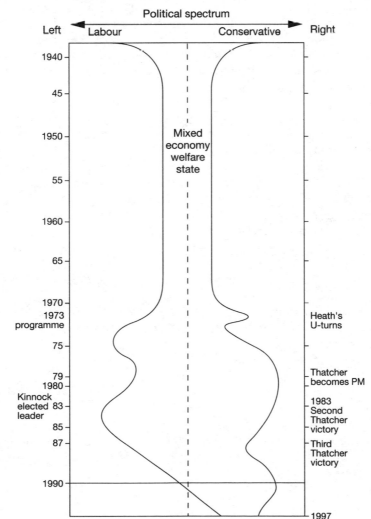

The centre parties

In the 1983 election the SDP–Liberal Alliance mustered 26 per cent of the vote, but following the botched merger after the 1987 election, the Social and Liberal Democrats, not to mention the rump SDP, had difficulty in articulating distinctive policies and getting their messages across. In 1990 the SDP formally came to an end but the Liberal Democrats inherited the mantle of the Liberals as the third party. In 1997 Ashdown's party did well, returning 46 MPs, but actually lost 1.1 per cent of its 17.2 per cent share of the vote in 1992.

The party retains a strong emphasis on liberty and individual rights; decentralisation (community politics); constitutional reform (proportional representation, devolution, elected House of Lords); and internationalism (a federal Europe and support for the UN). But its other emphases – on the mixed (social market) economy, less inequality rather than equality, multilateral nuclear disarmament, retention of Thatcherite trade union controls plus a less divisive class-war approach to politics – have been captured by 'New' Labour.

In 1995 Ashdown abandoned the policy of 'equidistance' between the two main parties in the event of a hung Parliament and admitted he would favour a Labour government. His position is uneasy following the 1997 election: he is naturally drawn to support Labour, especially over constitutional reforms (indeed he has been drawn into government itself as a member of a Cabinet committee on this subject). But he favours more spending on education and health and is more enthusiastic over Europe. The sticking point of co-operation may turn out to be the question of voting reform, over which Labour have promised a referendum.

The Greens

After a decade of fringe politics the Greens exploded into national politics with 15 per cent of the vote in the 1989 European elections. The Green, or ecological, prescription is by far the most radical of all those currently on offer in the political market-place. It is founded upon:

1. **A world approach.** All human activity should reflect appreciation of the world's finite resources and easily damaged ecology.

2. **Respect for the rights of our descendants.** Our children have the right to inherit a beautiful and bountiful planet rather than an exhausted and polluted one.

3. Sufficiency. We should be satisfied with 'enough' rather than constantly seeking 'more'.

4. A conserver economy. We must conserve what we have rather than squandering it through pursuit of high-growth strategies.

5. Care and share. Given that resources are limited we must shift our energies to sharing what we have and looking after all sections of society properly.

6. Self-reliance. We should learn to provide for ourselves rather than surrendering responsibility to experts and specialised agencies.

7. Decentralise and democratise. We must form smaller units of production, encourage co-operative enterprises and give people local power over their own affairs. At the same time, international integration must move forward rapidly.

The implications of such principles are far-reaching and involve major changes in lifestyles, e.g. a no-growth or shrinking economy, a drastic reduction in the use of cars and a new style of more primitive communal living. While most people now accept the need for strict control of pollution, their 'greenness' does not extend much beyond this. The other political parties have now all donned 'light green' policy clothing and appear to have marginalised the Green Party: in 1997 it polled less than 1 per cent of the vote.

Blundell–Gosschalk: an alternative classification to left–right

Traditionally, political ideas have been classified from left to right; left favouring State spending and economic controls and the right the free market. A report by the IEA, however (reported in the *Sunday Times*, 7 December 1997), suggested a more subtle approach. In collaboration with the pollsters MORI, the authors, Blundell and Gosschalk, distinguished five alternative categories: conservative (pro-free market but with strong controls on moral/ethical issues); libertarian (pro-maximum possible personal and economic freedom); socialist (big government and severe restrictions on the market); authoritarian (anti-personal/economic freedom); and centrist (in middle range economic/social freedom). Questions were posed to 1,700 respondents on topics designed to categorise them accordingly. The results were: conservatives, 36 per cent; libertarians, 19; socialists, 18; centrist, 15; and authoritarians, 13. A *USA Today* poll showed very similar findings for the US electorate, suggesting a close consensus between the two in the 1990s. In the 1997 election, Blair drew support from all five groups – only 23 per cent of conservatives to the Tories' 44, but a clear lead in all the other categories – indicating that the winning party in UK elections has to push the right buttons for a range of opinion groups and not just appeal to a limited constituency.

Further reading

I. Adams, *Political Ideology Today*, Manchester University Press, 1993.

I. Adams and B. Jones, *Political Ideas in Britain*, PAVIC Publications.

J. Blundell and B. Gosschalk, *Beyond Left and Right: The New Politics of Britain*, Institute of Economic Affairs and Market and Opinion Research International (MORI), December 1997.

C. A. R. Crosland, *The Future of Socialism*, Cape, 1956.

H. Drucker *et al.*, *Developments in British Politics*, Macmillan, 1990.

R. Eccleshall *et al.*, *Political Ideologies*, Hutchinson, 1984.

A. Heywood, *Political Ideologies*, Macmillan, 1992.

B. Jones (ed.), *Politics U.K.*, 3rd edn, Prentice Hall, 1997, Part Three.

L. Tivey and A. Wright, *Party Ideology in Britain*, Routledge, 1989.

Questions

1 Drawing upon this chapter, try to describe your own political beliefs.
2 Write brief explanations and critiques of: (a) Marxism; (b) conservatism; (c) socialism; (d) liberal democracy; (e) ecology.
3 'Politicians are either warriors or healers.' Discuss.

5

The changing party system

This chapter examines the changing assumptions about, and changes within, the party system. The two-party system has long been a cornerstone of most ideas of British politics. It includes such features as a one-party majority government, a dominant executive, class voting, stable administrations and the widely accepted authority of Parliament. Because these features are interrelated, it is not surprising that changes in one feature coincide with, and are causally related to, changes in others. Below we look at how we have changed from party system I (pre-1970) to system II (1970–92), and examine the prospects for further change.

Party changes

Party systems (i.e. the number and type of significant parties) usually change in response to one of three factors:

(a) *A party split*, e.g. the Liberals in 1885 or 1916.
(b) *A new issue*, which gives rise to a new party, e.g. Irish home rule and the Irish Nationalists after 1880, or nationalism in Scotland in 1974.
(c) *A change in the composition of the electorate* which allows new interests to be expressed, e.g. the rise of Labour after 1918 coincided with a significant growth in the number of working-class voters.

It is difficult, however, for new parties to break in. First, the established parties (Conservatives and Labour have been the two main ones since 1918) try and adjust to new issues and interests and thereby head off a new party. Second, the electoral system penalises minority parties (see below).

Popular assumptions and the changing reality

1. There are two parties and one-party-majority governments. This best describes the period 1945–70. For much of the twentieth century, there have been more than two large parties, and between 1929 and 1945 there were either minority or coalition governments. Between 1945 and 1970 the Labour and Conservative Parties together averaged 91 per cent of the vote at general elections. In 1974 this share fell to 75 per cent, falling more sharply outside England; rose to 80 per cent in 1979; then fell to a post-war low of 70 per cent in 1983; and has recovered to some 75 per cent since. But because of the disproportional electoral system, the two parties still managed to gain 95 per cent of seats in the Commons. So the two-party system more accurately describes the situation in Parliament than voting behaviour in the electorate.

2. The parties are national. Since 1974, however, there have been contrasting competitive line-ups in different parts of the UK. Ulster now has its distinctive system; in the south of England outside London, the Liberal Democrats until 1997 became the main rival of the Conservatives, and in Scotland the Nationalists rival the other three parties. After the 1983 and 1987 elections there were two party systems: in about half the seats Conservative and Alliance occupied the first two positions; in the other half Labour and Alliance or Conservative. It was difficult to talk of a general election giving a 'national' mandate. The differentiation was also seen in the variations in election swings in different parts of the country (see Chapter 8).

3. The electorate votes on class lines. In the absence of significant religious, regional or racial divisions, class has been the decisive influence (as Peter Pulzer has said, 'all else is embellishment and detail'). Again, this has changed sharply. Since 1974 the class alignments between the parties have declined, largely because of the reduction in working-class support for Labour. We might say that the changes above represent a shift from one party system (I) to another (II). The main contenders (Labour and Conservative) are still dominant, but their bases of support have weakened and the context of their competition has altered.

The two parties

1. Viewed in comparative perspective, the *Conservatives* have been remarkably successful. They have dominated the centre-right of the political stage, and, in contrast to major right-wing parties on the Continent, they are a secular rather than a largely religious party. They have been in office for much of the twentieth century and have earned the title of 'the natural party of government'. The party, like the major political, economic and social elites, has adapted to the rise of democracy and to social change and, compared with the political right on the Continent, it was not tinged with fascism in the inter-war years. Above all, since 1945 the party has managed to gain the support of about a third of the working class and has been opportunistic or pragmatic enough to embrace policies to secure that support. (For explanations of working-class conservatism, see Chapter 8.)

2. Apart from those in Scandinavia, *Labour* has also been more successful electorally than other socialist parties. It has monopolised the cause of the political left (compare the rivalry between Socialists and powerful Communist Parties in Italy and France), and the trade unions are more politically united than those in many other States. And much of the political consensus of the post-war period – the mixed economy, Welfare State and full employment – was the work of the 1945–51 Labour governments (see Chapter 1). However:

3. Until the mid-1990s Labour was clearly a party in decline, measured in terms of individual and trade union membership and electoral support. The 1983 and 1987 elections were the two worst results in over 50 years, and even 1992 was the third worst. It drew its main support from declining groups: the working class and the trade unions. The party's individual membership shrank from over 900,000 in the early 1950s to 274,000 in September 1992. Under Tony Blair the party has made a startling recovery. Individual membership rose to 420,000 by the end of 1996 and the party's electoral support in 1997 reached its highest level in over 30 years. But in becoming a radically reformed party, it has abandoned the traditional emphasis on public ownership and redistribution. It has decided that British society has changed so much – becoming more white collar and aspirational – that the party has had to shed much of its past in terms of policies, organisation and themes in order to become electable.

Explanations for the two-party system

1. **The electoral system.** The 'first-past-the-post', single-member-constituency system has played a part, particularly in penalising the Alliance parties in 1983 and 1987 and the Liberal Democrats in 1992.

2. **The social structure**, i.e. class. Yes, but the evidence suggests that this is now weakening (see Chapter 9).

3. **It is 'natural'.** There is an idea that political issues lend themselves to an 'either–or' treatment and that political argument is most appropriately dichotomised into government versus opposition. Duverger (*Political Parties*)

has suggested that this dualism is 'natural', but in reality the two-party system is a rare plant, hardly found outside Anglo-American societies. Most Western industrialised countries which are also liberal democracies have multi-party systems, proportional representation and coalition governments.

4. The British preference for strong government, i.e. a party with a clear majority in the Commons. It is questionable whether one-party government is necessarily 'stronger' than a coalition, or that millions of individual voters consciously co-ordinate their different votes to produce this outcome. At times of crisis (e.g. the two great wars and during the 1931 economic crisis) leaders have resorted to coalition.

Note that there are other parties. Since 1974 there has been considerable support for a centre party, formerly the Liberals, now the *Liberal Democrats*. In the 1997 Parliament there are 46 Liberal Democrats, the largest third-party total since 1929. Among the electorate there is clearly a three-party system; only the effects of the electoral system reduce the number of Liberal Democrat MPs from what a proportional system would give them. The party has had a distinctive agenda – constitutional reform, support for European integration (it is still the most pro-EU party), employee–employer partnership, and tax increases to improve health and school services. But Tony Blair's Labour Party has taken over much of this agenda and the co-operation between the two parties raises questions about whether the Liberal Democrats still have a distinctive role.

Consequences of two parties

The existence of disciplined, one-party-majority governments has made Britain distinctive (in comparison with the USA, with its separation of powers, and Western European States, which often have coalitions). The party system in Britain is associated with:

1. A strong executive. The Cabinet can rely, for the most part, on its disciplined majority in the Commons to pass legislation, and the ability of Parliament to resist ministers is accordingly weakened. But the strength of British government in relation to the Commons says little of its ability to impose its will on other groups. During the 1970s and early 1980s, successive Cabinets faced enormous difficulty in persuading major interest groups to agree to their policies. It is one of the measures of Margaret Thatcher's political success that she was able to overcome such opposition and sustain the tradition of strong, executive government at even higher levels. Tony Blair clearly wishes to follow this example.

2. Party government. British government is concentrated (a) in one party, and (b) in the Cabinet. In the absence of federalism, a written constitution, an independent legislature or coalitions, one party with a parliamentary majority enjoys virtually complete control over the law-making process.

3. Voters have a clear choice. Because parties are disciplined and programmatic there is a good chance that the majority party can enact its proposals. It can, accordingly, be judged on its record at the next election. In contrast, the separation of powers in the USA and the need for coalitions in much of Western Europe prevent the emergence of responsible party government (i.e. voters are unable to vote directly for one party to constitute the government and hold it responsible at the next election).

4. Consensus. During the 1950s and 1960s there was broad agreement between the parties on the mixed economy and the Welfare State. Because the parties were closely matched in votes and small swings decided the result, they pitched their appeals at floating voters in the 'moderate' centre. This encouraged a convergence of policies. In the 1980s, as we have seen, the consensus collapsed. The party which benefited from this was Margaret Thatcher's Conservative Party. After a series of crushing election defeats, the Labour Party moved to the new centre ground, largely defined by the Conservative Party. By the 1990s it was possible to talk about a new consensus again, one which largely supported Thatcherite policies on privatisation, low inflation, low rates of income tax, trade union reforms and the role of the market economy (see Chapter 4 and Box 5.1).

Why parties?

One may justify parties on several grounds. Below we examine four supporting arguments, together with the performance of British parties.

1. Representation and choice. Parties aggregate the preference of millions of voters and the interests of groups. For example, as issues associated with religion, free trade and nationalism waned and class became more salient after 1918, so Labour gradually replaced the Liberals as the natural alternative to the Conservatives.

In the 1980s, as class lost some of its influence on voting behaviour and the two main parties lost popularity, so the centre parties gained support.

However, the public are not always presented with a clear choice. The traditional lines of division between the Conservative and Labour Parties – in contrast to their leaders' rhetoric and the claims of manifestos – have not been so sharp, if one considers their record in office. That Conservatives were against public expenditure and anti-interventionist in industry and prices and incomes is belied by Mr Heath's government record; that Labour were

---

Box 5.1 A consensual party system

In their book, *British Political Parties Today*, Garner and Kelly discern a new 'social market' consensus comprising:

1. An acceptance that individual freedom, rather than equality, is the philosophical backdrop to modern political activity and that the role of the State must be strictly limited.
2. An acceptance that a modern economy must be based upon capitalist criteria, market practices and consumer choice.
3. An acceptance that the mixed economy of the 1970s has been remixed, irreversibly and justifiably, in favour of private enterprise.
4. An acceptance that trade unions should be mainly concerned with the needs of individual members and that any return to the status they enjoyed in the 1970s would be inappropriate.
5. An acceptance that the State retains vital responsibilities for the public's welfare (particularly health and education) but that they should be reworked to give more importance to consumer choice, cost-effectiveness, managerial efficiency and value for money.
6. An acceptance that macroeconomic management has been curtailed by European integration and a globalised economy.
7. An acceptance that the social and economic shake-up of the 1980s may have weakened social cohesion and that steps should now be taken to rekindle a certain type of collectivism, variously described as 'citizenship', 'unity values', 'stakeholder society' and 'one-nation Toryism'.

Source: Garner and Kelly, *British Political Parties Today*, Manchester University Press, 1998, pp. 29–34.

---

pro-nationalisation is hardly supported by the performance of the Wilson government in the 1960s.

In recent years many new issues – not easily accommodated within traditional party dogfights – have developed. On electoral reform, devolution for Scotland and Wales, welfare reform and Europe, particularly the single currency, the divisions within parties have been nearly as significant as those between them. The parties were never as monolithic or united as was indicated in the division lobbies.

2. Government. Parties are effective in staffing and organising the political part of the executive. But, when in government, how effective are they in realising their intentions? They may enact legislative proposals promised in manifestos, but what about the consequences supposed to follow from them – economic growth, better health care, more skilled workforce, etc.? Growing disillusion has been fuelled by a pervasive failure of British governments, e.g. membership of the Exchange Rate Mechanism, poll tax, and disappoint-ment with the results of institutional reforms in local government and the health service.

If parties in government have so little effect it may be because:

(a) *Parties are poorly prepared in opposition*. In opposition, policies are formu-lated with little consultation with the civil service and relevant interest groups. In office, ministers deal with permanent civil servants, who often have greater information and expertise. There are many examples of pro-posals which have been inadequately thought out (e.g. the Conserva-tives' poll tax). By applying tests of administrative (and political) practicability, civil servants confront ministers with 'on-going reality'. And when parties come into office, it is noted, they change only a hun-dred or so top decision-makers. Ministers usually lack the skills (man-aging a large organisation, policy-making), the permanence (they change every two years on average) and the partisan commitment to impose their will on the civil service.

(b) *Power is dispersed in the modern, complex British society*. In office, parties have to cope with the same major interest groups and the constraints imposed by economic resources and international commitments. Labour has to take account of business opinion and foreign holders of sterling to encourage investment and maintain confidence in the pound, just as Conservatives have to live with the trade unions. After 1976 Labour's economic policy was shaped in part by the agreement with the Interna-tional Monetary Fund which made a large loan available to help ster-ling, and John Major's government was constantly hampered by the need to agree policy with EU partners. Both parties have to deal with the same lobbies of pensioners, farmers, etc., and take account of agreements with international organisations. Much public expenditure is already spoken for by on-going programmes. So the 'realities' of group politics (Beer) again limit fundamental change. In part this explains why parties are less radical in office than they promised to be in opposition, and why the Labour left and the Conservative right, who want sharp change, feel aggrieved.

But consider the impact of Margaret Thatcher since 1979. It is interesting to consider the record of the Thatcher government in the light of the above argument. The government proclaimed its determination to break with many of the policies pursued by post-war governments. The rise in public spending and taxation as shares of Gross Domestic Product between 1979 and 1990 provides two measures of the government's failure. But in many other respects – e.g. privatisation, refusal to reflate the economy (even with unemployment at over 3 million), legislation on trade unions and industrial relations, rejection of bargaining with the social partners (unions and employers), reforms of the professions and its policies towards local governments – it showed that a determined government can impose many of its policies.

3. Participation. The two main parties now attract fewer members, voters and supporters (i.e. strong identifiers with them) than in the 1950s and 1960s, although Labour has recovered since 1994. The Labour and Conservative share of the electorate has slumped from an average of 72 per cent (1945–70) to about 50 per cent in 1997. In the past twenty years the proportion of strong identifiers with Labour or Conservative has fallen by half. Voters have turned away because of:

(a) *Social change*, e.g. the weaker class alignment. By 1997 less than half voted with their 'natural' class party.
(b) *The performance of the parties in office*, which has led to doubts about their competence, particularly Labour in 1979 and the Conservatives in 1997.
(c) *Dislike of the two main parties' policies* and their apparent identification with sectional pressure groups – business, in the case of the Conservatives, and the trade unions, in that of Labour before Blair.

4. Consent. Party government derives its legitimacy from being freely elected and being continuously accountable to Parliament.

'Ins' and 'outs'

A realistic perception of the parties must take account of the limits of what a party can achieve in government. There remain several continuities between them in actual policies and performance when they are in government. A party in opposition often presents a very different image from the government of the day and from what it itself did when last in office. It wants to oppose the government; it is relatively free to talk, to make promises and not to take tough and unpopular decisions. There is a change, however, when it is in government, faced by the same constraints and pressures as its much criticised predecessor. Might the significant difference between the parties be a consequence of 'ins' and 'outs', i.e. a matter largely of rhetoric and promises, lasting only as long as each is in opposition?

Party organisation

The Labour Party has a complex structure and its commitment to intra-party democracy has often proved troublesome for the leadership. The party Conference meets annually for five days; it represents the mass membership and in theory is the sovereign body. It elects the National Executive Council (NEC), which directs the work of the party on behalf of Conference. Until 1998, the twenty-nine members of the NEC included twelve members elected by the entire Conference, seven members elected by the constituency parties, one member for the Young Socialists, one member for the Socialist Society, and seats are reserved for the Labour leader and deputy leader of the party. In the 1970s the NEC and Conference came under left-wing control, and the left demanded that both bodies be given greater power *vis-à-vis* Labour MPs. Neil Kinnock gradually asserted his control over both bodies. He planned to reduce the roles of the trade union block vote and of Conference in making policy.

Tony Blair has carried Kinnock's project further and made Labour a leader-driven party. Blair has got his own way in the National Executive and at party Conference. The central theme of Blair's leadership has been *modernisation*, and he points to his reforms of the party as proof of his effectiveness. New proposals passed at the 1997 Conference will change not just the structure but also the culture of the party. The leadership is determined to prevent a return to the situation of the 1970s and early 1980s, when Conference and the NEC challenged the parliamentary leadership, even when Labour was in government. The adversarial format of Conference provided great scope for left-wing activists, and the bitter debates, covered by television, damaged the reputation of the party. The leadership is looking for a more deliberative style of policy-making, an NEC which is a partner to the parliamentary leadership and a Conference which provides more of a supporting rally. The Policy Forum, in which the initiative lies with the parliamentary leaders, will take more control of policy. The NEC has been increased from twenty-nine to thirty-two, with a maximum of three ministers and three MPs, to be elected respectively for ministers' and MPs' sections. Tony Blair has increasingly used the ballots of ordinary members to out-flank the party Conference and party activists. They approved by large margins his rewriting of Clause 4 of the constitution in 1995 and the early manifesto in 1996. In government there is a new Joint Policy Committee, chaired by the Prime Minister, with equal members from the NEC and government, who work together on policy developments and campaigns.

In the Conservative Party the authority of the party leader is clearer. The annual Conference discusses resolutions but its votes are not binding on the leadership. The leader has unfettered control over appointments to senior posts in Central Office (in Labour these are made by the NEC) and over the Shadow Cabinet (which is elected by MPs when Labour is in opposition). For more details, see Chapter 9.

The future

Possibilities include:

1. A return to the two-party normalcy of pre-1970. Elections will be a 'simple' either/or choice between Labour and Conservative. But a restoration of the 'old' two-party system assumes a substantial reduction in support for the Liberal Democrats, say to 12 per cent or less. In the four general elections (1979–92), Labour trailed the Conservatives by an average 10 per cent share of the vote. The 1997 election did not produce a return to competitiveness either, with the Conservatives now trailing Labour by 13 per cent of the vote and 179 seats.

2. Continued fragmentation, leading to minority governments like that of February 1974 and the deadlock of 1977–79. A government may be elected with a majority of seats on less than 40 per cent of the vote. Any of these outcomes is likely to encourage demands for electoral reform and may be more likely to follow its introduction. In 1997 support for third parties (i.e. voters who did not support the Conservative or Labour Parties) still accounted for over 27 per cent of the total vote and the 'other' parties returned a record number of seats. After 1992 many Labour MPs became more sympathetic to proportional reform because they thought it was the best way to oust the Conservatives. Since 1997 the Liberal Democrat and Labour Parties have worked together on a number of constitutional proposals and are committed to holding a referendum on proportional representation. Electoral reform has been agreed anyway for elections to the Scottish parliament and Welsh assembly.

3. Coalitions. In Britain these have been adopted for specific purposes (e.g. war in 1916 and 1940) and dissolved when the crisis passed. They have not been regarded as part of 'normal politics'. In summer 1997 Tony Blair invited a number of Liberal Democrats to join a Cabinet committee on constitutional issues. This has been seen as a version of the LibLab pact of the late 1970s. The good relations between the parties and the agreement on many policy areas mean that if proportional representation, or parliamentary deadlock, came about then the Conservatives could be out of power for a very long time. Some commentators see this as part of Blair's long-term project of making Labour the normal party of government by broadening its support and damping the left.

4. One-party government. It is a sign of the unpredictability of politics – or the short-termism of much political commentary – that we now focus on the decline of the Conservative Party and the possible hegemony of the Labour Party, after a decade of speculation that Labour was unlikely to form a government on its own again.

Further reading

A. R. Ball, *British Political Parties: The Emergence of a Modern Party System*, Macmillan, 1987.

S. Beer, *Modern British Politics*, Faber, 1969.

S. Beer, *Britain Against Itself*, Faber, 1982.

M. Duverger, *Political Parties*, Methuen, 1967.

S, Finer (ed.), *Adversary Politics and Electoral Reform*, Wigram, 1974.

R. Garner and R. Kelly, *Political Parties in Britain Today*, Manchester University Press, 1998.

S. Ingle, *The British Party System*, Basil Blackwell, 1987.

R. Rose, *The Problem of Party Government*, Macmillan, 1974.

Questions

1 Should there be more or fewer policy differences between the parties?
2 Consider the advantages and disadvantages of (*a*) coalition government, (*b*) minority government.
3 Analyse the pressures upon governments to move away from the policies they advocated in opposition.

6

The changing constitution

The terms 'constitution' and 'constitutional' usually refer to:

(a) an authoritative document or set of rules which describes the powers and duties of government institutions and the relations between them; or
(b) a spirit or style of politics, usually one in which there is a balance between the different institutions or which provides for a restraint on the holders of power.

Britain has a constitution, but not in sense (a). It is not unwritten but it is uncodified. Most written constitutions are adopted by States which are newly independent or have suffered a rupture in their evolution (e.g. France in 1958). In the case of Britain, we cannot date the system of government or set of rules as being constituted at one point in time. Rather, we talk about a system which has evolved over time.

The British system has been widely admired. Britain prepared written constitutions for many of the colonies when they became independent and many States, in drawing up constitutions, have tried to copy British features.

But the system, and therefore the constitution, came under stress in the 1970s. Most British political institutions and procedures faced some critical scrutiny in this period and the questioning spilled over to the constitution itself. The rise of Nationalist parties in Scotland and Wales and the collapse of British authority in Northern Ireland were examples of internal challenges to the constitution. Entry to the EC posed an external challenge. The Stormont parliament in Northern Ireland was suspended in 1972, and in 1979 Parliament passed bills to set up elected assemblies in Scotland and Wales, subject to referendum approval. Dissatisfaction has led to suggestions for other reforms, including a major constitutional settlement (e.g. by Lord Hailsham in the mid-1970s).

In the 1980s the large majorities enjoyed by the Thatcher governments to some extent weakened the pressure in the House of Commons for constitutional change. Nationalist support in Scotland and Wales did not increase, and support for the Alliance declined after 1987. Yet, paradoxically, the disproportional electoral system which gave Mrs Thatcher her large majorities in the Commons, and concern at the way her government used its majority, increased the Labour Party's interest in constitutional change – or limits on governments. The Charter 88 movement also helped to keep the issue prominent. Before considering reform proposals, this chapter looks first at the British constitution today.

Sources of the British constitution

1. Common law, or traditions and customs administered by the old common law courts, such as freedom of expression, which have come to be accepted as constituting the law of the land.

2. Laws:

(a) Statutory, or parliamentary, law overrides common law and provides a substantial written part of the constitution. It includes such measures as the Act of Union, 1707, successive Representation of the People Acts, the Bill of Rights, 1689, etc.
(b) Judges' interpretations of statute law, or 'judicial review', as it is called. Judges do not decide on the validity of laws duly passed by Parliament but on whether the law has been applied properly.

3. Conventions. These are rules which, lacking the force of law, have been adhered to for so long that they are regarded as binding. Examples include the resignation of the Prime Minister following defeat on a no-confidence vote in the Commons and the Sovereign's assent to a bill passed through Parliament. But the force of a convention depends on its being observed, and continued breaches – of the principle of the Cabinet's collective responsibility, for example – will weaken its strength.

Conventions loom large as an element in the British constitution: they are the key to its flexibility. Many essential features of the political system – e.g. ministerial responsibility, collective responsibility, occasions for a dissolution of Parliament and constitutional monarchy – are all largely the product of convention.

Consequences

1. The absolute and unlimited power of Parliament. An Act of Parliament is not constrained by any higher law; the courts cannot set aside, but only interpret, statute law; and there is no judicial review to compare with the role of the Supreme Court in the USA. Local and regional authorities only derive their powers from central government, and these may be rescinded (e.g. the abolition of Stormont in 1972; the abolition of metropolitan counties in the 1980s). The one exception to the absolute sovereignty of Parliament is, of course, *the provisions of the treaties which Britain has signed as a member of the EU*. These override domestic law.

2. The only check on the executive supported by a majority in the House is its sense of self-restraint and the need to bargain with groups, appease backbenchers and respect opposition rights in the Commons. In a famous lecture in 1976 Lord Hailsham argued that these checks were no longer sufficient: the decline of the Lords and the monarchy, the growth of party discipline and the more interventionist legislation, and Cabinet domination over the Commons meant that parliamentary sovereignty is actually an 'elective dictatorship'. Hailsham argued that a party-whipped House of Commons was no longer an adequate defender of the citizen's liberties and that a written constitution which ensures a legal limitation on the powers of Parliament might constrain the executive as the mixed constitution once did. When his party was in power, however, after 1979, Hailsham's enthusiasm for change faded.

3. The British style is not legalistic. It is pragmatic, intuitive, flexible and differs from the legalism found in some Western European States. Laws are often expected to follow behaviour, and the courts are expected to keep free from politics. But this is changing (see below). There are various pressures for a formal statement of the rules, i.e. a written constitution. The demand has been stimulated in part by a general dissatisfaction with the performance of the political system and the call for reform; in part by fear of a more interventionist government, against which citizens have little protection, and the spate of constitutional changes in recent years (see below). The latter illustrate the flexibility of the system but also reflect less agreement on the 'rules of the game'.

Innovations to the British constitution

Note the following recent innovations, either implemented or planned:

1. Referendums. So far these have been regarded as consultative, not binding; thus Parliament's formal sovereignty is preserved. But is there a need for rules on the occasions when referendums will be held and an authority to decide on the wording of the questions? The most powerful demands for referendums have been voiced in connection with constitutional matters, e.g. reform of the Lords in 1910–11, entry to and membership of the EC, and devolution for Wales and Scotland. It is interesting that party leaders have usually turned to them when their own party was divided on an issue, as Labour was over Europe in 1975 and on devolution in 1979.

But with the election of a new Labour government in 1997 referendums have become a part of the constitution. Within a few months referendums were held on devolution for Scotland and Wales, the election of a mayor for London, the peace agreement in Northern Ireland and further ones are promised over the electoral system and in the event of British membership of a single European currency. In the 1970s the decision to hold referendums was controversial; interestingly, today they do not excite any controversy. It is probably safe to say that no major constitutional change will now be made without prior approval by referendum.

2. Membership of the EU. This means that substantial elements of a written constitution are already part of the British system. Other British authorities now have to accept rules and regulations embodied in the original treaty, commitments flowing therefrom and further decisions taken by Community institutions. Note that all other EU States operate with written constitutions; Britain is the odd one out. And in cases of conflict between the British government and EU institutions, British courts will have to decide on the legality of Acts of Parliament.

3. Demands for a Bill of Rights that will be entrenched (i.e. Parliament either cannot override it or can do so only with great difficulty). One step is the planned formal incorporation of the provisions of the European Convention of Human Rights, which Britain ratified in 1951 but has not yet been enacted into law. This would enable citizens to take cases directly to British courts. It would also grant citizens the right of privacy and might be used against media intrusion. The new Labour government has said that it will incorporate the convention, but it may enter Britain anyway if the EU adopts it.

4. Tutelary law, which imposes codes of conduct. In contrast to the traditional British emphasis on negative liberty (see Chapter 3), governments have intervened more often to regulate formerly private areas of conduct, e.g. race relations, sexual discrimination and industrial relations.

5. Devolution. The failure of devolution to come about in 1979 made it a 'dead' issue in the 1980s. But under the Thatcher governments Scotland's sense of separation from England increased. Labour commanded a huge majority of seats in Scotland but trailed badly in England. Many Scots felt that they were ruled by an 'alien' (i.e. English) Tory government. There was much resentment at the fact that the poll tax was introduced early in Scotland and that Conservative governments showed little sympathy for demands for devolution or decentralisation. Labour, Liberal Democrats and a number of other groups organised a Scottish Convention to call for devolution, and opinion polls showed strong support.

The demise of the Conservative Party in Scotland (and Wales) in the 1997 general election showed how out of touch the Conservatives were. In September 1997 the Scots voted in a referendum by a clear majority for a Scottish parliament, which would have legislative and tax-raising powers. The 'yes' campaign was fought by a coalition of Labour, Liberal Democrat and Nationalist parties. The outcome in Wales was much narrower and was carried by a majority of less than 1 per cent. The powers of the assembly are more limited and confined to oversight of the powers of the Secretary of State for Wales. In the longer term, questions remain about what will happen in cases of conflict between Westminster and a parliament in Scotland and whether (as claimed by Conservatives) devolution will be a step on the road to the break-up of the UK. It is worth noting that Scotland (and Wales) already has more MPs than its electoral population justifies. There is also the so-called West Lothian question – the right of Scottish MPs to vote on UK legislation but the inability of non-Scottish MPs to vote on Scottish legislation. Some may also object to a continuation of Scotland (and Wales) enjoying a higher share of public spending per head than England, while also having its own parliament (see Box 6.1).

6. The House of Lords. The existence of hereditary peers in the House of Lords has long been opposed by many in the Labour Party. They have objected to it on democratic grounds (why should non-elected peers have voting rights?) and because hereditary peers are overwhelmingly Conservative. The new Labour government has pledged to abolish the voting rights of hereditary peers.

It is also considering further changes. The problem is that extending a Prime Minister's power to appoint life peers risks making the House of Lords an echo chamber of the House of Commons. On the other hand, an elected second chamber may threaten the democratic mandate of the House of Commons (see Chapter 13).

7. Multi-partyism. Coalitions are the norm in most Western European States. In Britain the Crown has only a minimal role when it comes to appointing a Prime Minister or granting a dissolution. This role may become more significant, and politically controversial, with coalitions or minority governments. Coalitions may also place collective responsibility under greater strain. The introduction of proportional representation is likely to reduce the prospects of any one party having a majority of seats in the Commons.

8. Northern Ireland. To date this has proved to be an insoluble problem. Governments have experimented: in the last twenty years there have been elec-

Box 6.1 Celtic fringe gets more cash than English regions

In 1976 a study revealed a bias in favour of Scotland and Wales in terms of calculated need in relation to money spent. In 1978 Labour's Chief Secretary to the Treasury, Joel (now Lord) Barnett, devised a formula to distribute public money fairly to the Celtic fringe. His formulation – basically, England 85 per cent, Scotland 10 per cent and Wales 5 per cent (with an adaptation for Northern Ireland allowing for security costs) – has been in place ever since except for minor adjustments in 1992. According to it, the substantially devolved functions – education, health, housing, local government funding, agriculture and (in Scotland) police, prisons and legal affairs – in Scotland and Wales received £14.3 and £6.9 billion, respectively, in 1995. In the early 1970s Scottish GDP per head was lower than the British average and it suffered from poorer health and housing, and higher unemployment. However, since then the Scots have fared better (see Figure 6.1) and have pulled up to near equality, though Wales still lags behind. In Cabinet, proposals to reduce funding were always overcome by the prediction that cuts would play right into the hands of the nationalists and that argument held sway throughout the Tory years. However, now devolution is a fact views are changing and tempers rising. Sir George Russell, Chairman of the Northern Development Company, which lobbies for overseas investment, complained in November 1997 that 'The Barnett Formula is no longer necessary or just. We [the North East] are now the poorest region in the UK.' But if spending levels in Scotland were reduced to English levels the new Scottish government would be £1 billion short annually. Admittedly, the new parliament can raise taxes by 3 pence in the pound but even this maximum provision would only produce £450 million. Unless the system of distributing public funds to the regions is fundamentally overhauled, progress towards devolution will run into severe political storms.

Figure 6.1   *Relative GDP per head, 1995*

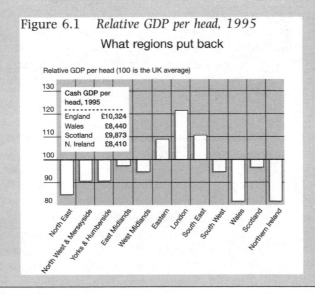

What regions put back

Relative GDP per head (100 is the UK average)

Cash GDP per head, 1995
- - - - - - - - - - - - - - - - -
England   £10,324
Wales   £8,440
Scotland   £9,873
N. Ireland £8,410

tions for a constitutional convention, a referendum and proportional representation elections. In each case these were constitutional innovations which no government envisaged for the UK. Their adoption reflected the politicians' awareness of the exceptional nature of the Ulster problem. Interestingly, during the years when governments have been prepared to consider greater devolution of decision-making for Scotland and Wales, they have moved in a different direction in Ulster. Four different forms of rule have been tried: (a) majority rule, pre-1972; (b) direct rule, 1972–74; (c) a power-sharing executive, 1974; and (d) direct rule again, 1974 onwards.

In April 1998 the lengthy peace negotiations in Northern Ireland concluded with an agreement which was approved in an all-Ireland referendum in May. This provided for a Northern Ireland assembly to be elected proportionally and voting proceedings in the asssembly designed to ensure that its decisions are taken on a cross-community basis. Policing and the criminal justice system are to be reviewed by independent bodies.

Other possibilities considered include:

(a) *Integration with the UK*, so that Ulster would be like, say, Liverpool or Birmingham. This would give the British government greater powers than it had before 1972, though it would provide Ulster politicians with more local self-government and probably rule out any possibility of an eventual united Ireland.

(b) *Integration with the Irish Republic*, with some guarantees for the Protestant minority. But Britain has pledged that it will consider this only if the majority support it (which they do not), and there is the probability that some Protestant groups will resist it by force, as they pledged to do before 1914.

(c) *A British withdrawal*. This would be a declaration of failure and impotence by the British government. It might lead to even more violence between Protestant and Catholic armed groups, or force the two sides to come to some political agreement in an independent Ulster.

(d) *Repartition of the border*, to give one or more of the six counties to the Irish Republic. This may lessen sectarian tension in Ulster, but it still fails to meet the goal of those who want a united Ireland.

In April 1998 a constitutional settlement was agreed by all parties to the conflict, but dissenting minorities posed a continuing threat.

How the constitution changes

In most States the written constitution may be amended through a formal process, e.g. by referendum or a vote by a two-thirds majority in the legislature. In Britain constitutional changes involving statute law are made in the normal way; e.g. altering the powers of the Lords in 1911 and 1949 was achieved via a simple majority vote in both Houses. Some changes have been controversial and politically divisive, such as reform of the Lords, extensions to the suffrage in the nineteenth century, Irish home rule and Ulster today, and devolution. They came about less by general agreement than by one party using its parliamentary majority to push a change through which was then gradually accepted. Changes in conventions tend to be more gradual and recognised as such only after the passage of time, e.g. that the Prime Minister should be in the Commons, not the Lords, and the weakening of the monarchy's political role.

Pressures for change

Because arguments for constitutional reform have often sought to place limits on a government's discretion and increase checks and balances, neither of the two usual parties of government, Labour and Conservative, have shown much interest. In the 1970s a number of Labour MPs regarded proposals for proportional representation and limits on government as part of an anti-Labour campaign.

In the late 1980s, however, some non-Conservative groups formed Charter 88, which revived the issue of constitutional reform. Demands for reform broadened beyond the Liberals and Social Democrats, and support now extends across much of the Labour, Liberal Democratic and Nationalist parties. Indeed, the constitution has emerged as a new divide between the Conservative and other parties. In the 1992 and 1997 general elections, the Conservatives ruled out any change to the Union (notably a parliament for Scotland) or to the electoral system. On the other hand, the Labour Party accepted much of the traditional Liberal reform agenda. In the 1997 election it was committed to devolution, reform of the House of Lords, a Freedom of Information Act, revival of local government and the protection of civil liberties. It is also prepared to hold a referendum on electoral reform. Tony Blair's programme of 'modernisation' includes reform of the political system. The Labour Party, largely because of its long period in opposition, became less attracted to the consequences of the first-past-the-post electoral system and the sovereignty of Parliament. For much of the twentieth century these two essential features of the British constitution have worked to the benefit of the Conservative Party.

It is also likely that the allegations and evidence of sleaze among MPs in the 1990s, improper behaviour of ministers uncovered in the Scott Report, and the appointment of political 'placemen' to quangos brought the political system into discredit. The recent appointment of the Nolan Committee and a code of conduct for MPs is one effect. Demand for constitutional reform is another. Since 1997, the Conservatives have been more open to constitutional reform.

It seems doubtful that constitutional change will end with devolution for Scotland and Wales. Over time, there may develop demands by the regions for greater self-government or even a *backlash by England*. In other words, once begun the process may lead in unanticipated directions.

The case for a written constitution

1. The view that power in Britain is too centralised and that the sovereignty of Parliament is open to abuse by any government. Demands for a written constitution are part of a broader belief that limited government is good *per se*, is under threat and should be safeguarded. Often, these demands are advanced by opposition politicians who do not like what the government of the day is doing. Governments, on the other hand, have little incentive to restrain their own powers. Constitutional reform includes electoral reform, devolution, revitalising local government, a Bill of Rights, safeguarding the House of Lords and other devices, which have the effect of promoting checks and balances against the government of the day (see reference to Hailsham above).

2. The need for statutory protection of individual liberties, e.g. by a Bill of Rights.

3. The need for certainty and clarity about the 'rules of the game'. At present in the matter of many conventions, the constitution is effectively what the government decides.

Objections to a written constitution

These may be advanced on grounds of:

1. Tradition. Having survived without one for so long, why start now?

2. Redundancy. The existing system works reasonably well. The 'rules' are widely understood, and the government's sense of self-restraint and awareness of its dependence on a parliamentary majority amount to a sense of 'constitutional morality'. There is no guarantee that a completely written constitution would be better.

3. Inappropriateness to the British style of conducting politics (see above) and the difficulty of agreeing on a new constitution (at the very least it would be enormously time-consuming). But the major barrier to introducing a written constitution is the hallowed principle of the sovereignty of Parliament, which backbenchers and governments defend as and when it suits them. No Parliament (and hence no law) can bind its successors. Neither of the two major parties has shown much interest in limiting its own power in this way.

4. Practical difficulties. The main problem in a new settlement is to find a set of rules which is acceptable to different viewpoints. This is crucial if a new set of rules is to be legitimate. The first step, presumably, would be to establish a Constitutional Commission, which in turn would submit proposals to a referendum. However, legislation affecting entry to the EC and devolution dominated parliamentary debate and the legislative timetable in the 1970s, and any future government is therefore unlikely to provide the legislative time necessary for constitutional reform. Moreover, it would give greater power to the unelected judiciary at the expense of the elected Parliament.

Further reading

W. Bagehot, *The English Constitution* (first published 1867), Collins, 1963.
Lord Hailsham, 'Elective dictatorship', *The Listener*, 21 October 1977.
Lord Hailsham, *On the Constitution*, HarperCollins, 1992.
P. Norton, 'Should Britain have a written constitution?', *Talking Politics*, 1988.
P. Norton, 'Europe and the constitution', *Talking Politics*, 1994.
P. Riddell, *Parliament under Pressure*, Gollancz, 1998.
F. Ridley, 'What happened to the constitution under Mrs Thatcher?', in B. Jones and L. Robins (eds), *Two Decades in British Politics*, Manchester University Press, 1992.

Questions

1 How might the achievement of the reformers' constitutional agenda in the 1990s change the style of British politics?
2 Explain the advantages and disadvantages of an unwritten constitution.
3 Comment on the view that a written constitution would place a further, major restraint upon a conservative country in great need of radical constitutional change.

7

The electoral system
and representation

This chapter examines the work of the electoral system and the cases for and against change. It also considers other problems about representation. Finally, it examines developments in campaigning.

The electoral system

An electoral system is a set of rules for translating popular votes into seats in the legislature. It is also the established method of electing representatives, e.g. a legislature, government or head of State. There are broadly two types of electoral system:

(a) *First past the post*, or the Anglo-American system. In this the candidate with the most votes wins, whether or not he or she has a majority of all the votes. This type of system is found, for example, in Britain, Canada, the United States and India.
(b) *Proportional representation (PR)*. Seats in the legislature are allocated in approximate proportion to the distribution of popular votes. There are many different forms of PR (see below).

The two types of electoral system exemplify two different ideals. The Anglo-American system emphasises majoritarianism, and usually produces a majority for one party or group of parties. In post-war Britain, except for February 1974, it has always yielded a majority of seats in Parliament for one party. The proportionality systems emphasise the importance of representativeness. The first system works best where there are two parties or a dominant party, and consent is more easily obtained from the minority if there are not sharp divisions in society (e.g. Northern Ireland). Another way of protecting the rights of minorities is to have federalism, a Bill of Rights or a separation of powers, as in the United States. The proportional system can also achieve a stable government, even though it may be a minority or a coalition government.

1. The working of the British system. There may be a marked disproportionality between seats and popular votes, and a bias which exaggerates the 'winning' party's share of the vote (see Table 9.2). The elections of 1951 and February 1974 were instances when the party with most votes did not have the most seats. Yet the second party is usually prepared to accept the outcome, because it has the chance of full power at the next election and because Britain has been largely a consensual society. In the 1970s and 1980s the rise in popular support for the Liberal and Alliance Parties produced more disproportional outcomes and fuelled demands for the introduction of PR.

2. Demands for electoral reform. PR was first raised in 1831 and attracted support throughout the nineteenth century. A Speaker's Conference recommended the adoption of the alternative vote (though not a proportional system) in 1917 and the proposal nearly gained a parliamentary majority. The Liberal Democrats, and their predecessor, the Liberals, have long campaigned for reform, because they always lost out under the present system. Pressure has grown in recent years from the EU. The Commission wants member States to move to a common electoral system for elections to the European Parliament. All States except the United Kingdom have a form of PR. Another pressure is from the Labour government plans for devolution for Scotland and Wales which include a list system of PR similar to that in Germany. Each elector will have two votes, one for a constituency MP elected under *first past the post*, and one for a *list* of candidates drawn up by the party. In the case of the Welsh assembly, forty will be elected under the first arrangement, twenty under the latter. For the Scottish parliament, seventy-three will be elected under the first system, fifty-six under the latter. The list members will be elected as additional members to bring a party's number of seats closer to its share of the vote.

The *additional member system* has the merits (for some) of retaining the link between an MP and the constituency, and it keeps power in the hands of party managers (to draw up the list).

Labour is also committed to hold a referendum in the 1997 parliament on the use of PR for Westminster elections. If PR is used for Scotland and Wales and perhaps for the European elections, the pressure is likely to increase for reform of the Westminster system.

The arguments examined

For the present system

(a) The single-member system allows the voter to choose a single representative. The link with the constituency MP is weakened if there are multi-member constituencies and the list of candidates is proposed by the national parties.

(b) PR may increase the bargaining or 'blackmail' power of a small party if it holds the balance in a deadlocked Parliament.

(c) PR may provide representation for 'extremist' parties (e.g. the National Front or Socialist Workers' Party). In 1997 the Front ran fifty candidates to ensure that it gained a broadcast slot on television.

(d) If there are coalitions, then delay, avoidance of tough decisions and the absence of coherent policies are likely. Coalitions also weaken the idea of responsible party government (see below).

(e) At present voters can vote directly for a team and a set of policies. But if there are coalitions the programmes will emerge only after bargaining and deals between the parties. In 1993, Italians voted by a large majority to change from a proportional system to a first-past-the-post system. They were tired of an electoral system which produced weak coalitions and a lack of clear electoral choice.

For PR

(a) Under the present system a government may exercise full power even though it is supported by a small minority of the popular vote, e.g. Labour formed a majority government in October 1974 with only 39 per cent of the vote.

(b) The present system is unfair when a party's share of the vote is markedly under-represented in its share of the seats, as always happens to the Liberal Democrats and in 1997 even to the Conservatives in Scotland. Their 17.5 per cent of the Scottish vote brought the party no seats at all.

(c) A majority government (probably a coalition) would be more representative of public opinion because it would have at least 50 per cent of the vote.

(d) PR would overcome the geographical bias of the present system in which the North and South are usually, respectively, Labour and Conservative strongholds. After 1983 and 1987 the Conservatives had 85 per cent of the seats in the South for only 50 per cent of the vote and Labour had 60 per cent of the seats in northern England and Scotland for only 40 per cent of the vote. At present only a handful of Conservatives sit for any of the great cities where many of Britain's social problems are at their most intense.

(e) Some critics have argued that the present electoral system fuels the adversary party system. It is argued that PR would be likely to encourage consensus and continuity of policy.

Barriers to change

Electoral systems raise questions of political power, and self-interest therefore dictates the reactions of most politicians. Given that no British party has gained 50 per cent or more of the popular vote in the past sixty years, either minority or coalition governments would be the likely outcome of a more proportional electoral system. Conservative or Labour leaders would have to bargain and dilute their programmes in search of coalition partners. An effect of such a change is easily illustrated: instead of dominating the House of Commons with two-thirds of the seats in the 1980s, Margaret Thatcher's governments would under PR have been in a minority with only 42 per cent of the seats. The same is true of Tony Blair's today.

The demise of the SDP after 1987 removed one advocate of PR from the political scene, but the Charter 88 movement helped keep the issue alive. Its most important success so far has been to make the Labour Party embrace some of its recommendations. Some in the party have complained about the waste of Labour votes in much of the South, where until 1997 the party had had few MPs outside of London. Others were influenced by their closer links with Western European socialist parties, most of which operate PR systems. Although some Labour influentials are still opposed to electoral reform, and Tony Blair has said that he is not persuaded of the case for change, he has established a commission under Lord Jenkins and promised to hold a referendum on the issue.

The Conservatives are adamantly opposed to any change in the Westminster electoral system, not least because in government they are unlikely to be supported by Nationalist or Liberal Democrat MPs. The line-up of parties at present is Conservatives: anti-change; Liberals: pro-change; Labour: considering.

PR, however, might come about if a third party regularly does well in the elections or has enough seats to deny a majority to one or other of the major parties. The introduction of PR would simply acknowledge that Britain has moved to a multi-party system. Yet one has to realise that in supporting the introduction of PR some MPs would be risking their seats. During the 1980s the over-represented Conservative Party would have lost many MPs under a more proportional system. After the 1997 general election, it is Labour which would have shed seats.

Possible effects

One can only speculate about the consequences of a move to multi-partyism, coalitions or deadlocked Parliaments, because the situations are hypothetical. Britain has had coalition governments to cope with crises, e.g. the 1931 economic crisis and the two world wars. The short periods of minority rule, as in 1974 or 1977–79, were regarded as temporary, with a speedy restoration of two-party 'normality' anticipated. If multi-partyism and coalitions were established the likely changes would include:

1. Individual electors would have to calculate their votes. It would no longer be a simple choice between the government and opposition. The opportunity for tactical voting would increase (e.g. Labour voters in a safe Conservative seat might vote for a second-placed Liberal Democrat as the best way of defeating the Conservatives), although if a form of PR was introduced the arguments about a wasted vote would lose their strength.

2. The House of Commons would probably become more independent towards the executive and MPs more independent of the whips. There are many reasons for the decline of the House of Commons' influence over the executive, but the dominance of the government over the legislative timetable and party discipline have been important factors. The passage of legislation has been virtually guaranteed because the government of the day is backed by a disciplined party majority. With a coalition, however, government leaders may have to bargain more for support from backbenchers.

3. A change in the role of the Crown. As noted in the discussion of the constitution (Chapter 6), if there is no majority for one party the monarch may become involved in the choice of a new party leader to form a government and deciding whether or not to grant a Prime Minister's request for the dissolution of Parliament. The important point is that multi-partyism would challenge many accepted principles of the constitution, increase uncertainty and might expose the Crown to charges of political bias.

4. The Liberal Democrats permanently in government. With a proportional system the Liberal Democrats would probably have a key role in providing Conservative or Labour with a majority of seats. If there was a convergence of policies – as there is at present between Labour and the Liberal Democrats – then the losing main party could be excluded from office for a very long time.

Problems with representation

It is worth noting some of the issues which have been raised by commentators about representation in Britain.

1. Mandate. The claim that elections give a winning party a 'mandate' for every item in their manifesto has long been suspect, because:

(a) many party voters do not know the party's policies on many issues; and/or
(b) they disagree with these policies. In the 1970s and 1980s there was a marked disagreement on a number of issues between Labour voters and the policies of the Labour Party.

As the manifestos of parties have become longer and more detailed since 1945, so it is less likely that voters are aware of any party's position on many issues. Moreover, the vote is a crude instrument: voters cannot pick and choose between rival parts of the programmes. But we can say that the party which wins the election may claim broad approval for its programmes. Perhaps a more effective mechanism for testing the preferences of voters on particular issues is:

2. Referendums. By the end of 1997 these had been held in Britain once, in Northern Ireland once, and in Scotland and Wales twice. They were all held on issues which raised constitutional questions and usually on which the Labour Party was divided. Referendums obviously raise problems about the status of collective responsibility and parliamentary sovereignty, although to date they have been only advisory. They are certainly difficult to graft on to the system of parliamentary sovereignty and responsible party government. As mentioned in Chapter 6, referendums are becoming part of the British constitution, given the new Labour government's promise to hold so many.

3. Local versus national mandates. The programmes of national government override the programmes of local government. But in recent years, particularly since 1979, there have been a growing number of clashes between Whitehall and local authorities. In view of the steady incursion by the centre of the independence of local government – particularly over local spending – the point has arrived, according to some critics, when local democracy has been seriously eroded (see Chapter 19).

Another case of a clash of mandates arises with:

4. Pressure-group politics. Pressure groups provide an ancillary form of representation, one that is more specific and perhaps more vital to the individual. Trade union leaders, for example, may be 'mandated' by their members not to accept an incomes policy that has been approved by Parliament. This clash of mandates was seen in 1974 when the miners broke the statutory incomes policy of the Heath government (see Chapter 17).

5. Party democracy. One criterion of democracy is that voters have a choice at periodic elections between different political parties. The critics of this view ask: what if the parties are run by elites or by leaders who are unrepresentative of members and supporters? They argue that there should be democracies within the parties as well as a choice between them.

In Britain this view is called a theory of intra-party democracy and it is associated with the Labour Party. It means that the party members actually decide the policy and elect and hold the party leaders responsible for their actions. Labour Party values include a great respect for the views of the grassroots, acceptance of decisions by majority vote and anti-elitism.

The members are represented at the party's annual Conference. This is the supreme policy-making body of the party, and motions approved by a two-thirds majority automatically become part of the party programme (see also Chapter 5). Critics and advocates of intra-party democracy claim that Conference is supposed to instruct the Parliamentary Labour Party (PLP). An early resolution (1907) said that MPs should carry out the programme but the method and timing would be left to the PLP. Many of these ideas about the subordination of the PLP were developed before Labour had a substantial number of MPs (after 1918) or first formed a government (1924).

Constitutionally, Labour has *three different centres of authority* – Conference, the National Executive Council (NEC) and the PLP. In government the PLP has usually had its way, and under Harold Wilson and Jim Callaghan the Labour governments ignored the demands of Conference for more public spending, more public ownership and unilateral disarmament. A number of commentators argued that Labour's constitution, which included the possibility of ministers being instructed by an outside body, was incompatible with the British constitution. As Labour ministers ignored Conference, so in the 1980s there was a demand from the left for greater control (by Conference) of the leadership. The critics managed to get the party leader elected by an electoral college representing trade unions (40 per cent of the vote), constituency parties (30 per cent of the vote) and MPs (30 per cent of the vote), and mandatory reselection of MPs between elections. The proportions have since been reduced by a third each. This procedure was designed to make MPs more responsive to pressure from local activists.

After 1983, however, the power of the left waned as Kinnock's drive for electoral respectability gathered pace (see Chapter 4), the 'entryist' hard left Militant Tendency having been countered and the idea of socialism itself discredited as communist regimes collapsed in 1989. The call for 'one member, one vote' became the dominant theme in discussions about Labour Party internal democracy. This was successfully achieved under John Smith at the 1993 party Conference. By giving moderate rather than active members more say in local decision-making, especially candidate selection, this argument also worked against the left. Having campaigned so loudly for intra-party democracy it was a difficult argument for the left to answer.

It also had implications for block voting by trade unions at party Conference. According to this practice, trade union leaders were able to cast votes representing the total of their affiliated members, thereby at one time commanding five-sixths of the voting strength and control over the composition of the NEC. The five largest unions voting together could deliver a majority for or against any policy. Union leaders, however, now find it difficult to justify the block vote; they were able to mount a rearguard action against its proposed abolition at the end of the 1992 Blackpool Conference. Although some big unions came out against the abolition of the block vote for selection of candidates, they lost the vote at the October Conference. In 1995 the unions' share of Conference votes was reduced to 50 per cent. Ironically, this development might backfire on the moderate leadership. Union block votes ensured Kinnock's success in shifting the party into the centre: a Conference of individual delegates might prove more volatile and difficult to manage. Reform also signalled the end of the trade union block vote in the selection and reselection of candidates and party Conference votes. A system of one member, one vote was brilliantly exploited by Tony Blair's use of ballots in his campaigns to reform Clause 4 of the party constitution in 1995 and gaining approval for the early election manifesto in 1996 (see p. 53).

The *Conservative Party* is spared the exhaustive business of internal democracy which has so occupied Labour. The Tory leader presents a clear focus of authority, controlling the party organisation, and appointing the party chairman and director of the research department. Together with senior colleagues the leader decides party policies; the Conference has no policy role. The simple structure limits the opportunity for disputes to exist, but this does not mean that they do not burst forth from time to time. Arthur Balfour (Conservative Prime Minister 1902–5) appeared to express this free hand given to leadership by the Conservative rank and file when he said that he would rather accept the advice of his valet than that of the Party Conference. Richard Kelly's study of the Conference, however, argues that beneath the determined applause and polite contributions, Conference rank and file delegates transmit important messages: the 'mood' of the party is conveyed and this has policy implications. This analysis certainly seemed to fit the post-1991 Conservative Conferences where the 'Euro-sceptics' (those opposed to further EC political and economic integration), led by an abrasive Lord Tebbit, fostered a mood of anger and rejection which John Major was hard pressed to contain. In 1997 grassroots hostility to MPs, for their disloyalty to John Major and association with sleaze, strengthened the case for giving party members a significant say in the election of the leader.

Election campaigns

New technologies and communication skills, often derived from the United States and commerce, are transforming election campaigning. In 1997, for instance, Labour overtook the Conservative Party in the use of computers, managing the media, targeting key voters, exercising discipline and 'staying on message'. Party managers insist that its spokespeople stick to the designated issue of the day and follow the party's 'line'. In this way they can shape the agenda for the media. Tensions with reporters build up if they carry other news. Both the Conservative and Labour Parties now use computers for rapid rebuttal – to provide immediate responses to boasts or accusations by another party. Computer and telephone canvassing are used in constituencies to identify target voters (i.e. potential converts in marginal seats) to whom direct mail and other messages are sent.

Parties also use opinion polls and focus groups to test themes, tactics, advertisements and election broadcasts. Because television is the most widely

Table 7.1   *Party spending on general elections, 1964–97*

*(a) Central party spending on general elections – 1964–97 in millions of pounds
(figures in brackets are in real terms at 1997 values)*

	Tories	Labour	Lib Dems	Combined	
1964	£1.23	£0.5	not known		(21)
1979	£2.3	£1.6	£0.2	£4	(11.5)
1983	£3.8	£2.3	£1.9	£8	(15)
1987	£9.0	£4.7	£1.75	£15.5	(24)
1992	£11.2	£10.6	£1.8	£24	(27)
1997	£28.3	£26.0	£3.2	£57	(57)

(b) Expenditure on central party advertising in elections in thousands of pounds

	Tories		Labour	
	Press	*Posters*	*Press*	*Posters*
1979	£766	£591 (cinema £144)	£260	£354
1983	£1,725	£843	£878	
1987	£4,532	£1,834	£2,144	£309 (cinema £86)
1992	£1,800	£4,000	£1,500	£1,768
1997	£3,158	£11,091	£900	£5,000

Source: Michael Pinto Duschinsky, *The Times*, 14 April 1998.

used and widely trusted source of political information, parties direct their efforts to it. Rallies, press conferences and photo opportunities are designed and timed to attract peak television coverage. A reflection of the importance of modern communication skills is the trend for the parties to employ advertising agencies to handle their campaign communications. These features are sometimes described as an Americanisation of British politics. Modern campaigning is more continuous and expensive than ever. Labour engaged in such campaigning for nearly three years before the 1997 election. In the twelve months to polling day in 1997 (see Table 7.1), Labour indirectly spent over £13 million and the Conservatives over £20 million on campaigning. In the spring of 1998, Lord Neil's Committee on Standards in Public Life addressed the subject of party finance.

Box 7.1 Local campaigning works

At the 1998 Royal Geographical Society Conference, Professor Ron Johnston told delegates:

> If you have a big majority in a big constituency, say in Huntingdon, then there is no point in campaigning. Best to move to a marginal seat where a few votes swing it. The Tories failed to understand this and failed to get their workers to move out of their home areas. Labour, on the other hand, did not bother with seats they knew they could win and picked up the marginals. Anyone who says local campaigning makes no difference is clearly wrong. And now it seems the electoral system works to Labour's advantage.
>
> In the last election Labour got 43.5% of the vote and the Conservatives 30.5% giving the party a 179 majority. If 6.5% of the vote was taken from Labour and given to the Conservatives then each would have 37% – but Labour would still have won the election by 82 seats.

Source: Guardian, 8 January 1998.

Further reading

A. Birch, *Representative and Responsible Government,* Allen & Unwin, 1964.
D. Denver, *Elections and Voting Behaviour in Britain,* Philip Allan, 1994.
P. Dunleavy *et al.,* 'The electoral system', *Parliamentary Affairs,* October 1997.
D. Kavanagh, *Election Campaigning. The New Marketing of Politics,* Blackwell, 1995.

Questions

1 Why do the main parties take different views about electoral reform?
2 What criteria should be used in assessing an electoral system?

8

Opinion polls

Opinion polls have become so familiar an aspect of our politics that it is sometimes hard to appreciate their effective provenance is so recent.

The word 'effective' is significant as there is evidence that 'straw' polls were used as long ago as the presidential election of 1824. The *Harrisburg Pennsylvanian* and the *Raleigh Star* asked selected groups of citizens to gauge the popularity of particular candidates. The polls showed Andrew Jackson leading John Quincy Adams by 335 votes to 169. The method was haphazard and polls did not significantly emerge again politically until the 1920s, when the US magazine *Literary Digest* sent millions of postcards to voters seeking their views on presidential candidates.

It transpired, however, that no matter how big the survey, the results were skewed in accordance with the 'sample': the magazine's mailing excluded working-class people for the most part. In 1936 nemesis arrived in the form of poll predictions that Roosevelt would lose to Republican Alf Landon. Particularly embarrassing for the *Digest* was that a new breed of pollster, the 'Father of Modern Opinion Polling' (see Box 8.1), George Gallup, challenged the magazine's findings. Along with Elmo Roper, Gallup had devised a new way of polling based on the interviewing of relatively small numbers of respondents, selected more scientifically and interviewed by trained people. Using these methods Gallup and Roper predicted a Roosevelt victory. Gallup went further and enraged the *Digest* by predicting, six weeks before it was published, that their poll would show 56 per cent for Landon and only 44 per cent for the Democrat. Given their past record of success, the editor dismissed these upstart claims; when his poll did appear, however, it predicted 57 per cent for Landon and 43 per cent for Roosevelt. In the election Landon secured only 38.5 per cent of the vote. The *Digest* selected names for its postal surveys correctly on a random basis, but its samples were not representative of the electorate as a whole (see below on sampling) as they were based on lists of telephone subscribers and car owners: better off people, more likely to vote for the conservative Republican Party. In 1936 of course, the Democrats offered policies targeted at lower-paid people who voted in numbers unde-tected by the *Digest* survey. The magazine, already in difficulties, never recov-ered from the 1936 debacle. The new polling agencies followed up by calling correctly the presidential winners in 1940 and 1944, but in 1948 came an embarrassing mistake when the polls predicted a comfortable win for Thomas Dewey over Harry Truman; some newspapers believed them and one even ran an early edition announcing a Dewey win. In fact, as Nick Moon argues in his *Opinion Polls and British Politics*, the error was not as great as the polls in 1936, but they had called the wrong winner and suffered a damaging loss of confidence as a result. An inquiry into the polls revealed they had stopped interviewing too soon before the election and had missed a late swing to Truman. Moreover, the samples used tended to over-represent Republicans, ironically repeating the mistake of the ridiculed *Digest* in 1936.

Box 8.1 Dr George Gallup, the 'Father of Modern Opinion Polling'

Dr Gallup was born in 1901 and did much to make the opinion poll the ubiqui-tous feature of modern life it is today. He became Director of Research at New York's Young and Rubicam advertising agency and held this post from 1932 to 1947. While there he founded the American Institute of Public Opinion in 1935, and soon his clients included politicians as well as business organisa-tions, universities, newspapers and broadcasters. His sampling methods were widely adopted by other pollsters and he, more than anyone, deserves the title of 'Father of Opinion Polls'.

Polling in Britain can be dated to the establishment of the British Institute of Public Opinion (BIPO) in 1937, effectively the UK branch of Gallup. In 1938 the BIPO predicted a Labour win in the solidly Conservative by-election seat of West Fulham and was correct to within 1 per cent of the votes received. In 1945 Gallup asserted, against the prevailing received wisdom, that Labour had a 5 per cent lead. Newspapers, however, were sceptical and the evidence was not given a high profile. Labour's landslide caused pundits to look more closely at this brand-new technique, but in 1948 as we have seen, its credibility was badly damaged by the failure to predict the results of the Dewey–Truman presidential election.

Sampling

This is the key element in polling, as the idea is to test a sample of the public which is truly 'representative' of the whole. The analogy often used is that of a 'spoonful of soup', as Moon explains:

'If someone places a bowl of soup in front of me, and asks me what kind of soup it is, I do not need to eat the whole bowl before I can answer the question. Unless it is an unfamiliar soup, the first mouthful will identify the flavour. I need to have a good mouthful to have a reasonable chance of picking up the nuances of flavour: if I had a tiny sip I might fail to spot that the mainly oxtail soup had a few mushrooms in it.'

To obtain such a 'spoonful' it is necessary to adopt a correct sampling strategy:

1. Quota method. This approach is based on dividing the survey into blocks which represent the nature of the overall population; so there would be quotas reflecting, for example, geographical region, sex, age, race and social class. However, interviewers are given some discretion in choosing members of their quotas. They have, for example, to identify a certain number of working-class men aged 25–35 or older women aged 55–70. However, this discretion can be taken too far and inaccuracy can enter the results; for example, interviewers might neglect to pursue respondents who are out when contacted or who live in inaccessible places. Also, some quotas might be inappropriate; for example, they might require a given number of council house dwellers at a time when such residents are in sharp decline; or they might posit a given number of trade unionists when these too are an endangered species.

2. Random or 'probability' method. In this method statisticians use special tables to achieve wholly random lists of numbers. When such an approach is used for poll sampling the result is better than the quota approach as no group is excluded from the poll's reach. However, this approach is less flexible; the validity of this approach is dependent on contacting the respondents identified and they may not be in or may refuse.

3. Margin of error. Experience and mathematics suggest that a sample size of 1,500 has a margin of error of plus or minus 3 per cent. A larger sample produces a smaller margin of error but not by much, so that most polling organisations use samples of 1,000 to 2,000 voters.

Functions of polls

Polls have burgeoned since 1950, when only one or two were used. In 1992 eight organisations produced fifty-seven polls in eighteen different media outlets. In addition, specialist polls occurred for target groups such as women and those in key constituencies. Polls have become popular and they exert massive influence.

First, they affect party morale fundamentally. When a party rides high in the polls, morale is buoyant and party workers enthusiastic; when low it can affect the internal politics of the party. For example, Alec Douglas-Home was politely deposed as leader by the Conservatives in 1965 after poor polling results on his leadership performance. Even more significant was the groundswell in 1990 against a Prime Minister who had won three elections; Margaret Thatcher, heroine of the Tories, was undermined when polls suggested she was so unpopular that she was unlikely to make it four in a row.

Second, polls are also the chief means by which the dates of general elections are fixed. Prime Ministers and their political advisers pore over the polls to calculate the most advantageous time to 'go to the country'. In 1970 the polls suggested to Wilson that he would win if he went a year earlier than he needed; he miscalculated though and lost. In 1978 Callaghan decided the polls were insufficiently encouraging and decided to wait; when his string ran out in May 1979 the 'winter of discontent' had already done for him. Campaigns are also affected by polls taken during them. Wilson used evidence from private polls to concentrate on prices and inflation and ignore the 'who governs' theme which motivated Heath to call the election in 1974. In 1997 Major risked calling for a debate with Blair; his poor showing in the polls told him he had nothing to lose by the gamble.

Third, parties depend on polls when formulating policies. In the old days they used experienced pundits or commentators with a 'feel' for what the nation was thinking. Polls are more precise and give more reliable information. Private polls did much to shift Labour away from a leftish standpoint and into the centre under Kinnock, Smith and Blair. Polls revealed voters were deterred by Labour policies on defence (unilateralism); spending and concomitantly high taxes; and its apparent preference for 'losers' dependent on the State rather than those who took opportunities to better themselves through hard work.

In recent years poll evidence for policy formulation has perhaps been usurped by so-called 'focus groups': gatherings of representative groups who react to suggestions or marketing initiatives. In late 1997 it was said the monarchy had assembled a focus group to help it keep abreast of public opinion, and on Saturday 10 January 1998 the *Guardian* published the results of its own focus group on the monarchy.

Finally, polls are crucial in by-elections. Voters are able to gauge which candidate is most likely to defeat the sitting member and vote accordingly in a tactical fashion.

Validity of poll results

There are other factors which affect validity apart from sampling: interviewers must check respondents know something about the topic upon which they are being questioned; questions must be 'piloted' for clarity and lack of bias; the form of questions must avoid implying a particular answer; and interviewers must be trained to avoid influencing the answers given. It always has to be realised that polls are a 'snapshot' of opinion at any one time; they do not indicate an unchangeable state of opinion and in politics many people are in any case undecided or 'don't knows'.

Notwithstanding these reservations, opinion polls have had a good record overall. From 1945 to 1992 they were reasonably accurate, rarely out by more than 1 or 2 per cent or 2 to 3 per cent in the predicted gap between the parties. In 1970 Labour was ahead in the polls at the start of the campaign but lost on the day, causing a sensation and the unsupported theory that it was voters 'punishing' the government for England's loss to West Germany in soccer's Mexico World Cup.

Close study of the data, however, revealed it was the decision of polling organisations to cease activity a few days before election day; consequently, they missed the late swing to the Conservatives (which some attributed to a poor set of trade statistics).

Much more important to the organisations was the:

'Debacle' of the 1992 election

Throughout the campaign the polls reflected an apparently close contest, with Labour shading the lead. The final forecasts before the election by the four main organisations – MORI, NOP, Gallup and ICM – revealed an average of 39.3 per cent Labour, 38.4 per cent Conservative and 19.3 per cent Liberal Democrat. Most commentators expected Labour to win after thirteen years in opposition and from the depths of a Conservative-created recession of awesome severity; if not an overall majority, it was expected that Labour would be the biggest party and at minimum would be the senior partner in a coalition with the Lib Dems. Once on a by-election programme Peter Kellner of the *Independent* said he was prepared to 'put his house' on the exit poll being right about the winner. On that occasion his property would have been secure but in 1992 he would have ended up homeless. The exit polls (based not on expectations but on how people said they voted after leaving the polling booths) registered a Labour lead and the BBC reporting operation built it into their other computer predictions. The results were, however, a sensational upset for the pollsters: 35.2 per cent Labour, 42.8 per cent Conservative and 18.3 per cent Liberal Democrat (see Table 8.1). Instead of being neck and neck with Labour, the result showed the Conservatives were over seven percentage points in front and had probably led from the outset. The polls were not just wrong, they were miles out and their credibility was seriously brought into question. Accurate polls might have led to an earlier election and would certainly have deterred the notoriously triumphalist rally

Table 8.1   *The opinion polls and the election, 1992*

Final (forecast) polls			Con. Maj.	Con.	Lab.	Lib Dem	Other
7–8 April 1992	MORI	*Times*	−1.0	38.0	39.0	20.0	3.0
7–8 April 1992	Gallup	*Daily Telegraph*	0.5	38.5	38.0	20.0	3.5
7–8 April 1992	NOP	*Independent*	−3.0	39.0	42.0	17.0	2.0
8 April 1992	ICM	*Guardian*	0.0	38.0	38.0	20.0	4.0
Forecast poll average			−0.9	38.4	39.3	19.3	3.1
		Result (GB)	**7.6**	**42.8**	**35.2**	**18.3**	**3.8**
Exit polls							
9 April 1992	Harris	ITN	5.0	41.0	36.0	18.0	4.0
9 April 1992	NOP	BBC	4.0	40.0	36.0	18.0	6.0
Exit poll average			4.5	40.5	36.0	18.0	5.0

Source: Professor Ivor Crewe, lecture to the Politics Association, 9 April 1997.

held by Labour in Sheffield when the Shadow Cabinet were introduced to cheering supporters as the 'next Home Secretary', 'the next Foreign Secretary' and so forth. The apparently close situation also possibly urged those still unsure about Labour to vote in greater numbers to prevent such a result.

The exit polls were 4.5 per cent out compared with the 7.6 per cent of the standard polls, but this was scant or no comfort to pollsters proud of their record, methodology and accuracy.

What went wrong?

A number of commentators went on record blaming sample errors, sample size, mode of interview and non-registration on the electoral register. Professor Ivor Crewe has shown all these arguments to be false. The post mortem by the Market Research Society in July 1994 was the most authoritative. Crewe picks out three main reasons for the pollsters' errors:

1. A late swing. The final polls on the Tuesday and Wednesday mornings had to meet an 8.00 p.m. copy deadline so interviewing had to be completed by lunchtime on Wednesday, leaving thirty-six hours for people to change their minds. This late swing was unusual as 80 per cent of voters have usually decided on their vote before the campaign even begins. About one-third of the disparity was caused by this factor.

2. Faulty quotas. This problem is explained above: the statistical bases for some of the quotas were out of date. Crewe suggests more appropriate quotas could have been devised: for example, newspaper readership – *Daily Telegraph* readers are more likely to vote Conservative and *Guardian* readers much more likely to vote Labour – and patterns of affluence – two-car families are more likely to vote Conservative. This too explained about one-third of the mistaken figures.

3. 'Spiral of silence'. This factor explains the final third of the error. It concerned Conservative voters but did not involve them lying, as so many have suggested. Rather, they either refused to answer the question, said they were a 'don't know' or refused the interview completely. Crewe explains this by judging that Labour had occupied the 'moral high ground' during the campaign, appearing to be caring and altruistic, while the Conservatives launched their appeal strictly to the wallet – low spending, low taxes – to the extent that even sections of the press were dismissive of them. Polls conventionally exclude from their results the 20 per cent who say they don't know or refuse to answer. It used to be assumed that these respondents were spread evenly between the three parties. Closer study revealed a disproportionate number of these people to be Conservative, the evidence provided by their answers to other questions such as saying Major would make the best Prime Minister or the Conservatives were more reliable on the economy. Crewe claims that some 65 per cent of the 'don't knows' eventually voted Conservative.

Remedial measures

The polling organisations were determined to re-establish their credibility in time for the 1997 election. The remedial measures included:

(a) polling right up to the last minute on the Wednesday afternoon, with a telephone check added to monitor any last-minute changes;

(b) improving quotas by utilising more accurate and up-to-date statistics;

(c) adjusting polls to take account of the 'spiral of silence' factor. Most of the main polls adjusted their final data to allow for this bias to Labour and against the Conservatives. ICM used a mock ballot paper in its interviewing technique and Gallup counted as Conservative anyone who refused to answer, said they were a 'don't know', or said Major was better than Blair or Conservatives better than Labour on the economy.

The new techniques were piloted in the 1994 European Parliament elections and proved successful. The unadjusted figures put Labour twenty-two points in the lead but when adjustments were made it was only sixteen ahead; this proved correct within a half of 1 per cent (see Table 8.2).

Table 8.2   *Final opinion polls for European elections, June 1994 (adjusted)*

	Fieldwork	Con.	Lab.	Lib Dem	Con. lead
Gallup	1–7 June	28	44	19.5	−16
ICM	6 June	29	43	20	−14
MORI	2–6 June	27	47	20	−20
Mean		28	44.5	20	−16.5
Actual result	9 June	28	44	16.5	−16.5
Discrepancy		−	+.5	+3.5	−

Source: Professor Ivor Crewe, lecture to the Politics Association, 9 April 1997.

The big test in 1997

The 1997 election was approached by pollsters with trepidation and care; if they were wrong once more their credibility would be badly damaged and their regular bread and butter income from commercial market research might suffer. During the long campaign the polls showed a big Labour lead and in retrospect it is astonishing how it was discounted, especially, though understandably, by Conservative leaders. Most commentators predicted the lead would narrow dramatically as the election approached. On election night exit polls still predicted a big Labour win, yet Michael Heseltine was confidently predicting a Conservative victory of 'sixty seats and nudging upwards'. Table 8.3 reveals how wide of the mark Heseltine was and how more accurate the polls, with their adjustments to avoid the errors of 1992, had proved to be. The major organisations were within a 3 or 4 per cent margin, with ICM coming closest. NOP however, Nick Moon's organisation, was furthest adrift, prompting, no doubt, further internal enquiries.

Table 8.3   *The results of the final opinion polls, 1997 (%)*

	Con.	Lab.	Lib Dem	Other
Harris	31	48	15	6
NOP	28	50	14	8
MORI	28	48	16	8
ICM	33	43	18	5
Gallup	33	47	14	6
Exit polls				
MORI/ITN	30	46	18	6
NOP/BBC	29	47	18	6
Result	31	44	17	7

Source: David Denver, 'The 1997 election results' *Talking Politics*, September 1997, p. 6.

Further reading

M. Abrams, 'Public opinion and political parties', *Public Opinion Quarterly* (27), 1, 1962, pp. 9–18.

I. Crewe, 'The opinion polls: confidence restored?', *Parliamentary Affairs*, October 1997.

I. Crewe and B. Gosschalk, *The General Election Campaign of 1992*, Cambridge University Press, 1995.

N. Moon, *Opinion Polls and British Politics*, Manchester University Press, 1998.

R. Worcester, *British Public Opinion: A Guide to the History and Methodology of Political Polling*, Oxford University Press, 1991.

A copy of Ivor Crewe's lecture to the Politics Association (9 April 1997), upon which this chapter draws, can be obtained from the Politics Association Resources Centre, Studio 16, Imex Business Park, Hamilton Road, Manchester M13.

Questions

1   Why did the pollsters fail so dramatically in the 1992 election?
2   Should opinion polls be banned before an election, as in France?
3   Is it better for polls to retain a degree of inaccuracy?

9

Electoral behaviour

In discussing the party system (Chapter 5) we noted the change from system I (to 1970) to system II (post-1970). Not surprisingly, this change is connected with changes in the behaviour of the electorate. The shift is:

1. from such 1950–70 features as:

(a) The great majority of voters were stable in their party loyalties.
(b) Constituency swings were largely uniform across the country, reflecting the 'nationalisation' of political loyalties.
(c) The Conservative and Labour Parties dominated the contests throughout the UK (gaining over 90 per cent of the votes between them).
(d) When one of the two main parties gained support, it was usually at the expense of the other party.

2. to such post-1970 features as:

(a) Volatility, or shifts in voting behaviour, because strength of party allegiance declined.
(b) Greater variations in the electoral behaviour of different regions. Scotland, from 1979 to 1983, swung to Labour, the North slightly to the Conservatives, and the South and Midlands on a much bigger scale to the Conservatives.
(c) The rise in voting support and – to a lesser extent – in parliamentary seats for the Alliance and the Liberal Democrats. This was marked in 1983 and to a lesser extent in 1987. There is also a differentiation in the choices in different regions. In many seats in the South a Liberal Democrat candidate was the runner-up to the Conservatives. In Scotland both Labour and Conservative have to compete with Nationalists.
(d) A turning away from both main parties, particularly from Labour.
(e) The sharp decline of the class basis of the two-party system. On average,

in post-war elections up to 1970, some two-thirds of the working class voted Labour; in elections since, the average has fallen to less than half. Middle-class support for the Conservatives has also fallen, from an average of four-fifths to less than three-fifths.

During the 1980s, polls suggested that the electorate had become more volatile, less predictable, and more fickle and critical, with a keener, more 'instrumental' (i.e. selfish) interest in issues.

How elections are decided

Elections are determined by the interplay of long-term and short-term factors. The former work, on balance, to stabilise voters' choices, the latter to change them. The factors include:

1. Long-term

(a) *Party identification* or loyalty. Some 70 per cent of voters identify to some extent with Labour or Conservative, and supporters, particularly strong ones, are likely to vote for the party in spite of misgivings about particular policies or leaders.
(b) *Social class*. For most adults their class position will not change. Historically there has been a relationship between social class and choice of party.

2. Short-term

(a) *Issues* associated with elections (see below).
(b) *Events* leading up to and during the election, e.g. the collapse of Labour support during the 'winter of discontent' in 1979, which destroyed the party's chance of electoral success; the successful campaign in the Falklands which transformed the Conservatives' prospects in 1983; the improvement in living standards which helped the Conservatives in 1987; the replacement of Thatcher by Major, which helped them after 1990, or the exit from the Exchange Rate Mechanism and cases of sleaze involving Conservative MPs, which damaged them in 1997.

In recent years the former factors have weakened and the latter have gained in strength. (The first two, until recently, also worked in Labour's favour.) Hence the volatility in electoral support for the parties.

The 1970s, and even more so the 1980s, were disastrous for Labour. After 1979 the party's fortunes nose-dived and over the four general elections, 1979 to 1992 inclusive, Labour trailed the Conservatives by an average of 10 per cent of the vote (Table 9.1). In 1997 that pattern was drastically reversed.

Table 9.1 *Conservative and Labour average shares of votes in post-war elections (%)*

Years	Labour	Conservative	Labour lead
1945 to October 1974	44.5	43.6	0.9
1979 to 1992	32.6	43.0	−10.4

In the next section we comment on: (1) the weakening attachment to the two main parties, and (2) the decline of social class as a basis for voting.

Party loyalty and social class

1. Loss of support. The proportion of voters identifying strongly with each of the two main parties fell from 38 per cent in 1964 to less than 20 per cent in 1997. Before 1970 swings were usually only calculated between Labour and Conservative, but in 1974 both parties lost heavily to the Liberals and Scottish Nationalists. Instead of a realignment there was a partisan dealignment of major party support in Britain. There is some evidence that support for the parties was already becoming more fragile and conditional in the 1960s. This increased in the 1970s. Voters were more 'instrumental', voting for and withdrawing support according to a party's performance and promises and generally becoming more volatile.

The declining support for traditional Labour principles – links with the unions, increased taxes to fund greater public spending on the social services, more nationalisation – continued in the 1980s. But to these were added dislike of the party's unilateralist defence policy, doubts about its competence to manage the economy, and worries over its divisions and extremism. The loss of support in the 1980s for the 'old' two-party system was largely a problem for Labour. It was connected with a sharp fall in working-class support for Labour and with:

2. Decline of the class alignment. Division between manual and white-collar workers has long been associated with the two-party system and its class basis. The great challenge to this association has been the large working-class Conservative vote and the party's successful electoral record in the twentieth century (in office either alone or in coalition for over seventy years since 1900).

That the traditional class alignment was waning became evident in 1974, and has been confirmed since. The decline has been explained by:

(a) *Television* as the main source of political communication for most voters; it tends to be more objective and balanced in its presentation than newspapers and, by exposing voters to different points of view, encourages a less partisan style.

(b) *Social change and affluence*, which have softened class differences and weakened class loyalties.

(c) *Complexity of social class.* The middle class, as noted, is divided between a growing proportion who work in the public sector (e.g. teachers, nurses and civil servants) and those in the private sector. The working class is divided into those who are in strong or weak trade unions, are in the public or private sector, are skilled or unskilled. In turn, the parties have difficulty appealing to a single social class because its interests are so diverse and sometimes contradictory.

Working-class conservatism

Why have so many working-class voters supported the party of the middle class?

Several explanations have been put forward. They include:

1. Political generations. The Conservatives have regularly enjoyed majority support among the old and have often been in a minority in the younger generation. This difference had less to do with people becoming more 'conservative' as they grow older than with how people acquire party loyalties. We have to remember that Labour became a major party only after 1918, at a time when many voters had already acquired loyalties to other parties.

The main reason why the old have been less likely to vote Labour than the young is simply that they were less likely to have had Labour parents or to have voted Labour the first time they voted. As these older voters died off in the 1950s and 1960s, and new working-class voters who grew up in Labour homes came on to the registers, so Labour gained a growing share of the working-class vote. But research showed, paradoxically, that (a) the class basis of voting was increasing in the 1960s, i.e. more workers were voting Labour, but (b) the intensity of class feeling – identification of the parties with class interests and perception of differences between parties – was declining.

2. Embourgeoisement. The spread of affluence and a middle-class lifestyle to workers was linked by commentators with the decline of Labour support two decades ago. It was effectively refuted by Labour's victory in the 1964 and 1966 elections. In the 1992 election, working-class Tories still refused to vote Labour in spite of the economic recession. In 1997, however, they switched to Labour in large numbers.

3. Social and political deference, or the belief that the Conservatives are innately more competent because of their 'better' social and educational background.

4. Policies. We should not ignore the fact that many workers have preferred Conservative policies or that during the 1980s Labour was out of touch with working-class opinion on a number of issues. This was true in the 1980s on taxes, trade unions, law and order, inflation and defence. Before the 1992 election Labour rethought its position on most of these issues and, according to the opinion polls, won back much working-class support. But on polling day, the votes did not materialise.

All the same, Labour has made gains among the growing middle class. There are two explanations:

(a) A good proportion of this class are now first-generation middle class, having come from working-class homes with Labour-voting parents. They have retained some of this partisanship.
(b) With the growth of public-sector employment, much of the expansion in middle-class jobs has occurred in local government, education and health. These services and the employees' salaries are paid largely by public expenditure. Traditionally, Labour has been more sympathetic to this expenditure, while the Conservatives have wanted to limit it and make room for tax cuts; these workers have more incentive to vote Labour.

Issues

1. 'Mandate'. The claim that elections give the winning party a 'mandate' for every item in their manifesto has long been suspect, because:

(a) many party voters do not know the party's policies on many issues; and/or
(b) they disagree with these policies.

2. 'Position' and 'valence' issues. American students of electoral behaviour have drawn a useful distinction between 'position' and 'valence' issues.

(a) *Position* issues are those on which voters and parties take different stands. The voter's choice of party is determined by his or her own preference and perception of which party will further it. In 1979 many voters turned to the Conservatives in the expectation of lower taxes, and in the 1980s that party gained votes because it was seen as providing stronger defence and law and order policies than Labour and as doing a better job in raising living standards.
(b) *Valence* issues, on the other hand, are those on which parties and voters

are largely agreed, e.g. maintaining full employment, securing peace abroad, building more houses. Here the voter is swayed by his or her perception of which party is more competent. In 1983, 1987 and 1992, for example, voters said unemployment was the main issue, and they preferred Labour's policy for tackling it. But Labour gained few votes because many voters doubted whether a Labour government would be effective. In 1997 the Conservative Party ran far behind Labour when voters rated the parties on such criteria as unity, integrity, competence and looking to the future, or suspected that its policies would have negative side effects, such as a steep rise in inflation.

The 1997 general election

Table 9.2   *The 1997 general election (%) (1992 figures in parentheses)*

	Votes	Seats
Conservative	30.7 (41.9)	25.7 (51.6)
Labour	43.2 (34.4)	65.2 (41.6)
Liberal Democrat	16.8 (18.0)	7.2 (3.1)
Others	9.3 (6.0)	1.9 (3.7)

Table 9.3   *How Britain voted, 1997 (%) (1997 vote, % change on 1992 in parentheses)*

	Con.	Lab.	Lib. Dem.
All Great Britain voters	31 (−12)	44 (+9)	17 (−1)
Men	31 (−8)	44 (+9)	17 (−1)
Women	32 (−11)	44 (+10)	17 (−1)
AB voters	42 (−11)	31 (+9)	21 (0)
C1 voters	26 (−22)	47 (+19)	19 (−1)
C2 voters	25 (−15)	54 (+15)	14 (−4)
DE voters	21 (−8)	57 (+17)	13 (0)
First-time voters	19 (−16)	57 (+19)	18 (−3)
All 18–29	22 (−18)	49 (+12)	17 (0)
30–44	26 (−11)	43 (+9)	17 (−3)
45–64	33 (−9)	43 (−2)	18 (−2)
65+	44 (−3)	34 (−2)	16 (+2)
Home owners	35 (−12)	41 (+11)	17 (−3)
Council tenants	13 (−6)	65 (+1)	15 (+5)
Trade union members	18 (−9)	57 (+7)	20 (+2)

Source: 1992 data ITN/Harris exit poll, 1997 data BBC/NOP exit poll.

The salient features arising from Table 9.3 are:

1. The election breaks with the patterns of (a) 1945–70, of competition between Labour and Conservative, and with (b) 1974–92, of Conservative dominance (Table 9.1). The election represents a remarkable comeback by the Labour Party, which had not reached a 40 per cent share of the electorate since 1970. Moreover, it flew in the face of many claims that social trends were dooming the party to irreversible decline.

The election broke many records:

- The biggest two-party swing, over 10 per cent from Conservative to Labour.
- Labour's largest ever number of seats.
- The Conservative Party's lowest share of the vote since 1832 and lowest number of seats since 1906.
- Labour's biggest ever parliamentary majority.

2. The Liberal Democrats could be disappointed. Their share of 16.8 per cent of the vote was well below the quarter that it was attracting in 1983 and 1987, and declined for the third successive general election. Yet they gained their biggest number of seats since 1929. It is also worth noting that the total third-party vote again exceeded 25 per cent and that the seventy-five third-party seats was the highest number since 1923. The Scottish Nationalist Party increased its share of the vote in Scotland by only 1 per cent but doubled its number of seats to six.

3. Anti-Conservative tactical voting proved important. Labour's vote rose by more than average where it started as second to the Conservatives and Liberal Democrat support fell by more than average. But Liberal Democratic support rose above average where the party started off second and Labour's vote rose by less than the average. This pattern of tactical voting helped Labour to gain a majority of 179, much greater than was anticipated. In 1964 Harold Wilson's Labour Party gained a majority of only four seats with a similar share of the vote.

4. In elections over the past thirty years there has been a growing North–South divide in British politics, one in which a predominantly Conservative South is pitted against a predominantly Labour North. In 1992 there was a modest reversal of this trend. Although there was an overall swing to Labour across the nation, in Scotland there was a swing to the Conservatives and the pro-Labour swing was actually higher in the southern half of Britain. One reason is that the recession had hit the South much harder than the North. 1997 continued this pattern. The trend to Labour was lower in its strong areas, namely Scotland and the North, and much higher across the South. The result is that Labour's support is now more evenly distributed across the country. But the regional imbalances still remain. The Conservative obliteration in Scotland and Wales, and its continued weakness in the cities, means that it is more than ever a party of southern England and the shires.

5. For the first general election ever, Labour drew as much support from the middle class as did the Conservatives. There was a remarkable 20 per cent swing to Labour among the C1 (lower middle class) voters, the party's biggest gain in any social group. But Table 9.3 also shows a class gradient. AB (professional and managerial class) voters are still twice as likely to vote Conservative as the DE (unskilled working class), while the latter are twice as likely to vote Labour as those in AB.

The election result was a vindication of Tony Blair's strategy of looking beyond the trade unions, council tenants and working class for support. These groups were too small and declining. He was determined to make Labour a people's or a catchall party, appealing across society and particularly among groups, such as the middle class and women, where it was weak. If changing the party's image and attracting these groups meant the party had to distance itself from the trade unions, policies of economic redistribution and high taxes, then so be it. New Labour wanted to attract the support of the middle class and prosperous working class; it wanted them to identify their aspirations with the party.

Box 9.1 But was it a landslide?
(asks John Curtice, University of Strathclyde)

The 1997 election result was immediately hailed as a Labour landslide. This was hardly surprising. More Labour MPs (419) were elected than ever before and Tony Blair had the biggest majority (179) enjoyed by any Prime Minister in postwar British politics.

Yet when we look at how the country voted, rather than how ballots were converted into seats, a more sober judgement is clearly necessary. True, the overall swing of 10.3% across Great Britain as a whole was by far and away the largest swing secured by Labour since 1945. But this is as much a measure of how badly Labour did in 1992 as how well it did in 1997. It is also worth looking at how the distribution of votes in 1997 compares with previous postwar elections ... One fact immediately becomes apparent: at 44.4% Labour's share of the vote was lower than that secured at any election between 1945 and 1966, including the three elections which the party lost in succession in the fifties.

It should also be noted that at 71.2% across the UK as a whole, turnout was lower than in previous postwar British elections. Indeed just three in ten of those registered to vote cast a ballot for a Labour candidate. Only the Labour governments which emerged from the two general elections in 1974 secured the keys to office on a lower share of the electorate than Tony Blair did this time around.

Source: 'Anatomy of a landslide', *Politics Review*, September 1997, p. 2.

6. Table 9.3 shows the continued Conservative strength among the elderly and Labour strength among the young and first-time voters. The election also produced a reversal of the long-standing gender gap: women were as likely to vote Labour as men for the first time since the 1950s.

Conclusion

1. Weaker attachment to the party (or parties) in government may further undermine support for unpopular government policies. The tendency since the mid-1950s has been for public opinion, as reflected in by-elections and opinion polls, to turn sharply against the government of the day once the initial honeymoon wears off, or when economic conditions are unfavourable. Governments have invariably recovered support when the economy has improved. The exception is 1997, where the steady improvement in the economy and the recovery in economic optimism did not translate into much improvement in Conservative support on polling day.

2. The new fragility of party support increases the likelihood that campaigns and events will actually switch votes. Class loyalty and party identification – the forces for maintaining party loyalty – have weakened. Voters may therefore respond more to the particular issues and candidates associated with each campaign.

Further reading

'Britain Votes', *Parliamentary Affairs*, special issue, October 1997.
D. Butler and D. Kavanagh, *The British General Election of 1997*, Macmillan, 1997.
D. Butler and R. Stokes, *Political Change in Britain*, Penguin, 1969.
F. Conley, *General Elections Today*, 2nd edn, Manchester University Press, 1993.
D. Denver, *Elections and Voting Behaviour in Britain*, Philip Allan, 1994.
A. Heath *et al.*, *Labour's Last Chance? The 1992 Election and Beyond*, Dartmouth, 1994.

Questions

1 Account for the changing importance of social class on voting behaviour.
2 Why did voters turn away from (a) the Labour Party between 1979 and 1987, and (b) the Conservative Party before the 1997 election?
3 How important are party leaders in election campaigning today?

10

Political recruitment

Among the questions to consider here are:

(a) Who are the people who enter national politics and get to the top?
(b) Is there a 'political class'?
(c) Have there been changes in recent years?

There are a number of 'rules' for identifying would-be politicians. First, they are likely to be drawn from those already interested and active in politics. This factor immediately reduces the pool of 'eligibles' to some 10–15 per cent of the adult population. Then they tend to come from those occupations most compatible with a political career, e.g. lawyers, company directors, teachers or trade union officials. The final two hurdles for would-be politicians are that they have to be selected for a constituency and, finally, be elected to Parliament.

There are several ways of recruiting people to office. The liberal democratic method, found mainly in Western States, depends on voters choosing between candidates of different parties at free competitive elections. Such election legitimises the politician's authority. However, many States are ruled by groups which have seized power. Military rule, for example, is often found in new (i.e. post-1945) States and in countries which are poor (i.e. have a low Gross National Product). In this case the army's claim to obedience rests on its monopoly of force. Another mode of recruitment is appointment by merit, as in the British civil service. Competence is demonstrated here by the possession of formal qualifications and by success in examinations.

In effect, British politicians are recruited through political parties and elections.

A political class?

It is well known that politicians in Britain, and in most other countries, are unrepresentative regarding their social and educational background. They are overwhelmingly male, middle-aged and middle class.

1. Historically, political leadership in Britain has been exercised by men of high birth and breeding. The combined effects of universal suffrage, organised mass political parties, increasing professionalisation of political life and the decline of the landed interest have eroded the political influence of the aristocracy. But men from an upper-class background have stubbornly retained a large toehold in Parliament and the Cabinet, via the Conservative Party. Forty-three per cent of the members of Cabinets from 1884 to 1924 (the year of the first Labour government) were aristocrats (born or married into titled families). Between 1933 and 1964 the figure was still an impressive 26 per cent. For the same two periods, the proportion of ministers educated at expensive public schools actually increased from half to three-quarters.

2. MPs are increasingly drawn from the managerial and professional occupations and from university graduates. This description fits some two-thirds of all MPs. The significant post-war changes are on the *Labour* side. Before the war the great majority of Labour MPs were from the working class. Since 1945, however, the average has been a third, and it is still falling (13 per cent in 1997). Between 1945 and 1992 the proportion of university graduates on the Labour benches rose from 32 to 66 per cent; over 80 per cent of Conservative MPs in the 1997 Parliament are graduates (see Tables 10.1 and 10.2). In part this reflects a change in society. Compared with the pre-war period, there are more white-collar or middle-class jobs, and the expansion of higher education has allowed more students from working-class families to gain degrees and enter the professions. To some extent, therefore, the embourgeoisement or social change of the Labour Party in Parliament reflects the decline in the working class and the increase in working-class graduates.

Table 10.1   *Education of Members of Parliament, 1951 and 1992*
        (% of MPs within each party)

	1951		1992	
	Con.	*Lab.*	*Con.*	*Lab.*
State school to age of twelve	1	26	–	3
State secondary school	23	53	38	82
Private ('public') school	75	20	62	15
Eton College	24	1	10	1
University	65	41	73	61
Oxford or Cambridge	52	19	45	16

Sources: David Butler, *The British General Election of 1951* (1952), Ch. 3; David Butler and Dennis Kavanagh, *The British General Election of 1992* (1992), Ch. 10.

Table 10.2   *Social background of Members of Parliament, 1951 and 1992 (% of MPs within each party)*

	1951		1992	
	Con.	*Lab.*	*Con.*	*Lab.*
Public professional				
University/post-eighteen teaching	1	8	2	14
School teaching	–	6	5	14
Armed services	10	1	4	–
Civil service/local government	3	3	3	6
Doctors	1	3	1	1
Private professional/business				
Barristers/solicitors	22	14	18	6
Company directors	24	3	11	–
Company executives	6	2	22	3
Commerce (banking, etc.)	6	4	3	–
Farmers	5	1	3	1
Other private professional	3	–	5	1
'Private means'	8	–	–	–
Public/private				
Manual workers	–	37	1	22
Misc. white collar	1	4	3	13
Politicians/political organisers	4	2	6	9
Totals				
Private professional/business	66	24	62	11
Public professional	15	21	15	35
Public prof. + 'public/private' groups	20	64	25	79

Sources: David Butler, *The British General Election of 1951* (1952), Ch. 3; David Butler and Dennis Kavanagh, *The British General Election of 1992* (1992), Ch. 10.

There have been fewer changes on the *Conservative* side, although there has been a reduction in the number of aristocrats, big landowners and Etonians, so that the party is becoming less upper-crust, as Labour is becoming less working class. Before the war, Edward Heath, Margaret Thatcher, John Major and William Hague would have been unlikely choices as Conservative MPs, let alone as leaders. However, three-quarters of Conservative MPs are still drawn from public schools and most of them are products of Oxbridge.

3. Although MPs are more middle class and better educated, differences between the two main political parties still persist. *Labour* MPs have usually attended grammar schools and 'redbrick' universities, and are engaged in teaching, lecturing or local government administration. *Conservatives*, as stated above, are usually from public schools and Oxbridge, and tend to be engaged in business or the law. *Liberal Democrats* in 1997 were drawn mostly from business and teaching.

In all parties MPs appear to be more full time, professional and ambitious. This may explain why they have become more rebellious over the past two decades. Traditionally there was a bloc of upper-class Conservatives 'from the shires' and a bloc of trade union Labour MPs who were strong party loyalists, neither with any great desire to make speeches or gain office. Riddell's book, *Honest Opportunism* (1993), looks at the jobs MPs did before they were elected; did they decide to become MPs after embarking on a career ('proper jobs') or did they take jobs 'entirely secondary to their main goal of winning a seat in the Commons?', for instance political advisers or researchers. He concludes that there has been a steady increase in those who were already 'full-time politicians' when elected: from 11 per cent in 1951 to 31 per cent in 1992. The number of MPs with proper jobs fell from 80 to 41 per cent over the same period.

4. Cabinet ministers are usually of higher social status than backbenchers. This has always been true of Conservative Cabinets but it has recently become increasingly applicable to Labour Cabinets also. Whereas half the Attlee Cabinets and Wilson's first Cabinet in 1964 were from a working-class background, this element had virtually disappeared by 1970. When James Callaghan won the Labour leadership in 1976 his six rivals were all Oxford graduates. Given the tendency of bright, working-class children to go on to higher education, there are not now many MPs from working-class families who have not gone to university and are of ministerial calibre (see Table 1 from Adonis and Pollard).

5. There has been a significant increase in the number of women MPs. In the 1997 election 120 were elected, compared with sixty in 1992. Of these 101 were Labour MPs. This was largely a consequence of the party's practice of women-only shortlists in 50 per cent of marginal and safe Labour seats. In 1996, when an industrial tribunal ruled that the practice was discriminatory and illegal, the party abandoned it. Both the Conservative and Liberal Democrat Parties are embarrassed at the failure of their local parties to select women and blacks. Black and Asian MPs increased in 1997 from five to nine; eight Labour and one Conservative.

Does social background matter?

Critics object that the emergence of MPs from a small segment of society makes Parliament biased towards middle-class interests. This charge assumes that knowledge about a person's background enables one to predict his or her behaviour and values. The evidence is not clear-cut, however. The Conservative Party probably does suffer more than Labour in terms of its image because its MPs are so uniformly male, middle class and public school in background. Marxists have always argued that people are the product of their particular class and cannot help but defend its interests.

Recruitment procedures for MPs

Labour

Party headquarters keeps two lists of approved aspirants. List A consists of candidates sponsored by trade unions which are affiliated to the party. The financial help that goes with sponsorship makes such a candidate attractive to hard-pressed local parties. List B consists of other candidates. A Labour candidate has to be nominated by a group affiliated to the local party. The choice is made by a vote among party members following the one member, one-vote rule change in October 1993. The new party rules also insist that at least one woman should be shortlisted.

Conservative

Before the war, nominations frequently went to wealthy candidates who offered substantial contributions to local party funds. The Maxwell-Fyffe reform (1948) imposed a limit on the amount which candidates and MPs could contribute in this way: henceforth constituency parties had to become financially self-sufficient. A central body, the Standing Committee on Candidates, maintains a list of 'approved candidates' from which the constituencies may select. Aspirants apply directly to the local executive, which compiles a shortlist. A general meeting of members then chooses the candidate.

Liberal Democrat

These procedures are similar to the Conservatives', but they insist that one woman be included in each shortlist of candidates.

Problems

The number of disputes that have arisen over the selection process is growing. By tradition, only exceptional circumstances prevented an MP from being renominated if he or she so wished. Although in recent years the most publicised cases have occurred on the Labour side, since 1945 there have also been difficulties over the reselection of MPs in the Conservative Party, as in 1997 over Tatton MP Neil Hamilton, the embarrassment of whom Central Office would rather have been without. If a Conservative association does not wish to renominate an MP, then (since 1973) the decision is left to a general meeting of all members. This step limits the opportunity for a small, unrepresentative group to manipulate the selection and has probably saved some MPs from dismissal. In the 1992 Parliament, such Conservative MPs as Sir Nicholas Scott, David Ashby and Sir George Gardiner were all deselected, usually because of behaviour which was considered to bring the party into disrepute.

Dismissing an MP is a lengthy and divisive business. The dismissed member may stand as an independent at the next election and help to lose the seat for the party. Indeed, because MPs defeated at a general election now receive three months' severance pay, they have a financial incentive to stand.

There is little central control of the selection process in the *Conservative Party*; it is a jealously guarded prerogative of the constituencies. The party headquarters has the 'passive' controls of maintaining a list of candidates and approving or vetoing the constituency's choice. Endorsement is rarely withheld from a nominated candidate. Conservative Central Office has long wanted local parties to recruit a more diversified set of MPs, but has had little success. Party leaders probably wished that controversial MPs such as Neil Hamilton and Piers Merchant had been disowned in the 1997 general election, but the centre had very little power. In 1998 the party HQ gained more control. *Labour* is more centralised. Under Neil Kinnock the Labour Party expelled Militant activists from key positions in local parties and took greater powers in the shortlisting of candidates for by-elections. This has been important in shortlisting candidates, and shortly before the 1997 election a number of MPs stood down and the leadership 'parachuted in' candidates.

Reforms

Criticism arises partly because small groups have such a large say in the selection and, because most seats are safe for one party, selection is often tantamount to election. Reformers suggest:

(a) *Primaries*, as in the United States, which allow the local party supporters to choose the candidate. This is impracticable because of the difficulties of scheduling primaries in the absence of fixed-calendar general elections, and because they may increase party divisions.

(b) *Participation by one-party members* in the selection and dismissal process, so making it more difficult for small groups to 'take over' a local party. Labour has introduced 'one member, one vote' selection procedures.

(c) *Making the MP more subordinate* (and accountable) to the local party. This was the objective of the introduction of mandatory reselection in 1981 (see p. 72). One objection here is that as local parties become smaller so they may become less representative of the party's voters. Activists in the Labour Party, often thought to be left wing, are frequently critical of the policies which Labour governments take up. The task of Labour leaders in Parliament would be made more difficult if 'loyalist' MPs could be more easily dismissed for not following contrary local pressures or Conference policies.

The procedure was substantially revised in 1993 when Conference decided that MPs with two-thirds or more of local nominations would be selected without a contest.

Ministers

In the twentieth century Cabinet ministers have on average served for fifteen years in the House of Commons before their first appointment. They usually ascend the ministerial hierarchy, working their way up from the junior posts to the major departments, such as the Treasury, Home Office and Foreign Office. If MPs wish to reach the political summit they are helped by entry to the Commons at an early age. This parliamentary background emphasises the skills of managing Parliament; this is inevitable as long as ministers are drawn as they are by convention in the UK, from Parliament. But some critics feel that more note should be taken of the recruitment methods of some other countries (which draw on civil servants, business executives and lawyers as well as parliamentarians for executive appointments). British ministers tend to lack the subject-matter expertise or skills in managing large organisations of many of their French, Dutch or American counterparts. British Cabinet ministers' average tenure of a department, at two years, is one of the lowest in Western countries and means that at any one time a number of ministers will be learning their jobs.

Party leaders

Conservative

Traditionally, Conservative leaders 'emerge' by a process of 'soundings' or consultations carried on by senior figures. In fact, because the party has so often been in office, the Crown's prerogative of selecting a Prime Minister has meant that the monarch has chosen the party leader as well. (Arthur Balfour, Andrew Bonar Law, Stanley Baldwin, Neville Chamberlain, Winston Churchill, Anthony Eden, Harold Macmillan and Sir Alec Douglas-Home were all chosen in this way.) Usually the party has chosen 'safe' consensus-seeking men. In 1963, when Sir Alec was selected, controversy broke out, partly because he was a peer and partly because there had not been an open, competitive election. The process was discredited.

The new rules of 1965 provided for a *formal election* of the leader. In order to win, a candidate required an overall majority and a lead of 15 per cent over the runner-up. In 1975 changes were made to the rules. First, provision was made for an annual election (providing an opportunity for MPs to dismiss a leader). Second, to be elected on the first ballot a candidate had to have an overall majority plus a lead of 15 per cent of *all those eligible to vote* (compared with 15 per cent of those voting, in 1965). Mr Heath, the first leader to be elected in an open competition in 1965, was also the first to be challenged and so dismissed in 1975. The Conservative method of electing leaders was broadly similar to Labour's until 1981. The adoption of formal election procedures strengthens the influence of backbenchers and has probably weakened the sense of hierarchy in the Tory Party.

Nevertheless, the decision of Sir Anthony Meyer – an Old Etonian of pro-European 'wet' political views (i.e. liberal on social and economic policies) – to take advantage of the annual opportunity to challenge the Conservative leader in the autumn of 1989 caused a sensation. Margaret Thatcher's political fortunes were at a particularly low ebb at that time and party leaders urged Sir Anthony to stand down lest the contest prove disastrously divisive. In the event, just over sixty Conservative MPs either voted for Sir Anthony or abstained: too few to bring the Prime Minister down, but enough to pose serious questions about her position. In November 1990 Sir Geoffrey Howe resigned from the Cabinet and his subsequent resignation speech in the House of Commons was a bitter attack on Margaret Thatcher. Prompted by this, Michael Heseltine challenged her for the leadership. On the first ballot Margaret Thatcher led Michael Heseltine by 204 votes to 142, two short of the required 15 per cent majority. After consulting her Cabinet one by one she quickly decided to withdraw. Douglas Hurd and John Major then entered the contest. The final result was Major 185, Heseltine 131 and Hurd 56. The last two candidates withdrew and pledged their support to John Major.

It is worth noting how unlucky Margaret Thatcher was in 1990. The election was held shortly after a particularly bad by-election defeat in the safe Conservative seat of Eastbourne. It coincided with a run of very bad opinion polls and continued evidence of the massive unpopularity of the poll tax, which was widely seen as 'Margaret Thatcher's tax'. A large number of Tory MPs were convinced that they would lose their seats at the next election unless Margaret Thatcher and the poll tax were removed. The resignation of Sir Geoffrey Howe raised questions about her management of the Cabinet.

The leadership election then followed, presenting a unique opportunity for Conservative MPs to force a change.

This lesson was learned by John Major. In the 1992 Parliament there was regular talk of critics mounting a leadership challenge to him. Rather than wait he seized the initiative by resigning in June 1995 and offering himself for re-election. He saw off the challenge of John Redwood by 220 votes to 89. But once we discount the 'payroll vote' of members of the government, it can be seen that about half of backbenchers voted for a change. As the government failed to recover popularity and backbench leaders ruled out another contest in the Parliament, so talk was of Major standing down. What is clear is that the ease with which the party leader can be challenged has had a *destabilizing* effect on the party in the last decade. By 1997 the party was considering changes which would protect the leader.

When John Major resigned as party leader in 1997, a number of established candidates, such as Michael Portillo, Malcolm Rifkind, Chris Patten and Michael Heseltine, were no longer available. The first three were not in Parliament and the latter withdrew after a recurrence of heart problems. William Hague trailed Kenneth Clarke in the first two ballots and Clarke also had the support of more constituency party chairmen (who supposedly reflected grassroots opinion). Hague, however, managed to win on the third ballot, by 90 votes to 70.

This election will be the last in which the Tory Party elects the leader by MPs only (see Box 10.1). The small (165) number of MPs meant that many seats in England had no formal voice and there were no seats from Scotland or Wales. The contrast with the participation of party members in the Labour and Liberal Democrat Parties is strong. In 1998 the party adopted proposals to establish an Electoral College which will give the vote to members who will choose from a short-list of candidates initially chosen by MPs. The party now has one member one vote democracy.

The kind of person chosen as party leader determines the type of Prime Minister. But who are the leaders? First, and most obvious, they are MPs. Second, they have long service in the House of Commons. This narrow background contrasts with experience in some other countries. It ensures that party leaders are well known to colleagues and, usually, are good parliamentarians and skilled debaters. The person who emerges as leader is usually not identified with a particular faction of the party. An important task is to preserve party unity.

But things are changing. Thatcher, Major, Kinnock and Blair were all elected as party leader in their forties and Hague was only thirty-six. They had significantly less experience in the Commons than their predecessors – e.g. Blair ten years, Hague eight years – and in Cabinet.

Third, we should note that political skill in Britain is shown within the parliamentary arena. Approval among this parliamentary elite is more decisive than a popular following in the country or party Conference in reaching the

**Box 10.1   Conservatives make their leadership election
system more democratic than Labour's**

In the *Observer* (11 January 1998), Andrew Rawnsley reflected on the decision
of the Conservatives to let the 'swinish multitude' in on the election of its
leaders:

> The MPs-only system of selecting a leader was discredited by the last Tory lead-
> ership contest. The ballot which produced William Hague to an indifferent or
> scornful world was not an advertisement for democracy the Conservative way.
> Mr Hague was not the first choice of the public: that was Kenneth Clarke. He was
> not the first choice of Tory activists: that was also Mr Clarke. Mr Hague was not
> even his own first choice as Tory leader. He initially agreed to lay down his ambi-
> tions in favour of Michael Howard, changing his mind after he had slept on it and
> the seductive effects of Mr Howard's champagne had worn off. Just 41 of those
> 164 Tory MPs voted for Mr Hague in the first ballot, making him the first pref-
> erence of only a quarter of his parliamentary party ... [Under the new system]
> Conservative MPs will retain the right to dispose of a failed leader ... What they
> will lose is the power of appointment. Tory MPs will effectively be reduced to
> selecting a shortlist of two or three leadership contenders from which the mem-
> bership will choose the ultimate winner ... The reform will make the Tory system
> arguably more democratic than Labour's electoral college.

top. For example, both Enoch Powell and Tony Benn have attracted
widespread grassroots support within the Conservative and Labour Parties,
respectively. But they attracted minimal support among MPs. Twelve of the
nineteen Prime Ministers in the twentieth century first assumed office without the sanction of a general election.

Labour

In its early years the party elected its leader annually. Indeed, it was so anti-
elitist that it preferred to call him a 'chairman' and give him limited powers.
As Labour grew in strength, so the leader (as a potential Prime Minister)
became more influential. Since 1922 a leader has been challenged only
twice: when Harold Wilson stood against Hugh Gaitskell in 1960 and when
Tony Benn challenged Neil Kinnock in 1988. When a vacancy occurred MPs
balloted until a candidate had an absolute majority. In 1976 James
Callaghan gained an overall majority only at the third ballot.

Until 1981 election for the Labour Party leader had no provision for participation by non-MPs. The leader was theoretically head of the parliamentary party, not the party as a whole. Change was finally achieved at the
annual party Conference in 1980 and a special conference in January 1981.
The special conference decided to establish an Electoral College to elect the

leader of the whole party. It gives the unions 40 per cent and MPs and local parties 30 per cent each of the vote. This particular scheme was opposed by the bulk of the Parliamentary Labour Party, who wanted at least 50 per cent for themselves. By and large the positions were determined by politics; the left, who were strong in the unions and constituencies, favoured a reduction in the influence of MPs; the right, a strong role for MPs (see Chapter 5). Commentators thought that the new system would strengthen the grip of the left in the party and the changes helped to drive some MPs into the SDP.

Michael Foot had narrowly beaten Denis Healey for the leadership in 1980, in an election held under the old rules. In 1983 Michael Foot stood down, having led Labour to a crushing electoral defeat. The so-called 'dream ticket' of Neil Kinnock and Roy Hattersley was elected to the positions of leader and deputy leader, respectively. The two men were overwhelmingly confirmed in their positions in 1988, when Tony Benn and Eric Heffer launched a challenge to them from the left. After another election defeat in 1992, Neil Kinnock and Roy Hattersley resigned. They were succeeded at a special leadership election in July by John Smith and Margaret Beckett. In 1993 Smith forced a change to the rules, so that the MPs, unions and constituencies each had one-third of the college vote.

When John Smith died in 1994 he was succeeded by Tony Blair and Beckett by John Prescott. Both Blair and Smith were elected by landslides in the Electoral College and each had clear majorities in all its sections. Both were firmly on the right wing of the party, an ironic comment on the effect of the reforms made by the left in the early 1980s. Moreover, it is now difficult to remove a Labour leader in government because a challenge has to be supported by two-thirds of the Conference. A further irony is that a Labour leader and, in particular, a Labour Prime Minister is now more secure than his Conservative counterpart.

Further reading

A. Adonis and S. Pollard, *A Class Act*, Hamish Hamilton, 1987.
J. Blondel, *Voters, Parties and Leaders*, Penguin, 1980.
D. Butler and D. Kavanagh, *The British General Election of 1997*, Macmillan, 1997, Chapter 10.
P. Norris and J. Lovenduski, *Political Recruitment*, Cambridge University Press, 1995.
P. Riddell, *Honest Opportunism*, Hamish Hamilton, 1993.
G. Thomas, *Prime Minister and Cabinet Today*, Manchester University Press, 1998.

Questions

1 Does it matter that MPs are not socially representative of voters?
2 Should Cabinets be elected by MPs?
3 Consider the arguments for and against positive discrimination regarding women candidates for Parliament.

11

The media and politics

'In today's world selective seeing is believing and in today's world television comes over as truth.' So said Margaret Thatcher during the run-up to the 1987 election. She proved it on her campaign bus in front of the cameras. She was clearly receiving good news; replacing the receiver she announced the release of a British hostage in Iran. In his book, *Live from Number 10*, Michael Cockerell reveals the Prime Minister had heard the news earlier: the phone call was just play acting (p. 326). Surveys show that 60–70 per cent of people cite television as their major source of political information, with the press a poor second at 25–30 per cent. But while the press is widely perceived as reflecting political bias, television (according to poll data) is usually believed to be fair and objective.

The media has forged a revolution in the way politics is conducted. In the early days of democratic politics, fiery speakers used to address crowds which nowadays could scarcely be crammed into Wembley Stadium, relying only upon their voices to transmit their messages. And they spoke at some length: during his famous Midlothian campaign (November–December 1879) Gladstone's speeches could last an hour or more. The popular press, emerging in the late nineteenth century, provided a new means of influencing political opinion and elevated newspaper owners into major players on the political stage. But the real communications revolution began in the 1920s. Stanley Baldwin (Prime Minister, 1923–24, 1924–29, 1935–37) was the first British politician fully to exploit the potential of radio: his cosy chats into the microphone carried his relaxed persuasive charm into the homes of millions of families. Churchill was also a master of radio broadcasting but proved hopeless when confronted with television. The huge potential of this latter instrument was first exploited in America, and successive developments of its use have crossed the Atlantic after an ever-diminishing time-lag.

The media: basic facts

The British press has a relatively large number of dailies, which to some extent reflect Britain's social stratification. Mass circulation tabloids – the *Daily Mirror*, the *Sun* and the *Star* – cater for the working classes; the *Daily Mail* and *Daily Express* for the lower middle classes; while the 'quality press' – the *Guardian*, the *Daily Telegraph*, *The Times* and the *Independent* – is bought by middle- and upper-middle-class group members. Indeed, readership of the quality press is about 80 per cent middle class while the same proportion of those who read the *Sun* and the *Daily Mirror* is working class.

As newspapers are big business and are owned predominantly by powerful businessmen, it is hardly surprising that six of the daily newspapers have traditionally been pro-Conservative with only two for Labour (the *Guardian* from a carefully guarded independent position). As Table 11.1 shows, political affiliations of tabloid readers are more evenly divided than those of the qualities' readership, suggesting that political news and comment is less important for the former group.

Broadcasting in Britain is controlled by the BBC and the IBA (Independent Broadcasting Authority). The BBC was established in 1922 and in 1927 became a public corporation. Funded by licence fees, it runs two television channels plus five national radio channels, as well as local and international radio services. The IBA was established in 1954 to regulate the activities of the fifteen advertising-financed television companies awarded regional franchises and those of Channel 4, established in 1982. In 1990 a new

Table 11.1   *Social class and political leanings of newspaper readership, 1992*

Newspaper	Party backed	% of readers in social class				Party backed by readers		
		AB	C1	C2	DE	Con.	Lab.	Lib Dem
Daily Mirror	Lab.	6	18	36	40	20	64	14
Daily Star	pro-Con.	4	14	38	44	31	54	12
Sun	Con.	5	17	35	43	45	36	14
Daily Mail	Con.	24	32	25	19	65	15	18
Daily Express	Con.	20	34	26	20	67	15	14
Today	Con.	12	26	37	25	43	32	23
Financial Times	No endorsement	57	30	8	5	65	17	6
Daily Telegraph	Con.	49	32	11	7	72	11	16
Guardian	Lab./Lib Dem	52	27	11	11	15	55	24
Independent	none	52	29	11	7	25	37	34
The Times	Con.	61	26	8	6	64	16	19

Source: Adapted from M. Harrop and M. Scammell, 'A tabloid war: the British election of 1992', in D. Kavanagh and D. Butler, *The 1992 General Election*, Macmillan, 1992.

authority, the Independent Television Commission, took over from the IBA. In addition a Broadcasting Standards Council was set up to monitor matters of taste and judgement on television programmes.

According to statute, television and radio must handle controversial political issues in an objective and balanced fashion. Unlike America, where politicians can buy television time to advertise themselves just like any other product, Britain, during election campaigns, allocates time free of charge to political parties on the basis of their strength in the country; currently parties are allowed ten minutes of television time for every 2 million votes received in the previous general election. Parties without parliamentary representation usually receive an allocation based upon the number of candidates fielded: in the 1980s five minutes per fifty candidates.

Party political broadcasts, however, provide only a small proportion of television's 'political' output even during campaigns: more important are news bulletins (about 20 million people regularly watch BBC's *Nine O'Clock News* and ITN's *News at Ten*) and current affairs programmes such as *Panorama*, *Newsnight*, *World in Action* and *Question Time*. On radio some 6 million people – including many key decision-makers – listen to Radio 4's early morning *Today* programme.

The impact of broadcasting on the political process

Broadcasting has transformed the political process over the last thirty years.

1. Broadcasting has reduced the importance of local party organisations. In the late nineteenth century political parties needed strong local membership to carry their messages into homes, encourage participation and sense of belonging, and get the voters out on election day. While the latter requirement survives, the former functions have been weakened by the ability of politicians to reach more people via two minutes on television than they could meet in a lifetime's door-to-door canvassing. This provides an important explanation for why both major parties have seen their active memberships decline drastically since the 1950s and it also helps to explain the reduction all parties have suffered in terms of highly committed support. Work by Patrick Seyd, however, at Sheffield University, detected a positive correlation between size of party membership and size of vote, especially in marginal constituencies. Seyd calculates that, if party membership had been twice Labour's level in 1992, the party would have won 40 per cent of the vote and consequently have won power. Media messages, however, tend to be more centralised and seek to exploit the nationally known political leadership. The novelty and hopeful rhetoric of a new party attracted intense media interest when the SDP was launched in 1981. In consequence it virtually dominated British politics for over a year without any well-established grassroots branch network. However, such media-based success can be short-lived: the SDP never recovered after the Falklands War shifted the spotlight elsewhere.

2. The role of the House of Commons has been usurped by the media. The media have dislodged the House as the focus of popular political attention. Some research showed Margaret Thatcher ignoring the House, when Prime Minister, but not television: her crucial performances were more likely to be on *Panorama* than at the Dispatch Box. Similarly, ministers are more interested in announcing new initiatives direct to a mass television audience than to a poorly attended House. This and other arguments were deployed for over twenty years in support of televising the House's proceedings. Dire warnings that the unique and intimate nature of the parliamentary process would be forever sullied by the vulgar gaze of the cameras had proved wrong in the case of the House of Lords – televised since 1985. And so it has proved, to the satisfaction of most commentators, with the Commons after television was finally allowed in on 21 November 1989.

Extracts from televised statements, debates and particularly Prime Minister's Question Time have now become a normal part of news broadcasts. However, the 'bear garden' atmosphere of PM's Questions which the cameras encouraged led Blair, after May 1997, to substitute a single half-hour session for the previous two fifteen-minute ones. Through television the House has won back some of its lost ground, but as a forum for political debate BBC's weekly *Question Time* has an audience many times larger. Perhaps more important in the long term is the prominence which television can now give to hitherto neglected aspects of the parliamentary process, such as select committee hearings or late-night adjournment debates. On 19 July 1990 televising the House was made permanent in a free vote of 131 to 32.

3. The form of political communication has altered. Gladstone's magisterial addresses have been replaced by relaxed television performances where politicians strive to persuade us of their competence, commitment and sincerity within the time constraints of television schedules and audience attention spans. To be successful requires special attributes and skills possessed by few politicians. Margaret Thatcher was carefully coached by (now Sir) Gordon Reece to lower the tone of her voice, wear non-fussy clothes and change her make-up and hairstyle. She was still undeniably herself on television but training helped play down her weaknesses and emphasise her strong points. Attendance at a television 'charm school' has now perhaps become a requirement for ambitious politicians. However, if a politician has not got the potential to perform well on television, it is unlikely in these days that he or she would even think of entering this insecure profession.

4. Political leaders must be good on television. Attlee and Churchill were cheerfully dismissive of the little box; Eden and Macmillan were more attentive and responded to its demands; Wilson and Callaghan deployed their relaxed folksiness to good effect; Heath tried hard but when Prime Minister could never relax; and Margaret Thatcher triumphed over her shortcomings, as we have already noted. Michael Foot, however, elected Labour leader in 1981, scored badly on a number of important counts: his clothes and spectacles were wrong, he looked frail and elderly, he had a number of nervous twitchy mannerisms, and he tended to ramble and waffle instead of answering questions confidently, concisely and persuasively. Hitherto Labour had tended to resist television coaching as too close to the business or capitalist advertising world but after Foot attitudes changed; Neil Kinnock was chosen as his successor principally because he was believed to be good on television. John Major was widely thought to be poor on television, lacking passion and a gift for language. However, he was able, through his manner, to communicate his qualities of relaxed friendliness, modesty and cheerfulness: quite possibly these were crucial factors in his shock 1992 election victory.

5. The government has made more use of television to sell its policies. Under the influence of Lord Young, annual spending on government advertising increased from £35 million to £150 million between 1979 and 1989. Television was used extensively to sell privatisation and other policies and under the more centralised control of Alastair Campbell (Blair's Press Secretary) it is unlikely that Labour, after 1997, will be significantly different.

6. The media have transformed the conduct of elections.

(a) *Political hustings* where candidates met voters of all parties and displayed their political talents by dealing with hecklers have largely died out. Political meetings involving party leaders are now all-ticket affairs with everything choreographed and carefully rehearsed for the television cameras. The leader arrives to ecstatic cheers from a crowd bedecked in party colours and rosettes. He or she steps up confidently to the microphone to deliver (in Margaret Thatcher's case, with the assistance of the invisible one-way autocue first used by Ronald Reagan) a speech in which carefully written passages have been strategically inserted for media attention. Campaign organisers hope to create the impression of a united party, a charismatic leader, a euphoric unstoppable march to victory. They hope the cameras will briefly capture this essence for news bulletins, together with one or two of the prepared 'sound bites'.

(b) *Campaigns have become presidential.* Because television news conveys political news in such an abbreviated form, it is inevitable it should focus upon party leaders, who also inevitably have come to represent their party's brand image. The emphasis is increasingly upon the person rather than the party: whatever the leader says or does is, perhaps too slavishly, reported. Packs of reporters consequently form royal processions behind the party leaders, who have learnt to eschew potentially dangerous impromptu press conferences in favour of symbolic 'photo opportunities' involving them in activities such as driving a tank (tough on deterrence), playing with disabled children (caring on social policy) or visiting retraining workshops (concerned about unemployment). However, if leaders do make gaffes, as they did in both 1987 and 1992 (e.g. Neil Kinnock's muddled message at the end of the campaign over reforming the voting system), they are leapt upon with delight by the media and loudly exploited. The Conservatives allegedly chose a long six-week campaign in 1997 as they believed the pressure on Tony Blair would force him to crack. Heseltine even claimed Blair was failing to cope, sweating before speeches and about to suffer a breakdown. This proved far from the truth as Blair handled all the big tests with consummate professionalism; ironically it was Heseltine's health which suffered a breakdown just after the election.

(c) *Campaign and media managers now play crucial roles.* The Conservatives have tended to take the lead in employing advertising agencies such as Saatchi & Saatchi and media advisers such as Gordon Reece and Tim Bell. Labour, however, soon caught up, appointing an ex-television producer, Peter Mandelson, as Communications Director. Mandelson's media skills soon became legendary and the Tories' nickname for him, The Prince of Darkness, a reflection of the fear he inspired within them. Once in government Mandelson became a minister and, according to some, continued to exercise his black arts in the business of maintaining Labour's favourable image in power. Blair's Press Secretary, Alastair Campbell, has also been criticised for excessive 'spin doctoring' and for insisting on a highly centralised system of information management.

(d) *Personal attacks* in the tabloid press have grown in frequency and intensity. In 1987 especially, the private lives of certain politicians were subjected to an inquisition perhaps more merciless than during any previous election. Many criticise this as dishonourable and unjustifiable – which it mostly is – but most people are interested in the peccadilloes of others, especially those in the public eye, and there is much evidence from both sides of the Atlantic to suggest that the victims of such character assassinations also suffer in the ballot boxes.

The media influence voting behaviour

Research into this topic is inconclusive and a little confused. One school of thought is that the media merely reinforce voter preferences because of the 'filter effect': people tend to watch, listen and read what they want to hear

---

Box 11.1   Martyn Lewis and good news/bad news

In March 1993, Martyn Lewis, the BBC's most popular newsreader and author of a book on cats on television, himself made the news with a lecture in the USA. In it he berated broadcasters for delivering an excessive diet of bad news: 'a relentless culture of negativity'. It was time, he said, to 'treat both good and bad news with an equal degree of seriousness'. He suggested 'a shift in the overall balance of good and bad news of between 10 and 15 per cent a year'. The public seemed supportive but his fellow professionals poured contempt over his suggestions. As well as Paxman, MacDonald and Humphrys, Peter Sissons commented: 'It is not our job to ... make people feel better.' But Michael Grade, Head of Channel 4, defended Lewis: 'Here is a guy actually trying to do something with his life and the cynical journalistic response is to sneer.'

Were the sneers justified?

Certainly the news is gloomy fairly regularly, but this is no more than a reflection of the wars, famines and disasters which afflict the world constantly. To replace the reporting of such things with deliberately upbeat items would be irresponsible and misleading. Such 'good news' would also favour the government of the day, always keen to foster a 'feel good' consciousness. But it is true that news is not an accurate reflection of the real world: it is merely the artificial construct of reporters and editors. There are hundreds of items competing for inclusion in each bulletin and it would not be difficult to leaven the misery with more 'good news'. The current mix is dictated by conventional ideas, borrowed from Fleet Street, of what the public wants, i.e. 'news values' or stories which concentrate on personalities rather than issues; shocking revelations; and disasters, natural or otherwise.

---

and remember what they want to remember. While this may well be true of newspapers, in that people tend to read those which coincide with their views, it ignores the role which newspapers might have over time or on people whose views are undecided. It also ignores the more balanced treatment provided by television. It is impossible for viewers of *Question Time*, for example, to be oblivious to the arguments put forward by representatives of parties with which they disagree.

Professor Ivor Crewe often argues that 20–30 per cent of voters can switch parties during an election campaign and media messages almost certainly play a causal role in influencing them, especially 'new' and uncommitted voters. But it is hard to disentangle the media from the other causal factors, such as family, work, region and class, and it is hard to separate the media from the message. For example, Hugh Hudson's film on Neil Kinnock in the 1987 election was a clear case of the form of media creation having a massive impact. However, the 1992 film about Jennifer Bennett's ear operation (seriously delayed, while a similar operation on the daughter of a well-off family was performed at once in a private clinic) appealed to a myriad of

Box 11.2   Spin doctors: (a) John Major's July 1995 leadership contest, and (b) the 'overspinning' of the EMU, October 1997

(a) In July 1995 John Major caused a sensation by challenging his opponents to stand against him in a leadership contest. Having consulted widely, he perhaps expected his challenge to go uncontested by any major figure. However, he counted without the resolution and ambition of John Redwood. In the ensuing contest commentators wondered how many votes Major needed to be seen to have bested his opponent. Party rules state that to win in the first round a contestant needs to win an overall majority of the Conservative MPs plus 15 per cent more votes than his or her nearest rival. In the Channel 4 documentary *Bye Bye Blues* (5 October 1997), Lord (Jeffrey) Archer, as one of Major's campaign team, explained his strategy: 'We had various plans in connection with different results – 100 or 130 and he's back on the bus to Brixton. 200? Well that's tricky. After the result [218] was announced we knew the key time was from then for the next twenty minutes. I knew exactly what I was going to say: "No other leader in Europe has received a 67 per cent vote of confidence. Imagine Kohl getting this, this is far higher than I expected, it's overwhelming!" The four of us (including John MacGregor, Michael Ancram and William Waldegrave) moved in a circle and covered twenty-one programmes in seventeen minutes. By then the die was cast; I heard the *Sun* editor say "Major could still go" after the result, but after twenty minutes it had been accepted.' Archer thus described one of the most audacious and effective spin-doctor operations in the history of British politics. It was definitely not certain that Major could survive with one-third of the party withholding its support – after all, in 1940 Chamberlain had resigned when only eighty of his vast majority abstained – but after the smart grab for the microphones by Archer and Co. in the immediate wake of the announcement, Major's position was validated and he could continue as Premier for nearly another two years.

(b) In October 1997 the Labour government faced a dilemma over the single European currency. To remove the rumour of tension between Blair, thought to be against, and himself, thought to be for, Gordon Brown briefed the press one way but his advisers or 'spinners' briefed another; as Ewan McAskill wrote in the *Guardian* on 20 October: 'The confusion has been created by a gap between what ministers, including Mr Brown, are saying in public, and what spin doctors are saying in private. Ministers are hinting that Britain will stay out until after the next election while refusing categorically to rule out entry before that.'

emotions focusing on the universal emotive appeal of suffering children and parental concern to do their best for their children's health. Common sense tells us that a medium which can sell so many products should surely be able to sell politicians. Politicians clearly agree, otherwise they would not spend so much money on the activity – at the very least they fear they will lose by default if they fail to use television while their opponents do – but the precise impact of the medium defies accurate measurement.

Political control of the media

The widely accepted pluralist theory of how our democracy should (and to some extent does) work predicates media which are independent, free of sectional interest and thus able to give fair and accurate reportage. Given the power which the media clearly have, this is an important political issue.

The independence of the press

The press is independent of government control in that all newspapers in Britain are privately owned. However, it is widely asserted that because the press is owned by big business concerns which exist to make a profit, the press is bound to favour the party of capitalism, the Conservatives. About 80 per cent of newspaper circulation is in the hands of three big conglomerates. The late Robert Maxwell and Rupert Murdoch have been modern-day press barons, taking an interventionist editorial line. Maxwell dictated a pro-Labour line for the *Daily Mirror* but he was unusual. The majority of daily and Sunday newspapers urge readers to vote Conservative at elections, from the raucous populism of the *Sun* to the more sedate but no less committed injunctions of the *Daily Telegraph*. Murdoch was a confidant of Margaret Thatcher and a strong supporter of right-wing policies. There is some evidence of co-ordination of editorial policy during elections between Conservatives and sympathetic newspapers, but usually the support is so strong that no encouragement or direction is needed. The 1997 election was extraordinary in that a number of key Conservative-supporting newspapers, such as *The Times*, the *Daily Mail*, the *Sun* and the *Daily Telegraph*, bitterly criticised Major for weak leadership and pro-Europeanism. Even more astonishing was that the Murdoch-owned press dramatically switched to Labour just before the campaign got under way. Cynical commentators suggested that Blair had done a deal during his publicised lecture to Murdoch's staff, whereby Murdoch agreed his support in exchange for favours to be delivered by Blair in government.

The effect of the lobby system

Some critics claim that the lobby system tends to favour the government of the day – whichever party is in power. One hundred and fifty Westminster journalists belong to this organisation, whereby unofficial confidential briefings are given by ministers and information officers, provided no specific attribution is made. Often information is transmitted via this system which would not otherwise have seen the light of day but, argue critics, it is inimicable to democracy in that it enables the government to manage the news and set the political agenda. It also encourages laziness among journalists who come to prefer dictated government briefings to challenging, investigative journalism. In 1997 secrecy was relaxed and the Premier's Press Secretary, Alastair Campbell, became less invisible.

Television

Television comes much closer to the requirements of a democratic system in that it is legally required to avoid bias and offer a balanced treatment of political issues. It is still possible for the government to influence television, however, and both Labour and Conservative governments have striven to do so. Harold Wilson was convinced of an anti-Labour bias within the BBC and fought an extended battle with its governors and staff. Margaret Thatcher was likewise convinced that the BBC and some independent television companies, especially Granada Television, were strongholds of leftish sentiment. In common with her predecessors, she sought to apply pressure in the following ways:

1. Power of appointment. Advised by the Home Secretary, the Prime Minister appoints the Chairmen of the IBA and the BBC, together with Board members for given periods of office. The appointment of Marmaduke Hussey, ex-Chairman of *The Times*, as Chairman of the BBC was widely interpreted as Margaret Thatcher's attempt to 'sort out' a supposedly leftward-leaning BBC. Shortly afterwards Alasdair Milne, the Director-General with whom Margaret Thatcher had been in dispute, was fired. But experience suggests that even political supporters, once appointed, can oppose the government, as Hussey did over a number of issues, including the restrictions on reporting from Northern Ireland.

2. Financial support. Several governments have used their control over the licence fee as a lever with which to pressurise the BBC. Margaret Thatcher was known to favour the introduction of advertising to finance the BBC, but the Peacock Commission on the financing of television failed to produce the hoped-for recommendation. As part of the move to deregulate independent television and reduce the power of the IBA, the regional franchises were sold to the highest bidders. This, however, had more to do with Margaret Thatcher's free-market principles than with any attempt to influence editorial control over news and current affairs programmes.

3. Opposition to particular programmes. The BBC has come in for much criticism, especially in relation to programmes concerned with defence, the security services and Northern Ireland. During the Falklands War some Conservative MPs actually accused the BBC of 'treason' because their reports of the action were couched in objective rather than committed or patriotic terms. The Corporation fought its corner on this and other programmes such as the *Real Lives* series on Northern Ireland in 1985, but was forced to give substantial ground; the sacking of Alasdair Milne over the Zircon Satellite programme in 1987 badly hit morale in the Corporation. Independent television companies have also come under intense pressure. The government did its best to prevent the broadcasting of Thames Television's *Death on the Rock* in 1989, which suggested that the SAS shooting of three IRA terrorists in Gibraltar was part of a shoot-to-kill policy. The IBA resisted and the programme was shown. The government was doubly furious when an inquiry headed by Lord Windlesham, a Conservative ex-minister, exonerated the programme and the reporting techniques employed.

4. Political campaigns. In 1986 a monitoring unit was set up in Conservative Central Office and in the summer of that year a critical report of the BBC's coverage of the American bombing of Libya was published, together with verbal onslaughts from the then Conservative Party Chairman, Norman Tebbit. BBC executives complained of 'intimidation' in the run-up to the election and, despite their claims to the contrary, they were almost certainly affected by the pressure. In January 1990 another Conservative Party campaign became evident when the early morning *Today* radio programme was accused of giving Conservative ministers the third degree while Labour spokesmen were subjected to much milder inquisitions. On the eve of the 1992 election campaign, the Home Secretary Kenneth Baker warned the BBC that the government would be looking carefully at its political coverage. The presenters denied any bias and pointed out that the party which actually disposes of power, the government of the day, will naturally attract the toughest questioning from any medium which is truly independent. Similar shots across the bows of the BBC were fired as the 1997 election approached.

Do the media favour the left or the right in British politics?

As we have seen, Conservative politicians and commentators perceive the BBC as a stronghold of left-wing and post-war consensus points of view. They point out that the present generation of senior management began their careers within the BBC during the radical 1960s, and cite any number of news, current affairs and radical dramatic productions in support of their case. Indeed, at one time among Conservative MPs a belief in the left-wing bias of the BBC was virtually a litmus test of Thatcherite orthodoxy. The left can mount a powerful rebuttal. Indeed, the case that the press has a right-wing bias is virtually undefended, but the issue of bias among broadcasters is more controversial. Bryan Gould argues that 'Everything is referred to a presumed standard of normality and therefore anybody who is outside the mainstream, who takes a different view, who is a bit radical, inevitably looks on television or radio to be something of an eccentric or a maverick.' This tendency to marginalise left-wing points of view, in Gould's opinion, is 'not their fault, it is just intrinsic to the way that they operate' (interview on Tyne Tees TV, April 1986). The Glasgow University Media Group, however, in a book called *Bad News* and successive volumes, argue that in some areas, especially the reporting of industrial relations, television producers reflect a right-wing bias: as members of the upper middle class they have a vested interest in presenting working-class arguments in an unfavourable light.

Marxist critics go a step further (not to mention the influential US intellectual, Noam Chomsky). They argue that the media are just one element in the complex web of mystification which the ruling economic group in society utilises to buttress its position. Just as the educational system, Parliament and the government bureaucracy implicitly transmit dominant values, so also do the media.

Which argument is more persuasive? At the party political level there may well be something in the case for the BBC as a repository of consensual views, but when they are not being paranoid, party politicians are often playing a shrewd political game in which they believe advantage can accrue from attacks upon the media. The Marxist critique is more difficult to answer, but while it may contain elements of truth, British broadcasters are surely not the supine instruments of capitalist propaganda. Recent history reveals that they jealously guard their independence and successfully resist a great deal of pressure to conform from politicians of all persuasions.

Further reading

D. Butler and D. Kavanagh, *The British General Election of 1992*, Macmillan, 1992, Chapter 9.

N. Chomsky, *World Order, Old and New*, Pluto Press, 1994.

M. Cockerell, *Live from Number 10*, Faber, 1988.

J. Curran and J. Seaton, *Power Without Responsibility. The Press and Broadcasting in Britain*, Routledge, 1988.

Glasgow University Media Group, *Bad News*, Routledge, 1976.

Glasgow University Media Group, *More Bad News*, Routledge, 1980.

M. Harrison, *TV News: Whose Bias?*, Hermitage Policy Journals, 1985.

B. Jones, 'The pitiless probing eye: politicians and the broadcast political interview', *Parliamentary Affairs*, vol. 46, January 1993, pp. 66–91.

B. Jones *et al.*, *Politics UK*, Philip Allan, 1991, pp. 588–606.

D. Kavanagh, *Election Campaigning: The New Marketing of Politics*, Blackwell, 1997.

B. McNair, *An Introduction to Political Communication*, Routledge, 1996.

B. Miller, *The Media and Voters*, Clarendon Press, 1991.

M. Moran, *Politics and Society in Britain: An Introduction*, Macmillan, 1989, Chapter 6.

R. Negrine, *Politics and the Mass Media in Britain*, 2nd edn, Routledge, 1994.

P. Riddell, *Parliament under Pressure*, Gollancz, 1998.

P. Seyd and P. Whiteley, *Labour's Grass Roots*, Clarondon, 1992.

C. Seymour-Ure, *The Political Impact of the Mass Media*, Constable, 1974.

D. Watts, *Political Communication Today*, Manchester University Press, 1997.

J. Whale, *The Politics of the Mass Media*, Fontana, 1978.

Questions

1 Do you think that the impact of media advisers and 'charm schools' has enabled politicians to mislead the public as to their true natures?
2 Assess the impact of televising the House of Commons.
3 Do you think the impact of television has overall been beneficial for democratic government?

12

The monarchy and the House of Lords

This chapter deals with the 'dignified' parts of the political system, i.e. those which outwardly look the most impressive but in reality have least effect. Arguments for and against each of these ancient institutions are considered. The Queen dubbed 1992 her '*Annus horribilis*' as a result of the marital scandals surrounding her son Andrew and the heir to the throne, Charles. Much worse was destined to come in future years with a gradual cooling of the public's enthusiasm for the institution itself. In 1997 the nadir appeared to have arrived with the death of Diana, Princess of Wales; in the wake of this event the nation seemed to express grief at her death and hostility to the monarchy in equal measure.

The monarchy

The development of a constitutional monarchy

Over a thousand years ago monarchs' right to rule was absolute; they dominated all the functions of government. Parliament existed to advise, endorse and provide revenue for monarchical needs. But as their needs became greater Parliament began to sell its support more dearly. A great struggle for power ensued between monarch and Parliament which only a civil war could resolve. Finally, the 1832 Reform Act gave the electorate the ultimate deciding power and the monarch was now forced to act, in accordance with the developing party system, upon the advice of ministers commanding a majority in Parliament. By Queen Victoria's time the monarchy had been gently eased into a position which had dignity and occasional influence but no power.

In the wake of Diana's death, arguments for and against the monarchy raged as never before.

Arguments against the monarchy

1. Heads of State should be elected. Inherited titles, it is argued, cannot be justified in a democratic age. In most other developed countries, heads of State are popularly elected.

2. It reinforces conservative values. The monarchy is not non-political, in that it reinforces Conservative values such as inherited privilege and wealth, deference to social status and tradition, and support for the status quo. The Queen may be non-partisan but her influence and advice are bound to reinforce the values which sustain the position of the traditional ruling elite.

3. It is expensive. The Queen used to receive an annual grant of nearly £6 million – the Civil List – to meet the expenses of the nearly 400-strong royal household.

In July 1990 a new arrangement was introduced whereby the Queen receives an agreed sum over a ten-year period, with more money being made available in the early years (£7.9 million in 1991–92). Similar arrangements were made for other members of the Royal Family.

Critics argue that the State should not have to pay the Queen's personal expenses, let alone those of royal hangers-on, when the Queen is the richest woman in the world. (The *Sunday Times* (8 April 1990) calculated her personal fortune at £7.0 billion, though this was dismissed by the Palace as wildly excessive.)

4. The absurdity of the honours system. The Queen is the cornerstone of what is often called an absurd system of elevating some men and women above their fellows. Mainly on advice from the Prime Minister, who can use such patronage to strengthen his or her own position, the Queen dispenses honours such as peerages, knighthoods and sundry medals.

5. Its functions are meaningless. In theory there are many things the Queen can do without consulting Parliament – declare war, conclude treaties, grant pardons – but in practice these powers do not exist. Moreover, it is argued, most of the other functions are meaningless:

(a) The Queen's annual opening of Parliament is a time-wasting ceremonial; even her opening speech is written by the Prime Minister.
(b) In theory the Queen can select her own Prime Minister, but in practice she always chooses the leader of the majority party.
(c) The Queen has a large number of appointments at her disposal – ministers, permanent secretaries, bishops, Lords of Appeal, the governors of the BBC – but in practice they are prime-ministerial nominations usually arrived at through some measure of consultation with the bodies concerned.

(d) The Queen can refuse to sign Acts of Parliament, but for some 200 years no monarch has seriously attempted even to delay legislation.

6. The royal prerogative has been usurped by the executive in virtually every respect. While Parliament can influence ministers, anything done in the name of the Crown is immune from democratic parliamentary control, nor can it be challenged in the courts. Thus, for instance, NHS hospitals are run by the State (in theory by the Crown) so they cannot be prosecuted if their kitchens are a health hazard. The left-wing Labour MP Tony Benn has long campaigned against the government's usurpation of the royal prerogative and for greater accountability to the Commons.

7. Following the death of Diana in August 1997 public support for the monarchy seemed to be ebbing and many commentators – e.g. Jonathon Freedland in the *Guardian* and Andrew Rawnsley in the *Observer* – called for the ending of the monarchy and the establishment of a republic.

Arguments for the monarchy

1. It is a unifying influence above party. Elected heads of State usually have a party colour, while the Queen is a permanent, non-partisan symbol of national unity. The British system also offers an advantage over the US system, where the President has to combine onerous chief executive functions with time-consuming head of State duties. The Queen is able to perform hundreds of engagements and overseas visits each year. She is a full-time head of State and is very experienced and skilled at her job.

2. The Queen tenders non-partisan advice to the Prime Minister. Bagehot wrote of the sovereign's 'right to be consulted, the right to encourage and the right to warn', and most Tuesday evenings the Queen discusses matters of State with the Prime Minister for over an hour. We are told she takes an active interest in Cabinet business, and perhaps her long experience of public affairs – she has advised ten Prime Ministers – proves of value. The Queen is scrupulously neutral in party political terms but occasionally she does hint at personal views; in June 1986, for example, it was rumoured that the Queen disapproved of Margaret Thatcher's opposition to economic sanctions against apartheid in South Africa.

3. The ceremony of monarchy 'legitimises' government. Some argue that solemnity and symbolism are essential ingredients in public life in that they strengthen awareness of national identity and respect for the authority of government. According to this view, most people are not so rational that they remain unmoved by the splendour and mystery of the monarchy.

4. It provides representation abroad. Connected with this the Queen makes a superb ambassador abroad. As one of the few remaining 'splendid' monarchies, representatives of it are extremely popular and draw huge crowds.

5. Loyalty of military. In some countries the military is a powerful political force and can threaten to take over the State; in Britain the strong allegiance of the armed forces to the monarch works against this.

6. It is a touchstone of social behaviour. The Queen's personal and family life are above reproach and, it is held, act as a model for the nation. She lends her moral weight to countless charities and good causes. The death of Diana may have injured the monarchy severely (see below).

7. The monarchy is popular. Opinion polls regularly show high endorsement of the monarchy: the Jubilee celebrations in 1977 and the royal weddings in 1981 and 1986 gave spectacular evidence that support had never been higher (but see below and Box 12.1).

8. Head of the Commonwealth. As a ceremonial head of the Commonwealth, the Queen acts as a focus and a binding influence for this loose association of States. Her constant contacts with other heads of State must be of value to the government.

9. The monarchy generates money. Thousands of tourists are attracted to London by the pageantry and glitter of the monarchy, thus earning valuable foreign currency. In addition, the Queen makes superb 'public relations' visits abroad. Hundreds of thousands flock to see her, and business deals often follow in the wake of these visits.

10. The monarchy is good value. It may cost more than its equivalent in Holland or Scandinavia but the essence and appeal of the monarchy lie in its more 'splendid' nature. After all, said its defenders in the 1980s, spending by the NHS on appetite suppressors alone exceeded the cost of the Civil List.

Lessening enthusiasm for the monarchy

At the beginning of the 1980s there was widespread support for the institution; ecstatic Jubilee celebrations had been held only a few years earlier. However, since those halcyon days the monarchy's reputation has plunged disastrously. Bagehot observed that the essence of the monarchy's appeal was its mystery. It followed that aiming the light of publicity at it would destroy such an elusive quality. Perhaps unfortunately this is what the Royal Family decided to do, starting with a documentary study shown on television in the late 1960s and later the full glare of media attention on the weddings of Charles and his brother Andrew. When these marriages began to go wrong and scandal surrounded the actions of Sarah Ferguson, Duchess of York, and Diana, Princess of Wales, not to mention the admitted adultery of Charles himself, the monarchy seemed to be transformed into a sleazy tabloid soap opera.

Diana's death

Throughout all this criticism the Queen survived relatively immune; it was widely felt she had retained her dignity and sense of duty while her children had behaved irresponsibly and selfishly. However, even this fig-leaf of legitimacy was removed in the wake of Diana's death. Then it was felt that the Queen had not shown sufficient warmth towards the beloved Diana; had been partly responsible for Charles's inadequacies as a husband through an emotionally repressed upbringing; and had been cold and unfeeling towards Diana's death (Box 12.1).

Table 12.1 shows the huge loss of support for the Queen and Prince Charles since 1981: 71 and 58 per cent ratings plunging to 10 and 5 per cent, respectively.

Box 12.1 The death of Diana and its aftermath

When Diana, Princess of Wales, died in a car smash in Paris in the small hours of Saturday 30 August 1997 the Princess precipitated a crisis in the Royal Family as severe as any she had caused when alive. Initially it seemed the Queen was unwilling to make any public expression of sadness; it was rumoured that she was so disaffected with the Princess – linked to a number of lovers and a prominent critic of the royal ways of conducting family life – that her very name was forbidden to be spoken in her presence. However, the royals had miscalculated the national mood; millions expressed their sorrow in a near hysterical week of national grieving at someone who, though controversial, had been able to touch people's hearts in a unique way and to win widespread support for the many charitable causes she championed. The Queen was more or less forced to make a broadcast expressing deep sorrow at the death of her daughter-in-law to win back some public sympathy. The Prime Minister, Tony Blair, was the only public figure who found the words and the sensitivity to express the nation's feelings. At the funeral, a massive State affair despite the fact that the Princess was technically no longer a royal and had been stripped of her HRH title by the Queen, the Royal Family was bitterly criticised by Earl Spencer, Diana's brother: the spontaneous applause which washed into Westminster Abbey from the crowds outside reminded the royals it was Diana who had captured the nation's hearts and not Charles or his mother.

Table 12.1   *Public attitudes towards the monarchy in the wake of Diana's death*

1. How many marks out of 10 would you give the Queen as Britain's head of State and Prince Charles as Prince of Wales for the way they carry out their roles?

% giving 10 out of 10	1981	1997
Queen	71%	10%
Charles	58%	5%

2. Which of these options would you prefer:

(a) The monarchy should continue in its present form	12%
(b) The monarchy should continue but be modernised	74%
(c) The monarchy should be replaced with a republic when the Queen dies	5%
(d) The monarchy should be replaced with a republic as soon as possible	7%

3. Assuming that the monarchy continues, do you agree or disagree with each of these statements?

	Agree	Disagree
(a) The Royal Family should become much more informal and less concerned with preserving their traditional ways	81%	15%
(b) The Royal Family is out of touch with ordinary people in Britain	79%	17%
(c) The Royal Family should not take part in field sports such as fox hunting and grouse shooting	62%	23%
(d) The Queen should start to give interviews like other public figures	49%	39%
(e) The Queen should give up functions such as signing new laws, opening Parliament and formally appointing a Prime Minister and stick to purely ceremonial duties	37%	57%

4. If the monarchy does continue, when the Queen dies, do you think the Crown should pass to Prince Charles or straight to Prince William?

Charles	38%
William	53%

Source: Observer, 21 September 1997.

Reforming the monarchy

1. Finance. In 1990 it was agreed that the Civil List should be set at £7.9 million a year until 2000. However, the costs of four castles, the royal yacht, the royal train and the Queen's Flight add up to over £57 million annually. In 1988 40 per cent of respondents in a poll reckoned the monarchy 'cost too much' and two years later a MORI poll showed three-quarters favoured taxing the Queen's income. On 11 February 1993 John Major announced that the Queen would pay income tax from April that year, though with a huge allowance and exemption from inheritance tax for the Prince of Wales.

2. Change the succession. Table 12.1 shows over half the respondents in the ICM poll for 14 September's *Observer* favoured skipping a generation and making Charles's son William King instead of him. However, as Andrew Rawnsley pointed out, this would be a horrendous weight to place upon a still grieving son.

3. 'Modernise' the monarchy. This Blairite word was used a great deal in the wake of the death of Diana to reflect the widespread feeling that the monarchy should become cheaper, more accessible and less stuffy, though still continue with its present duties. The ICM poll revealed a massive majority in favour of this option and only a minority in favour of a republic.

The future of the monarchy

Many commentators have pointed out that the monarchy has passed through periods of great unpopularity before – for instance, during the Abdication Crisis in the 1930s – and still survived. It would seem that, despite the sleaze and its poor showing after Diana's death, there is still a plentiful well of support for the institution. But the signs are unmistakable: to survive it must adapt and change and become closer to the people, rather like the popular monarchies of the Scandinavian countries.

The House of Lords

In 1407 Henry IV ruled that agreements on funds spent by governments were to be initiated in the Commons, but throughout the Middle Ages the House of Lords was able to use its influence to control the Commons through its widespread control over elections and nominations to Parliament. Relative harmony between the two Houses in the nineteenth century was shattered in 1832. The Great Reform Act ended the Lords' control over the Commons by extending the vote to the lower middle classes and removing the Lords' ability to nominate members. The Commons now came to represent wider interests than the landowners who sat in the Lords – the growth of the Liberal Party reflected the change – and these conflicting interests were manifested in a series of clashes between the Liberal-controlled House of Commons and the Conservative-dominated Lords.

In 1909 the Liberal Chancellor, David Lloyd George, introduced a budget which declared 'implacable warfare on poverty and squalor' via a package of tax increases. The Lords threw it out, 350 votes to 75. Two elections in 1910 reaffirmed the Liberal majority in the Commons and when the new King, George V, threatened to create sufficient non-Conservative peers to shift the balance of power in the Lords, the diehards caved in. The Parliament Act of 1911 reduced the Lords' power over legislation to one of delay only for a period of up to two years after the second reading of a bill. In 1949 Labour's Parliament Act halved the period to twelve months.

In 1958 the Life Peerages Act made it possible for men and women to be elevated to non-hereditary peerages for their own lifetimes. The Peerage Act of 1963 made it possible for hereditary peers to give up their peerage and become eligible for the lower House. These two measures have helped transform the Lords: average attendance has doubled since the 1950s to about 300 a day, and average length of sittings has increased from three and a half to six and a half hours per day.

Harold Wilson stopped creating hereditary peers in 1964 but Margaret Thatcher renewed the practice after 1983, though on a very limited scale – three in all. In November 1988 there were 784 hereditary peers, 353 life peers (by far the most active element in the chamber), 24 bishops, 2 archbishops and 22 Law Lords. Total membership was 1,183 (of whom 65 were women) but when those who declared they wished to take no part in proceedings are excluded, the potential actual strength of the Lords is reduced to 932. The political complexion of the Lords breaks down as shown in Table 12.2.

Table 12.2   *The House of Lords, by political allegiance*

	number	%
Conservative	538	45.4
Labour	117	9.9
Liberal	60	5.1
Social Democrat	25	2.1
Communist	1	0.1
Independents		
Crossbench	220	18.6
Non-party	54	4.5
Non-political affiliation	168	14.2
Total	1,183	100

These strengths, however, are somewhat theoretical. Shell (1990) shows that while a majority of Labour, Liberal and Social Democrat peers attend at least one-third of sittings, the figure for Conservatives and crossbenchers (peers not aligned with any one party) is only 30–40 per cent. The Conservatives' Chief Whip in the Lords therefore, when in government, could never count on a majority when opposition peers united with crossbenchers.

Indeed, while Margaret Thatcher's governments suffered only three defeats in the Commons, she sustained scores in the Lords.

Box 12.2 The composition of the House of Lords

Tony Blair has little sympathy for the Lords. In reply to Lord Cranbourne's (the Tory leader in the Lords who can trace his line back to the Cecils) assertion that the chamber he graces is often in touch with the common man, he derisively asked about the 'three generations of the Brocket family: the first had bought his title in the early part of the century, the second was a Nazi sympathiser and hated Scottish landowner, and the third was detained at Her Majesty's pleasure for making a claim on Ferraris he had concealed in a lake' (Ewan MacAskill, *Guardian*, 8 January 1998). The Lords certainly does not reflect the common man: only 5.7 per cent of members can claim to be working class; 58.6 per cent are professional; and 44.4 per cent are from the business world. In terms of education, 47 per cent went to Eton and 40 per cent to Oxbridge.

Arguments for and against the House of Lords

1. The hereditary principle

For. Enoch Powell defends the hereditary principle as no worse than any other method of appointment. John Stokes, former Conservative MP, admired hereditary peers: 'their behaviour is impeccable. They are trained for the job from youth onwards and they are truly independent, being answerable to no constituents' (*Hansard*, 10 April 1981). Those of a practical rather than romantic frame of mind point out that the services of their lordships – hereditary and life peers – are given cheaply: they are not paid a salary but are entitled only to an attendance allowance of up to £112 (per day) plus £33.50 per day secretarial expenses (1998 rates).

Against. It is argued that: (a) The hereditary principle is totally indefensible in a democracy: legislators should be accountable to society as a whole. Hereditary peers in any case have a poor attendance record compared with life peers. (b) It represents outdated values such as inequality, inherited privilege, wealth and the right to rule. No one would deny that the Lords is heavy with respect for tradition and the established way of doing things.

2. The constitutional function

For. The House of Lords still retains an absolute veto over any proposal to extend the lifetime of a Parliament beyond the present limit of five years. Supporters of the Lords argue that its powers of amendment and delay provide a useful check against ill-thought-out or over-radical legislation, particularly when the government is elected with a thin or no overall majority. The 1949 Parliament Act has never been formally used to overrule delay by the Lords: in a dispute the Commons has usually reached a compromise with the upper chamber.

Against. It is argued that it is indefensible for a body of non-elected peers to frustrate the will of the elected chamber. Moreover, the Conservatives have a permanent majority over Labour (though not overall) and if necessary can increase their number by summoning less regular attenders (or 'backwoodsmen'). This enables the Conservatives to delay and amend for party political reasons, particularly in the later years of a Labour government.

3. Useful for the Prime Minister

For. The Lords provides ministerial personnel, though mostly for managerial/political reasons. Because it is necessary to pilot bills through the Lords in the form it wishes, it requires ministerial representatives. This usually means two regular members of the Cabinet – Lord Chancellor and the Leader of the House – and sometimes up to two more. In addition, ten to fifteen additional ministers plus seven whips are appointed from the upper chamber. Moreover, it provides a useful way for the Prime Minister to recruit ministers from time to time directly, without an election/by-election. In addition, of course, it is an honoured resting place for politicians who have retired or who need to be moved to one side.

Against. Because peers can be appointed to government office, it is argued that ministers should be accountable to the Commons and that the patronage of the Prime Minister is already dangerously excessive. Moreover, the majority of life peers are past retirement age and even the active members are elderly. It is not unusual to see their Lordships hobbling about with difficulty or dozing off in the somnolent atmosphere: younger blood is needed to make it effective.

4. Deliberative function

For. The Lords represents a protean mix of wisdom and experience. Its thoughts upon certain public issues, unfettered by constituency or party pressures or the harsh timetable and restrictive procedures of the Commons, are often illuminating and occasionally provocative. Televising debates has generally been judged a success; about half a million on average watch the daily 'highlights'.

Against. It is pointed out that, however excellent they may be, few bother to read reports of Lords debates, nor do viewing figures tell us how attentive the television audience is.

5. Legislative function

The Lords does not interfere with bills concerned primarily with finance (about one-quarter of all legislation) but it has a key role in other respects.

(a) *Non-controversial legislation*

For. By introducing non-controversial legislation, particularly in connection with local government, the Lords relieves the burden on the overworked Commons. About 40 per cent of all government legislation was introduced via the Lords during 1974–79.

Against. Sometimes controversial bills are introduced in the Lords for tactical political reasons. In this way MPs were denied first consideration of sweeping proposals under Michael Heseltine's Local Government Planning Bill in 1980.

(b) *Revision and amendment*

For. The Lords revises and improves bills on their way to Royal Assent, and the government often uses this stage of the journey to introduce its own amendments and improvements. The Labour Party, which often when in office has a 'large and contentious legislative programme, probably gains more than it loses from the second chamber in terms of valuable and relatively non-partisan scrutiny of its bills, the anomalous composition of the House notwithstanding' (Drewry, in Walkland and Ryle, p. 106). During the 1987–88 session the Lords made amendments to legislation originating in the Commons, all but 1 per cent of which were subsequently agreed by that body.

A final argument is that because the Lords has no representative role in principle, it is better able to concentrate on the detail of its revising/amending function.

Against. It is sometimes argued that a reformed chamber would perform this task more effectively.

(c) *Select committee work*

For. It is often overlooked that the Lords has a European Communities Committee with a wider remit than its Commons equivalent. Sixty to seventy peers are involved in its six subcommittees and its reports are widely read and perceived as influential. The Lords also sets up a number of ad hoc committees on specific topics. All take particular care to consult expert opinion.

Against. Once again, a reformed chamber with younger members might perform these tasks more effectively.

6. The judicial function

For. The House acts as the highest court in the land, but this function is performed by the Law Lords, who include the Lord Chancellor, ex-Lord Chancellors and Lords of Appeal in Ordinary (including those retired). They do not pass judgement but rather clarify the law and give their opinion upon appeals.

Against. Critics point out that this function could be performed by a separate institution completely unconnected with a second legislative chamber.

Reform or abolition?

Since the 1950s, the Lords has undergone something of a renaissance. The injection of life peers into the work of the upper House has transformed its work rate, so that 525 peers spoke at least once in the 1985–86 session compared with 283 in 1957–58; 631 questions were placed for oral answer compared with 184; 1,182 questions were placed for written answer instead of 48; 250 divisions were called instead of 19; the House sat for 1,213 hours instead of 450; and average daily attendance was 317 instead of 136. In June 1990 the Lords roused itself to reject emphatically the Nazi War Crimes Bill (to facilitate the prosecution of war criminals living in Britain) after the Commons had passed it equally emphatically on a free vote. In spite of this vigour, or in some cases because of it, many people agree that the chamber should not remain as it is.

Opinion, however, is divided. Some want to abolish it and end for good its ability to interfere with the decisions of the Commons. Others believe that the functions at present ill-performed by the Lords are of crucial importance and would be done better by a reformed chamber.

The Labour Party and the Lords have had a long and difficult relationship. In 1918 Conference resolved to abolish the second chamber and Labour's 1935 election manifesto promised to carry this into effect. In power after 1945, however, Labour found legislative revision in the Lords valuable and its 1949 Parliament Act was only a mild reform. In fact, Labour politicians have always willingly sat in the Lords and taken part – though when Ramsay MacDonald offered him a peerage, R. H. Tawney (left-wing intellectual, 1880–1962) replied, 'What harm have I ever done the Labour Party?' Richard Crossman's 1969 proposals were embodied in the Wilson government's Parliament (No. 2) Bill, but an 'unholy alliance' between the Labour left (led by Michael Foot), who feared a strengthened chamber, and the Conservative right (led by Enoch Powell), who opposed the direction of the changes proposed, led to the withdrawal of the bill.

In 1976 Labour's difficulties over the Lords reached a new climax. Denis Skinner's bill for abolition was defeated 168 to 153 in the Commons, but the party Conference in 1977 voted overwhelmingly for it. During Question Time on 3 August 1978, James Callaghan denounced the unelected Lords as having no legitimate authority, but it was he who insisted that a commitment to abolition be withdrawn from Labour's 1979 election manifesto. Reaction within the party helped strengthen the left, and at the 1980 Conference Tony Benn urged immediate abolition by a new Labour government, even if it meant creating a thousand Labour peers to vote for their own extinction.

According to the eminent lawyer Lord Denning, in his 1980 Dimbleby lecture, the Lords has a constitutional safeguard against such action. While allowing that Parliament had the right to reform the Lords, he doubted whether it could lawfully abolish the second chamber altogether, at least without a referendum. 'I would expect any such legislation to be challenged in the courts.' This view was strongly challenged by the law professor John Griffith, among others.

Labour's 1983 election manifesto contained a pledge to abolish the Lords. By 1987 this had been dropped, and in 1989 Labour's policy review proposed the establishment of a reformed upper chamber, probably called a senate. Members would be elected to it possibly via a different system to election for the Commons. The role of the chamber would be to scrutinise legislation, especially that relating to the EC, and to delay bills which altered citizens' fundamental rights for the lifetime of a Parliament. During the 1992 election campaign the Conservatives defended the efficacy of the present House; the Liberals offered to replace it with a hundred-strong senate, elected by single transferable vote (a proportional voting system – see Chapter 7) and with the ability to delay legislation for up to two years; and Labour favoured an elected second chamber with powers of delay, in some cases for the lifetime of a Parliament. Labour set up a committee in 1998 to examine the manifesto commitment to reform the Lords. A bill to abolish the powers of hereditary peers will provide 'stage 1' of the reform. However, 'stage 2' – the new shape of the chamber – is still in question at the time of writing. Critics attack this phased approach and argue that the whole thing should be done at once. Certainly, if the hereditary peers are abolished it will leave the Lords staffed only by nominated life peers, making it the biggest quango in the country and, arguably, without any democratic basis to be part of the legislature. Neil Kinnock believed it would be foolish to try during a first term of office for Labour. Changing constitutional arrangements is exceptionally time-consuming and the new Labour government will find it hard to create the necessary legislative time.

This impasse is not unfamiliar. The House of Lords is one of a series of structural political questions, like electoral reform or devolution, which are so contentious and divisive that they are left untouched. One of our fundamental political problems seems to be the system's inability to reform itself even when there is a strong consensus in favour. Because reform has implications for devolution and the voting system, the upper House is likely to be with us in its present shape for a little longer yet. No one believes it to be particularly useful, relevant or efficient, but the truth is that attempts at change carry short-term penalties. In Britain bad reasons can always be found to defend the status quo, and more than good reasons are needed to change it.

Conclusion

Enoch Powell believed that the House of Lords is 'at worst a useful device' but one of its members, Lord Foot, is not convinced. 'It really can do very little. It performs a minor useful function of looking at matters in detail which the Commons has not got the time to do but that is no satisfactory bicameral system' (*Hansard*, 18 November 1980). From 1979 to 1990 the Lords voted down Margaret Thatcher's legislation over 150 times. Government defeats themselves are not unknown: Edward Heath suffered twenty-six between 1970 and 1974, and Labour 355 between 1975 and 1979. What made this state of affairs unusual, of course, is the preponderance of Conservatives in the Lords and the severity of some of the defeats. They included the exclusion of special cases from the council tenants' Right to Buy scheme; the rescinding of transport charges for schoolchildren in rural areas; and, possibly most important, the reform of local government. The Commons, of course, can reverse Lords' amendments and do so when the issue is deemed sufficiently important, e.g. in 1988 over proposed increases in dental charges and charges for eye tests, and in 1998 over university tuition fees.

This record suggests that the Lords – free of constituency and re-election pressures – do take their role seriously as guardians of the constitution. The huge Conservative majorities after the 1983 and 1987 elections gave added point to this concern that an 'elected dictatorship' should not 'railroad through any old measure which takes the fancy of the Prime Minister' (Beavan). Ironically, the Lords became, in some ways, more important as a counter to Margaret Thatcher's government than the generally weak opposition in the Commons.

Further reading

A. Adonis, 'The House of Lords since 1945', *Contemporary Record*, vol. 2, no. 3, 1988.

A. Adonis, *Parliament Today*, Manchester University Press, 1990.

J. Beavan, 'At bay in the Lords', *Political Quarterly*, autumn 1985, pp. 375–81.

P. Hennessy, *The Hidden Wiring*, Gollancz, 1995 (Chapter 5 on monarchy).

J. Morgan, *The House of Lords and the Labour Government*, 1964–70, Oxford University Press, 1975.

P. Riddell, *Parliament under Pressure*, Gollancz, 1998.

D. Shell, 'The House of Lords', in D. Judge (ed.), *The Politics of Parliamentary Reform*, Heinemann, 1983.

D. Shell, *The House of Lords*, Philip Allan, 1988.

D. Shell, 'The evolving House of Lords', *Social Studies Review*, March 1990.

S. A. Walkland and M. Ryle (eds), *The Commons Today*, Fontana, 1981.

P. Whitehead, *The Windsors: A Dynasty Revealed*, Hodder, 1994.

Questions

1 Should the monarchy be abolished or reformed?
2 Argue the case for abolition of the Lords.
3 Discuss Enoch Powell's view that the hereditary principle is no worse than any other method of appointment to a legislative chamber.
4 Construct your own plan for a reformed upper chamber.

13

The House of Commons

In October 1997 the Henley Centre published a report which revealed that only 10 per cent of respondents declared a 'great deal of confidence' in Parliament, while large majorities registered faith in Kellogs (84 per cent), Boots (83 per cent) and Heinz (81 per cent). Of course, the survey did not compare like with like and the functions are very different in each case, but the low figures must be a cause for concern. This chapter traces the decline in the power of the House over the last century and considers the substantial functions it retains, together with proposals for reform.

The development of the House of Commons

In theory Parliament, comprising the House of Lords and the monarchy as well as the House of Commons, is the ultimate source of power in British government. A majority vote in both Houses endorsed by the Queen's signature can make or change any law; there is no written constitution to place limits to this power (see Chapter 6).

It is often said that Britain has the 'Mother of Parliaments'; its history dates back to the Witan, the council of the Anglo-Saxon kings. Its subsequent history has been one of struggle against the power of the monarchy, with Parliament winning the battle by the eighteenth century, and struggle between the elected House of Commons and the hereditary House of Lords, with the former gaining dominance in the nineteenth century when a series of reform acts increased the number of people with the right to vote.

The idea of 'representative government', as elaborated by J. S. Mill and others, replaced the notion of an inherited right to rule. According to this view, ultimate authority would rest with an educated public electing representatives who would control the process of government in the interests of society as a whole. In the mid-nineteenth century, with a small electorate, loose party discipline and MPs with private incomes who did not rely heavily upon party affiliation for re-election, theory accorded closely with reality. The House 'sacked Cabinets, it removed individual Ministers, it forced the government to disclose information, it set up select committees to carry out investigations and frame bills and it rewrote government bills on the floor of the House' (Mackintosh, p. 613).

The decline of the House of Commons

Since those days the power of the House has been lessened by:

1. Expansion of the electorate and growth of a disciplined party system. Political groupings in the House realised that the new mass electorate responded to a coherent programme and that co-ordinated voting enabled them to pursue such policies more effectively. Parliamentary government became party government. Typically, two large parties competed for the popular vote, striving to achieve an overall majority of MPs which would enable them to govern for the maximum term. MPs ceased to play the same intermediary role: the executive bypassed Parliament and dealt more directly with the electorate. Opportunities for free debates virtually vanished as the timetable was geared to the achievement of manifesto programmes; the majority of amendments and even many private members' bills could now succeed only with the support of government. The MP's role was now dominated by support for his or her own party and opposition to others. Debates ceased to unseat governments, and the real debates took place offstage in the meetings of the majority parliamentary party. Strict party discipline was enforced: MPs knew that without a party label endorsement their re-election would be virtually impossible.

2. Growth in the power of the Prime Minister. As the role of backbench MPs has diminished, ministerial office has become an even more fiercely sought-after prize. The Prime Minister has control over the hundred or so Cabinet and junior ministerial appointments that are made from within the majority party, and MPs are loath to jeopardise Prime Ministerial favour by acting independently. There is some justification for Neil Kinnock's jibe that the House has become 'little more than an Edwardian fan club for the Prime Minister' (see Chapter 13).

3. Extension of government activities and growth of the bureaucracy. The numbers employed in the civil service have grown enormously as government responsibilities have expanded in scope and complexity: under 50,000 were employed at the turn of the century compared with some half a million at present. The number of ministers has only doubled during the same period, and the relatively temporary part-time, amateur politicians have found it increasingly difficult to challenge, or even critically assess, the advice offered by their highly professional permanent civil servants. A growing volume of legislation, moreover, is now 'delegated'; Parliament agrees a framework and the often important details are worked out by civil servants.

4. Loss of control over finance. Historically the House controlled the purse strings of government, but this function has passed almost wholly into the hands of the executive. Even in the late nineteenth century, debates on supply – which in theory consider proposed expenditure – had degenerated into party political exchanges over economic policy. The old Estimates Committee, set up in 1912 (and reformed in 1971) to scrutinise spending proposals more closely, never exerted more than a minimal check. For MPs to exert control over a sum representing about half the Gross National Product was difficult enough, but it became more so in 1961 when the executive (government) began to plan public spending five years in advance via the work of the Public Expenditure Scrutiny Committee. The legislature (Parliament), in contrast, still strove to 'approve' expenditure on a twelve-monthly basis.

5. The growth of pressure-group influence. As government's powers and responsibilities have increased it has come to rely upon pressure (or 'interest') groups for advice, information and co-operation in its day-to-day running. Moreover, new legislation is often formulated jointly by ministers, civil servants and pressure-group representatives before Parliament has any chance to see it. The capacity of MPs to challenge the corporate wisdom of this 'triumvirate' is limited.

6. The increasing influence of the media, particularly television, has distracted public attention from the floor of the House. In an hour-long interview with the Prime Minister, broadcasters have more chance to probe and challenge than the elected chamber has in most weeks. (The televising of the Commons since November 1989 has helped to redress the balance – see below.)

7. Membership of the European Community since 1972 has caused many decisions affecting the UK economy and way of life to be taken by Community institutions rather than the House of Commons (see Chapter 20).

8. Challenges to Parliament, such as Clay Cross council's rebellion against the 1972 Housing Finance Act and the trade union refusal to accept the 1971 Industrial Relations Act, brought the authority of the elected chamber into question.

9. The referendum was used in 1975 by Harold Wilson as a device to counteract opposition in the House – mostly in his own party – to continued membership of the EC. The devolution referendums in 1978 were again an extra-parliamentary device, though, interestingly, this time used by MPs who wished to frustrate government legislation on devolved powers for Scotland and Wales. Referendums on devolved assemblies for Scotland and Wales were both held in September 1997 and both endorsed the proposals.

Critique of the Commons

By the mid-1970s some commentators felt that the House had reached a nadir of impotence (e.g. Walkland and Ryle, pp. 279–304), pushed offstage into a peripheral, almost ritual role, regarding the formulation of government policy, the control of public expenditure, the passing of legislation and informing the electorate about public affairs. According to this view, the democratic chain of accountability from the electorate to the legislature to the executive and back again to the people had been hopelessly short-circuited. Instead of helpfully collaborating with the chamber to which they were accountable, ministers, once appointed, behaved purely defensively, aided and abetted by civil servants and pressure-group representatives.

According to this view, ready-made legislation is presented by ministers for Parliament's formal imprimatur; opposition attempts to alter or amend are resisted as a matter of course, and any dissatisfaction within the government party is branded as disloyalty; and debates have become a futile series of party political assertions and counter-assertions.

One study calculated that of the forty-eight government bills passed in 1967–68, only 12 per cent were 'substantially amended' (Rush, p. 81). Professor John Griffith reported that during three sessions in the early 1970s, 99.9 per cent of government amendments to bills were passed, while only 10 per cent of government backbench and 5 per cent of opposition amendments were approved. MPs allegedly responded by deserting debates after the opening speeches, and the public by low electoral turnouts and withdrawal of support from the two main parties. Having spent centuries winning its independent powers from an executive dominated by the monarch and the nobility, the House had meekly surrendered its powers to an executive controlled by its own representatives; governments had become in effect an 'elective dictatorship', in Hailsham's phrase. This is a powerful critique, but it oversimplifies and neglects the considerable functions which the House still performs.

Functions retained by the Commons

1. It sustains government. Its efficacy may have declined but it is still elections to the House that decide the political complexion of the government, and it is the majority party in the House that provides its publicly endorsed support. Ironically, the mid-1970s critique was followed by a period when Labour's lack of an overall majority injected vigour and significance into the Commons' activities. Ultimately the House defeated the government in March 1979 on a vote of no confidence – the first time this had happened since 1841. True, it was due to an unusual distribution of seats and in the May 1979 general election the traditional pattern was reasserted, but MPs had proved that the way they vote can still defeat governments.

2. It sets limits to government action. It follows that when governments frame legislation they have to be aware of what is acceptable. Apparently loyal voting often masks bitter divisions within parties, and what the majority party will accept from its leaders sets the boundaries within which policy is made. Government whips play a crucial mediating role here in reconciling what the government wants with what the party will accept; the difficulty of their task is just one measure of democracy in the House. Furthermore, the prospect of a violent reaction from the opposition, with associated delaying tactics, may also deter governments from taking certain decisions.

Finally, the government has to explain and defend its policies convincingly in the Commons; it cannot afford to lose the argument regularly or its credibility will be threatened and the morale of its supporters diminished. This was well illustrated by a comment in the (Conservative-supporting) *Daily Telegraph* (17 June 1990) on some recent lack-lustre parliamentary performances by Transport Minister Cecil Parkinson: 'It is dismaying to notice that Mr John Prescott, Labour's front bench spokesman, has sounded considerably more convincing than his government counterpart in his analysis of the transport issue this week.' The House's reaction does matter.

3. As a 'sounding board of the nation'. Some argue that the House is unfit for this task in that it is unrepresentative. Former Conservative Cabinet minister Enoch Powell believed, however, that the House's good geographical representation is more important and that MPs in close contact with their constituencies can accurately reflect what the country is thinking. They can represent these views in a wide variety of ways: in major debates, on Ten-Minute Rule Bills, in emergency debates under Standing Order No. 9, in adjournment debates, via private members' bills and motions, and through written and oral questions. They can also see ministers privately, publicise their views in the media or demonstrate them through abstention or cross-voting in a division.

4. Legislation. Most legislation passes through Parliament as the government wishes, but on a significant number of occasions MPs do rouse themselves to say emphatically, 'No'. The defeat of the Wilson government over House of Lords and trade union reform in 1969 is well known, but the Heath government suffered six defeats in 1970–74, and the Labour governments in 1974–79 no fewer than forty-two. Even Margaret Thatcher's large majority did not prevent Conservative backbenchers from rebelling on numerous occasions, over MPs' pay, proposed increases in parental contributions to student grants, and the Shops Bill, when they inflicted a humiliating defeat on the attempt to fulfil a manifesto commitment to Sunday opening. And Tony Blair's huge majority after May 1997 did not prevent groups of dissident backbenchers complaining about failure to spend more on welfare services and the proposal to charge parents a proportion of their children's university tuition fees.

Moreover, the hurdles placed in the way of private members' legislation have not prevented a number of resourceful MPs from clearing them and contributing towards an important body of law, on issues such as divorce, homosexuality, capital punishment and the disabled (see Morris, 1981).

5. Financial control. Scrutiny of public expenditure was improved by the introduction in 1971 of an annual White Paper with an accompanying debate and by the replacement of the Estimates Committee by the strengthened Expenditure Committee: further reform of select committees took place in 1979 (see below). While these innovations have increased the House's influence rather than its control over expenditure, far greater control is exerted over the taxation proposals in the Chancellor's budget speech. Often unpublicised, many concessions are made to special interests during the legislative stages of the Finance Bill.

6. Recruitment and training of ministers. All ministers must be Members of Parliament, and so service in either chamber is a form of apprenticeship for ministerial office. As the executive has become so powerful, the recruitment and training of the hundred or so government ministers and the smaller number of opposition Shadow spokespersons (offered as an alternative government team) is one of the House's most important functions. MPs usually have to serve several years – making their mark in debates, select committees, etc. – before being rewarded with junior ministerial office. It is in the Commons that the ambitious MP still has to establish a reputation, e.g. Gordon Brown in debates against Chancellor Nigel Lawson in 1988–89. The skills of the parliamentary performer are not necessarily those of the able minister, but the House can undoubtedly be a testing stage. Speakers must be in command of their subject and their audience and have a ready wit.

The House is also a socialising influence. It has a curious mixture of formality and informality – rather like the gentlemen's club it is often compared with. The dignity of the Speaker's procession at the start of the day's proceedings contrasts with noisy interruptions and occasional uproar during debates. Similarly, MPs who oppose each other bitterly in debate may be on first-name terms outside the chamber.

Whatever the differences, there is a strong sense of belonging which, in time, seems to affect even the most radical new members. After a few years this influence becomes as important as, if not more so than, any previous background a member may have had.

7. Political education. Despite the encroachments of the media, the House still plays an important role in political education. The various stages of debate – formal first reading, second reading debate, committee stage, report back, third reading debate and then a similar process in the Lords – provide opportunities for informing the public and for challenge and scrutiny. Ministers have to justify their actions on the floor of the House or in the standing committee rooms. Few people read the verbatim *Hansard* reports, but edited extracts appear in the quality press and on the radio. In addition, much of the content of news stories and features draws upon the proceedings of Parliament, and the media seem almost lost when it is in recess. 'Parliament remains,' according to David Wood (*The Times*, 7 August 1980), 'the great democratic educator, the sounding board without compare.'

8. Private grievances. Each of the 650 MPs represents a constituency – usually around 60,000 voters – and anyone may contact their MP. MPs can write to government departments to seek explanations, lobby ministers or meet them on their constituents' behalf, put down questions for a written or oral answer, or raise the topic on a motion for the adjournment (i.e. instituting a half-hour debate at 10.00 p.m.). If the issue relates to maladministration by a government department for which a minister is directly responsible, an MP may refer it to the Parliamentary Commissioner for Administration, or 'Ombudsman', as he or she is popularly called (see Chapter 14).

9. The House 'legitimises' political decisions. All societies seem to adopt some formal procedures for publicly endorsing government decisions. The House is particularly appropriate for this function in that its ancient traditions and esoteric procedures lend it a special mystique.

10. Scrutiny of the executive.

(a) *Question Time*

(i) *PM's Question Time*: This used to occur for two fifteen-minute sessions every Tuesday and Thursday and attracted perhaps disproportionate interest as the Prime Minister took on the Leader of the Opposition in gladiatorial combat, with supporters on both sides baying and crying for blood. When elected Prime Minister, Blair reformed the system in an attempt to take the noisy passion out of the event. Now it takes half an hour and occurs only once, on Wednesday afternoons.

(ii) *Question Time*: Monday to Thursday, ministers reply to oral questions for some thirty minutes. MPs are allowed one supplementary question and a clever MP can put a minister on the spot, but this is rare; briefed by civil servants most ministers can take on allcomers with confidence.

(b) *Party committees*. All parties have a wide range of committees, for the most part shadowing government departments. They are frequently addressed by ministers, and backbenchers have considerable chances to challenge and influence. Similar opportunities arise during the twice-weekly party meetings.

(c) *Select committees*, as opposed to standing committees (which scrutinise legislation during its committee stage), usually have an investigative remit into a particular area of government, with power to collect evidence and summon witnesses. About a third of all MPs are involved in them. The most powerful is the Public Accounts Committee. Its task is to ensure that government funds have been properly spent and its existence is thought to deter inefficiency or malpractice by civil servants (see below). Of the other three dozen or so committees, some relate to internal or procedural matters, but since 1978 most of the remainder now have concentrated on either a particular function or a department of government (see below).

The power of the Commons

If power has shifted away from the House over the last century, it does not mean that no power, influence or worthwhile role remains. The House is far from being a rubber stamp, and indeed underwent something of a renaissance in the late 1970s. John Major's slim 1992 majority of twenty-one placed many measures – especially those concerning the EU – in the thrall of factions within his own party. Just eleven dissenters could bring about the defeat of the government. On 22 July 1993 European disagreements came to a head when 'Eurosceptics' in the Conservative Party voted with Labour on a motion to ratify the Maastricht Treaty. Major won the next day, but only after threatening his rebels with a possible dissolution of Parliament and a general election.

Assessment of this changed role depends very much upon the balance thought desirable between the legislature and the executive. If one takes a minimalist view of Parliament as a forum for public debate on the activities of government, with the power to influence occasionally when it thinks fit – a passive watchdog – then its present functions fulfil, or even exceed, the requirements. However, if it is expected to perform an active interventionist role, then it will still be found wanting. Those who support the former view argue that the functions of government in running a complex, changing technological society while performing a wide range of welfare roles have properly placed more power in the hands of ministers supported by expert advisers. The government, according to this view, must be allowed to govern, and the House should recognise that it best serves the public when it occupies a responsible, supporting, watchful, but essentially secondary, role. Borrowing Norton's terminology, the UK Parliament is not a policy-making legislature, nor is it a mere piece of constitutional window dressing; rather, it is a 'policy influencing legislature', one which can 'modify and sometimes reject measures brought forward by the executive but cannot formulate and substitute policy of its own' (Norton, 1997, p. 245).

However, there are those who, while accepting that the House can never regain its former eminence, have argued strongly that the balance has shifted too far in the direction of the executive. They believe that the House needs to be strengthened to ensure that the nation's elected representatives have a greater say in executive decisions and that government is more answerable to them.

Box 13.1 'Parliament doesn't exist'

Tony Wright, the political scientist and Labour MP, argues (Wright, 1997) that Parliament as a forum for national policy debate does not really exist. 'What exists is Government and Opposition, locked in an unending election campaign on the floor and in the committee rooms of the House of Commons.' He discerns eight functions in theory performed by Parliament: sustaining and providing government; sustaining and providing opposition; making laws/ legislating; holding government to account (e.g. questions); investigation (select committees), debate forum; redress of grievances; and legitimation. However, he does not think that any are performed especially well and that reform is long overdue: 'There is no institution in more need of reform ... the reform agenda has been sitting there for years ... Parliament does not exist – but the task is to make it exist.'

The overworked House of Commons

The foremost academic expert on the House of Commons, Professor (Lord) Philip Norton of Hull University, has pointed out (in Jones and Robins, 1991) how desperately overworked the House of Commons has become. He explains how the pressures on the lower chamber have expanded from a number of sources, including the government itself, pressure groups (enormously) and constituents (in the early 1980s about 10,000 letters a month were written by MPs to ministers on behalf of their constituents; by the end of the 1980s the figure had reached 15,000). Other sources of work which have grown include increased pressure-group activity (see Table 13.1);

membership of the European Community, which has imposed a massive amount of legislative scrutiny work upon the Commons; and other members via select committees, written and oral questions, and so forth. Norton argues that the facilities in the House of Commons are woefully inadequate to cope with these increased democratic pressures. A MORI poll of MPs in 1990 revealed that 58 per cent of those who responded considered the House to be a 'fairly poor' or 'very poor' place to work. There is evidence to suggest that most MPs also consider that select committees are not sufficiently serviced to give an efficient scrutiny of departmental activities.

Table 13.1   *Organised groups: contact with Parliament*

Type of contact	No.	%
Regular or frequent contact with MPs	189*	74.4
Presented written evidence to a select committee	166*	65.5
Regular or frequent contact with peers	148*	58.7
Presented oral evidence to a select committee	124*	49.0
Contacts with all-party groups	120*	47.6
Contacts with party subject groups or committees	103*	40.9

Note: Based on questionnaire to 253 organised groups. *One respondent did not answer.
Source: M. Rush, *Parliament and Pressure Politics*, Oxford University Press, 1990, p. 14

Reform of the Commons

The movement for reform gained momentum in the 1960s, when a number of academics – Crick, Hanson, Wiseman and Mackintosh – adopted it and wrote widely upon it. In the House, Richard Crossman carried the banner for Labour and Norman St John Stevas for the Conservatives. Throughout its history, however, the movement has been vitiated by a number of fundamental contradictions.

1. There is a tacit agreement between the government and ambitious MPs who, while wishing to assert the power of Parliament, do not want to limit their own freedom when they themselves become ministers.

2. The champions of parliamentary power are split between those who favour the growth of small specialist committees and those who resist this tendency as a distraction from the floor of the House, where, it is maintained, the great issues should be publicly debated (see below).

3. Proposals for reform generate great dissent and absorb valuable legislative time. In the 1960s and 1970s, House of Lords reform and devolution both obsessed Parliament for years and both ultimately failed.

4. Reformers often support conflicting aims. Walkland points out (p. 285) that Labour reformers have tended to favour strong executive government to achieve socialist objectives while urging that Parliament be strengthened. They cannot have it both ways, e.g. in the late 1970s the House's enhanced effectiveness was won at the expense of the Callaghan government's authority.

Recent reforms

In 1978 the Select Committee on Procedure reported that the relationship between the House and the government 'is now weighted in favour of the government to a degree which arouses widespread anxiety and is inimical to the proper working of our parliamentary democracy'. The report signalled a sea change in the attitudes of MPs. Party politicians they may all be, but there is also a collective sense in which they are all legislators and share a concern that Parliament should be more than a rubber stamp to executive action. A number of reforms followed this watershed report.

Two minor reforms recommended in the report were adopted in 1980: Friday sittings now begin at 9.30 a.m. instead of 11.00 a.m. and, in an attempt to curb garrulity, the Speaker was empowered to set a ten-minute limit on speeches during second-reading debates from 7.00 p.m. to 9.00 p.m. Other reforms since 1978 have included:

1. House of Commons Commission. Set up in 1978, this body gave the House a greater measure of political and financial control over its own administration and personnel appointments. The Speaker is its ex-officio chair, and it comprises the Leader of the House plus three backbench MPs.

2. The National Audit Office (NAO) and the Public Accounts Commission (PAC). These two bodies were set up as a result of a private member's bill steered through by Norman St John Stevas in 1983. The NAO was established to replace the Exchequer and Audit department of the Comptroller and Auditor-General – the agency entrusted with the task of ensuring the government has spent its money properly and effectively. Now the Comptroller and Auditor-General operates independently of Treasury control, and on the basis of statutory authority, not convention, as hitherto. The PAC was also established as an independent body to help supervise the NAO. It comprises the chair of the PAC, the Leader of the House and seven – usually senior – backbenchers.

3. 'Special' standing committees. In 1980 the House agreed to a new type of standing committee – the ad hoc groupings of MPs which scrutinise bills in detail during the committee stage whereby four two-and-a-half-hour hearings could precede normal business so that evidence could be taken and witnesses heard. Only five committees became 'special' in the years up to 1983. In the event they were generally regarded as a successful experiment, but no substantial follow-up can be discerned.

4. Estimates days. In July 1983 it was agreed that three days would be allocated each session for the debate of specific items of proposed expenditure (estimates), to be chosen by the Liaison Committee (comprising chairs of select committees).

5. Opposition days. Traditionally, twenty-nine Supply days were made available each session for debates on topics to be chosen by the leader of the opposition. However, several of these days were always taken up by regular subjects such as the armed forces and Europe. In 1981 the regular topics were accordingly allocated to government time and the Supply days reduced to nineteen. In May 1985, the number was increased to twenty, but three were now placed at the disposal of the leader of the second largest opposition party – at that time the Liberals.

6. Televising the House of Commons. In 1966 the proposal that the House of Commons be televised was heavily defeated, chiefly on the grounds that such an intrusion would rob the House of its distinctive atmosphere. Successive votes in the 1970s sustained this position. In the 1980s Margaret Thatcher's opposition helped tip the balance against the cameras until November 1989, when the House finally bowed to the inevitable. Contrary to dire predictions, the world did not end and a limited experiment was transformed into established practice. Severe restrictions on what the camera could show were relaxed somewhat as early as February 1990. The Labour Party had hoped the cameras would show them to advantage, but initial surveys showed Margaret Thatcher (despite her nervousness at the prospect) outpointing the then opposition leader, Neil Kinnock.

The biggest hit of the televised proceedings was initially the twice-weekly clash between Thatcher and Kinnock at Prime Minister's Question Time. These clashes even interested audiences in the USA, but UK audiences were perhaps less easily impressed. Only 150,000 people used to watch the summarised highlights at 8.15 a.m. on BBC. Much more important, however, are the extensive excerpts used in the major news bulletins which are watched by up to 20 million people each day. Despite the politicking for good exposure, few have suggested that the House's distinctive character has been seriously affected by the televising process.

7. Select committees. This reform, set in train by the 1978 report, has been the most significant and far-reaching. Previously, select committees – charged with investigating areas of government activity of their own choice

– had been regarded lightly for the most part, and their reports were regularly ignored by other MPs, press and government alike. The new broom in 1979 abolished most of the old committees and fourteen new ones were established – for Agriculture, Wales, Defence, Education, Employment, Energy, the Environment, Foreign Affairs, Home Affairs, Trade and Industry, Social Services, Transport, Treasury and Civil Service, and Scottish Affairs. All have eleven members, except the last, which has thirteen; 156 MPs in all. Since 1979 the committees have been busy, producing over 400 reports on a whole range of topics – some of them very broad, such as the Treasury Committee inquiries into economic policy, and others more specific, such as the Home Affairs report, which prompted the abolition of the 'sus' law.

Opponents of the new system argue that:

(a) It has further diverted attention from the floor of the House, contributing to sparse attendances.
(b) MPs are being choked with information.
(c) It imposes strain upon civil servants and ministers.
(d) Committees concentrate upon neutral consensus topics and deflect MPs from winning the really important debates in the House and the country.
(e) Many of the committee reports are still ignored, and real legislative power is still controlled by party whips and leaders.
(f) Members fail regularly to attend meetings and others ask ill-informed questions.

Supporters reply that:

(a) The committees have achieved some real successes, e.g. the repeal of the 'sus' law.
(b) They have extracted much more information from government departments than would otherwise have been divulged.
(c) Ministers and civil servants have been forced to defend their policies before skilled and informed questioning and have consequently become more accountable. Before the reform, ministers frequently ignored committee requests to give evidence with impunity: now they usually comply.
(d) The widespread publicity which their reports receive helps inform the public and influence the climate of opinion.
(e) Chairs of committees have enhanced their authority and stature: MPs have been given an additional way of acquiring expertise and proving themselves. An example of this was the outrage expressed by maverick MP Nicholas Winterton when party whips relieved him of the chair of the Social Affairs Committee. Gerald Kaufman, veteran Labour backbencher, once opposed the select committee system, but once the prospect of a ministerial post receded he accepted the chairmanship of the Heritage Committee and performed his duties with skill and relish.

(f) MPs have been encouraged to find common cause as legislators and cross the often artificial party lines on specific issues.

(g) The televising of the Commons has won a national audience for select committee work. It is true that select committees do not command legislative power, but they have done a great deal to redress the imbalance of power in relation to government. In the wake of the Westland crisis the Defence Committee held the limelight for some time, especially when it probed the facts surrounding the famous leak of the Solicitor General's letter, but the limitations of select committee power were also revealed. Margaret Thatcher refused permission for two of her key aides to testify, and in their evidence Sir Robert Armstrong (Secretary to the Cabinet) and Leon Brittan (former Industry Secretary) were shamelessly evasive or unforthcoming. The government's response to the Committee's scathing July 1986 report was to rule the questioning of civil servants out of order in future. However, the report was debated in the House, and the Liaison Committee gained government recognition that Westland was 'an aberration'. Business has proceeded more or less as normal.

As the work of the select committees has become more important, leaks of papers and conclusions have proliferated. Calls have also grown for better professional support. In May 1990 the Social Services Committee gained attention by revealing that government statistics had been wildly overestimating the extent to which poor people's standard of living had improved during the early 1980s. It was able to do so through a commissioned report by the Institute for Fiscal Studies.

Further reforms

1. Devolution. Implementing its manifesto promise, Labour held referendums in the autumn of 1997 to test Scottish and Welsh enthusiasm for devolved assemblies to be elected by a species of proportional representation. Scotland voted heavily for the idea and also for some limited tax-raising powers for the assembly. Wales voted only narrowly, however, for its assembly. Once in operation the assemblies will have considerable implications for Westminster as they will become powerful voices for their respective regions and possibly for a federal structure for the UK in the future.

2. Proportional representation would enable small parties with thin national support to gain representation in Parliament which reflected their support. The big parties jealously guard the simple majority system, which benefits them, but growing minorities now favour change.

Box 13.2 Neil Hamilton and 'cash for questions'

This episode began with an article in the *Guardian* on 20 October 1994 which accused the then junior trade minister Hamilton of taking up to £2,000 from Mohammed al-Fayed, the owner of Harrods, to ask questions in the House. His co-accused, Tim Smith, admitted the offence and resigned, but Hamilton and lobbyist Ian Greer both sued the newspaper for libel; five days later Lord Nolan's Committee on Standards in Public Life was set up. In November the Members' Interests Committee considered the case of Hamilton's undeclared stay in al-Fayed's Paris Ritz Hotel, but by spring 1995 the Conservative majority could not decide what to do either about this or the cash for questions issue; in June it concluded that Hamilton was 'imprudent' not to have registered the stay but no further action was advised. In November 1995 al-Fayed, in testimony to the Standards and Privileges Committee, said he gave cash payments to Hamilton. A year later, in September 1996, Hamilton and Greer dropped their libel case and paid some of the *Guardian*'s costs; the next day the paper's headline was 'A Liar and a Cheat' above a photograph of the former minister. Hamilton said the inquiry undertaken by Sir Gordon Downey, the Parliamentary Commissioner for Standards, set up in the wake of the Nolan Report (May 1995), would exonerate him. Tim Smith stood down as a candidate in March 1997 but Hamilton insisted he would continue (possibly because being an MP was the only major source of income left to him). BBC war reporter Martin Bell decided to stand against Hamilton in Tatton as an 'anti-corruption' candidate. After a sensational campaign, Bell romped home with an 11,000 majority. Hamilton claimed Downey would prove his innocence but when it appeared in July 1997 it found 'compelling evidence' that Hamilton took cash from al-Fayed. Hamilton dismissed the report as the 'view of one man' and fought on. In October the Committee on Standards and Privileges refused to re-open its investigation into the matter and on 6 November endorsed the Downey findings. The final irony in this saga was provided when Hamilton appealed to his MP, Martin Bell (whom he had himself accused of 'corruption' during the election), to assist his attempts to appeal. Bell promised to do what he could.

---

3. Full-time members. Many MPs carry on their parliamentary duties without giving up their normal jobs, and in consequence fewer than half could be called full-time members. Labour MPs tend to favour measures which would discourage a second occupation, e.g. morning sittings, but others, such as the Conservative Sir David Renton, are opposed to MPs being full-time, which would tend to produce 'an inward-looking ... and rather narrow-minded Parliament. It is far better that we keep our contacts with life.' The marked tendency of certain (mostly Conservative) MPs to accept outside consultancies which could influence their role as MPs has intensified calls for stricter controls over such activities.

4. MPs' pay and facilities. In the autumn of 1997 MPs received £43,000 per year plus up to £40,000 Office Costs Allowance. Some MPs claim this is not enough if they are to do their job properly, and cite German and Japanese MPs, who receive twice their incomes. But judged by market forces, they arguably receive too much: after all, scores of applicants compete for every nomination!

5. More resources. As we have seen, some reform proposals focus on more resources for MPs, and better working conditions and more resources for Commons committees.

6. Labour's reforms. Once in power Labour established the Select Committee on the Modernisation of the House of Commons. Leader of the House, Ann Taylor, set out the government's four priorities on 22 May 1997: superior legislation through the publication of more draft bills and more extensive consultation; holding ministers to account through the hourly afternoon sessions for questioning the Prime Minister and other ministers; improving the monitoring of delegated legislation, much of which currently passes relatively unscrutinised; and the ceremonial procedures often criticised as time-consuming and unnecessary.

7. Peter Riddell, in his excellent study 'Parliament under Pressure', concluded with ten reform proposals for the House:

1 Central features of the constitution should be entrenched, e.g. changes in the voting system; maximum length of a Parliament. There should be a permanent Electoral Commission to administer referendums and reforms.
2 Law Lords to judge whether law is inconsistent with the European Convention of Human Rights, but otherwise to cease any active legislative role.
3 The remaining prerogative powers of the Crown exercised by ministers to be made subject to parliamentary control. Major public appointments to be considered by the relevant Select Committee and then approved by Parliament.
4 Number of paid ministers and whips serving in the Commons to be fixed at a maximum percentage of the whole House, e.g. 8 per cent would mean a reduction from the present eighty-nine to fifty-three.
5 Chairmen of Select Committees to be paid an appropriate salary, e.g. £10–15,000 per annum.
6 Select committees to report each year on expenditure programmes of their respective departments plus their related agencies and quangos.
7 All bills to undergo lengthy consultation procedures with Green Papers and draft bills considered by select committees. All bills to go to a special standing committee to hear witnesses. All bills to be timetabled with present annual cut-off ended.

  8 Scrutiny of European legislation to be improved via strengthened European Legislation Committee; better contacts between Westminster and the European Parliament.
  9 Nolan rules need to be strengthened, e.g. MPs who claim their commercial activities are not connected with being an MP when they clearly are. The Parliamentary Commissioner for Standards to be enabled to publish reports independently of the Standards and Privileges Committee.
10 Size of House and its sitting time to be reduced; fewer ministers plus devolution should enable a reduction from 659 to approximately 500 to be made.

Further reading

A. Adonis, *Parliament Today*, Manchester University Press, 2nd edn, 1992.

K. D. Ewing and C. A. Gearty, *Freedom under Thatcher – Civil Liberties in Modern Britain*, Oxford University Press, 1990.

Hansard Society, *Making the Law: Report of the Commission on the Legislative Process*, Hansard Society, 1993.

B. Jones, 'Select committees and the floor of the House. Du Cann v. Kilroy Silk', *Teaching Politics*, September 1982.

Labour Party, *Meet the Challenge, Make the Change*, Labour Party, 1989.

J . P. Mackintosh, *The British Cabinet*, 2nd edn, Hutchinson, 1977.

J. P. Mackintosh, *The Government and Politics of Britain*, 4th edn, Hutchinson, 1977.

A. Morris, 'The Chronically Sick and Disabled Act', *Teaching Politics*, September 1981.

P. Norton, *The Commons in Perspective*, Martin Robertson, 1981.

P. Norton, 'A decade of change in the House of Commons', *Teaching Politics*, January 1986.

P. Norton, 'The House of Commons: from overlooked to overworked', in B. Jones and L. Robins (eds), *Two Decades in British Politics*, Manchester University Press, 1992.

P. Norton, 'Reforming the Commons', *Talking Politics*, Autumn 1991.

P. Norton, 'The House of Commons', in B. Jones *et al.*, *Politics UK*, 3rd edn, Prentice Hall, 1997, Chapter 17.

E. Powell, 'Parliament and the question of reform', *Teaching Politics*, May 1982.

P. Riddell, *Parliament under Pressure*, Gollancz, 1998.

M. Rush, *Pressure Politics*, Oxford University Press, 1990.

S. Walkland and M. Ryle (eds), *The Commons Today*, Fontana, 1981.

A. Wright, 'Does Parliament work?', *Talking Politics*, Spring 1997.

Questions

1 'In the House you can say what you like but you do as you are told.' Is this a fair description of democracy in the House of Commons?
2 Can a socially unrepresentative House still be a democratic one?
3 'Parliamentary government in Britain was designed for the nineteenth century and is wholly inappropriate to the twentieth.' Discuss.
4 Comment on Labour's prescription for a reformed House of Commons.

14

The redress of citizens' grievances

The citizen has many opportunities to try to influence the government, e.g. by voting, joining a pressure group, writing to his or her MP, etc. Indeed, the opportunity to choose the government (via elections) and to influence it is an essential feature of a democratic system.

But what protection does the citizen have against the government, civil servants or the activities of other groups? Another feature of a liberal democracy is that there are limits on what a government or a majority of the population can do, and rights or liberties are guaranteed for individuals and groups. In contrast, there are few formal limits on what a totalitarian government may do.

Some countries with written constitutions (e.g. the USA, France) give citizens formal guarantees of freedoms – from arbitrary arrest, the right of free speech, the right to a free trial, etc. Such a Bill of Rights is often part of a larger constitutional settlement.

There is no such settlement in Britain, and the Bill of Rights, dating from the seventeenth century, deals largely with the rights of Parliament against the monarch. At the time it was a far-reaching check on the monarchy or executive. For example, it declared that in peacetime an army could be raised only with the consent of Parliament. In Britain we rely on the rule of law, or the rights enshrined in common law and upheld over time by judges, and the general culture or climate of public opinion. If there are few guaranteed rights for individuals, there is a general freedom to do as one wishes, as long as it does not transgress the law or interfere with the rights of others. Many of our freedoms (speech, organisation, demonstration, etc.) exist as long as, and to the extent that, they do not infringe the law. No particular freedom is absolute, because if it is pushed to the limit it may limit the freedom of others. Freedom of speech is limited by laws against defamation, obscenity and slander.

Protections for the citizen

There are many ways in which the citizen may be protected against the exercise of arbitrary power by the government and other public authorities and his or her freedoms maintained. They include:

1. The rule of law. The basic idea of this concept is that governors as well as the governed should be subject to clear and promulgated law, and that government cannot act in an arbitrary manner. Its most famous exponent was the nineteenth-century constitutional lawyer A. V. Dicey. He suggested that the English constitution rested on three major principles which amounted to a 'rule of law':

(a) The equality of all before the law, with disputes decided in ordinary courts.
(b) No one is punishable except in the case of a distinct breach of the law. No one is above the law.
(c) The laws of the constitution, especially the liberties of the individual, are the result of judicial decisions. The rights of the individual do not derive from the constitution but precede it, and are backed by the law.

Dicey claimed that this rule dominated the constitution in the sense that the principles were the result of judicial decisions made under common law. In other countries these rights were granted by the written constitution and could be withdrawn.

But Dicey's formulation is now widely criticised. First, it is hardly compatible with the sovereignty of Parliament, which means, as some observers have noted, that it is unchecked (see below). Parliament may choose to give the government arbitrary powers, as in wartime or in Northern Ireland. In 1972, when a High Court decision left doubt about the legality of the army's actions against civilians in Ulster, the Home Secretary introduced a bill to legalise them retrospectively, and it became law the same day. In 1983 the government withdrew the right of workers at GCHQ, the military surveillance centre, to belong to a trade union. The decision was later upheld by the courts on the grounds that only the government could decide whether national security was endangered. An appeal was considered by the European Court of Human Rights but was rejected. One of the first acts of the New Labour government of 1997 was to restore trade union rights at GCHQ. Many public authorities (e.g. ministers and the police) have special powers, and until the 1980s trade unions enjoyed special immunities, e.g. from claims for damages by firms or other groups due to breach of a contract while acting in 'furtherance of trade dispute'.

So Dicey's principles may be important as ideals rather than a guide to actual practice. And the courts may bring the executive to order, as they regularly overturned decisions of ministers in the 1990s.

2. Letters to MPs. MPs receive weekly a large postbag of letters – maybe 200–300 – from constituents requesting support, help or redress of various kinds. MPs usually do their best to assist, mindful of the fact that a reputation as a good constituency MP secures the support of their local parties and promulgates a reputation which, in a marginal seat, can mean the difference between re-election and defeat. Tony Wright (Labour, Cannock and Burntwood) believes this function is conscientiously performed by MPs: 'You'll see in late night adjournment debates individuals' cases being aired and debated in the nation's forum. We may be discussing Mrs Jones of 14 Railway Terrace. There's only one MP and the minister there but nevertheless, Mrs Jones has had her grievance ventilated, possibly redressed in the House itself' (Wright, 1997, p. 204).

3. Questions in the Commons or approaches by an MP to the minister concerned. The minister (according to the convention of ministerial responsibility) is accountable for the actions of his or her civil servants. But with the growth in the activity of the State and the number of civil servants, many doubt the efficacy of this procedure today.

4. Appeal to the Ombudsman. The Parliamentary Commissioner for Administration (PCA) (1967) was modelled on Scandinavian practice. He or she deals with private citizens' complaints that the authorities have not carried out the law or have not observed proper standards of conduct, e.g. in income tax assessment or the conduct of an eleven-plus examination. Examples of maladministration would include such features as bias, delay and arbitrariness in making a decision. Initially the complaint must be channelled through an MP. Many of the complaints which the Ombudsman receives prove to be outside the terms of reference, e.g. about the police, local authorities or the health service, all of which have their own complaints procedures. (Indeed, the last two and Northern Ireland have their own Ombudsman.) In investigating a complaint, the PCA is empowered to call for the relevant files of the department concerned. If he or she finds a case of maladministration, the department is invited to rectify it. (A successful case was the Sachsenhausen claim, in which the Foreign Office belatedly agreed to pay compensation to former inmates of that prison camp.) If the department refuses, then the PCA lays a report before Parliament and a select committee will consider the case. The PCA finds maladministration in about 20 per cent of cases, usually affecting the Inland Revenue and the Health and the Social Security Departments.

Some critics have complained about the narrowness of the remit; they say it is too concerned with maladministration, i.e. failure to follow the established procedures and rules. Critics want the PCA to comment on the rules and policies themselves if he or she thinks they work unfairly, and apart from dealing with procedural errors to deal with cases of unfairness. In Sweden and New Zealand the Ombudsman has broader scope. To date, most holders of the office have been former civil servants. Critics allege that this limits the PCA's independence; defenders claim that personal experience of administration and of how the government machine works helps the Commissioner's judgement and ability to operate effectively.

5. Administrative tribunals. Breaches of civil rights can clearly be dealt with by the courts (see above). But in the twentieth century the growth in the size of government (e.g. regulations, laws and civil servants), and its intervention in society and the economy, together with the proliferation of duties and rights among citizens, have led to problems. Many regulations and statutory instruments are left to civil servants to work out, applying administrative discretion.

In the event there are many disputes: about planning permission for motorways and slum clearance, hospital treatment, the allocation of housing rents, dismissal from work, and entitlements to pension, unemployment and National Insurance benefits.

The ordinary courts would be overwhelmed if they had to decide on the details of all these cases. Adjudication of queries and complaints is therefore left to the appropriate administrative tribunals, e.g. on Supplementary Benefits on benefit matters, or Commissioners of the Inland Revenue on tax matters, or local valuation courts on rates queries. Members of tribunals are appointed by the appropriate minister, who usually accepts their advice. But critics say that this form of appeal still falls short of providing an effective check on civil servants' possible abuse of their discretion.

6. European Court of Justice. It is possible for citizens to take their case to this, the highest European Union source of legal wisdom for a judgment. Usually it is concerned with arcane matters relating to constitutional questions and relations between member States and EU institutions, but it can also relate to individual matters. Steven Malcolm Brown, for example (case 197/86), brought a case against the Secretary of State for Scotland, challenging restrictions placed by the UK government on the eligibility of students and migrant workers from other member States for admission to higher education and maintenance (see also Chapter 20 on Europe).

Rights

These include, for example:

1. Freedom of meeting, subject to laws on obstruction, nuisance and trespass.

2. Freedom from arbitrary arrest and imprisonment. This includes such principles as a person's presumed innocence until he or she is proved guilty, the right to a fair trial and no detention without trial (i.e. a person has to be charged with a specific offence if he or she is to be detained and brought before a magistrate within twenty-four hours – but this does not apply to IRA terrorists).

3. Freedom of speech, subject to laws on blasphemy and obscenity. A further limit has been imposed in the form of the Race Relations Act, which forbids statements to be made in public which are designed to stir up racial hatred.

4. Freedom of conscience, e.g. to practise religion or exclusion from military service on grounds of conscientious objection.

The above are *civil* rights. In recent years Parliament has been active in promoting *social* rights, e.g. to work, against unfair dismissal from work, and to abortion, and has also given some protection to women, consumers and racial minorities. But many rights are not absolute. They may conflict with other rights, e.g. the freedom to join a trade union versus the freedom not to be a member and retain one's employment (the 'closed shop' may be inconsistent with the latter), or the freedom of some strikers to picket in large numbers and the freedom of others to work. The police have had to face growing physical attacks and political criticisms for protecting strike-breaking workers and meetings organised by the National Front. In the case of the latter, how does one strike a balance between the NF's freedom of speech (however objectionable the views) and the disorder and obstruction to which NF meetings invariably give rise?

Reform

A combination of such trends as (a) the growth of bureaucracy, (b) more interventionist government, (c) the subordinate role of the courts to Parliament, and (d) the imbalance in the constitution, particularly the power of a party majority of the House of Commons (see Chapter 7), has led some to call for a Bill of Rights, or even a written constitution, to provide greater protection for the individual's rights.

One of John Major's initiatives was to establish the Citizen's Charter (launched in 1991). This was designed to improve public services by giving greater rights to consumers and making producers and providers more aware of their responsibilities and duties. The users include students, patients, rail travellers and taxpayers. Steps included providing improved complaints procedures and publishing information about performance (e.g. the records of schools in examinations and truancy, and waiting lists at hospitals). The former nationalised industries, now privatised, have independent regulators which have various powers, including promoting customer satisfaction. They include OFGAS (for gas), OFWAT (for water) and OFTEL (for telecommunications).

There has been growing all-party support for a Freedom of Information Act, so that there may be greater information about the work of central government. The 1996 Scott Report into the Matrix-Churchill case (minister misleading Parliament over illegal sale of arms to Iraq) revealed that ministers used security provisions to cover up potential embarrassments. In 1998 the government proposed legislation which will provide greater openness except for certain categories of information covering national security and financial gain. It will also set up an Information Commission to rule on cases. The new Labour government has also introduce a bill to incorporate the main provisions of the European Convention on Human Rights (see below). It should become law in 1998.

European Court of Human Rights

There has been support, too, for the incorporation into British law of the European Convention of Human Rights. The convention is enforced through the European Court of Human Rights, whose jurisdiction Britain recognises. However, appellants have to pursue their cases in Strasbourg. To date, more appeals have been received, registered (i.e. regarded as suitable for the court) and upheld against Britain than against any other member State. About a quarter of all cases in which a breach of the convention was found involved Britain. The court, for example, has ruled against the use of torture in Northern Ireland and telephone tapping, and in favour of prisoners' rights to correspond in confidence with their lawyers (see Box 14.1). As noted, Tony Blair's government has incorporated the convention into British law. In doing this, it will overturn traditional Labour scepticism about giving more power to the courts and (unelected) judges.

Box 14.1 European Court decisions bearing on the rights of British citizens

The European Court:
- criticised treatment of suspected terrorists interned in Northern Ireland;
- allowed prisoners the right to correspond with their lawyers, MPs and the press;.
- condemned corporal punishment in schools;
- upheld the rights of workers against closed shops;
- declared British immigration rules to be unlawful because they discriminated against women;
- criticised ineffective judicial protection of a detained mental patient.

Source: B. Coxall and L. Robins, *Contemporary British Politics*, Macmillan, 1989, p. 347.

Further reading

A. Davis, 'The political role of the courts', *Talking Politics*, 1993.
C. Pilkington, *Britain and the European Union Today*, Manchester University Press, 1995.
P. Riddell, *Parliament under Pressure*, Gollancz, 1998.
F. Ridley, 'British approaches to the redress of grievances', *Parliamentary Affairs*, 1984.
H. Street, *Freedom, the Individual and the Law*, Penguin, 1982.
A. W. Wright, 'Does Parliament work?', *Talking Politics*, Spring 1997.
M. Zander, *A Bill of Rights*, Sweet and Maxwell, 1997.
M. Zander, 'UK rights come home', *Politics Review*, 1998.

Questions

1 Write a critical appraisal of the role performed by the Ombudsman in the political system.
2 Consider the arguments for and against a Bill of Rights.
3 Do you consider that opportunities for the redress of individual grievances are adequate?

15

The role of the Prime Minister

Much, probably too much, of the analysis of the Premier's role has been devoted to his or her 'power', and whether it has grown to such an extent that we should now talk of 'Prime Ministerial government' rather than Cabinet government. Critics of this development claim that it is unconstitutional if the Cabinet is being bypassed.

Power

The claim that we have moved into the era of Prime Ministerial dominance rests on a number of arguments: the Prime Minister is leader of the majority party and *de facto* head of the civil service; the media increasingly portray politics and elections in terms of personalities; and the Prime Minister is invariably a central figure in most of the major policy areas.

It could also be added that the sheer increase in the volume of work facing the Cabinet (the overload phenomenon) has limited the scope of collective discussion. The Cabinet meets only weekly, but decisions have to be taken all the time. Increasingly matters are left to the departments or to the Prime Minister, with the Cabinet less important as a decision-making body.

This line of argument intensified under Margaret Thatcher's stewardship at No. 10. She was seen, and to some extent presented herself, as a figure apart from her Cabinet. Many of the resigning ministers, notably Michael Heseltine (1986) and Sir Geoffrey Howe (1990), complained that she had been dominant to the point of behaving unconstitutionally. Margaret Thatcher and a small group of ministers allowed the American bombers to fly from British bases and bomb Libya, and decided to purchase Trident; she alone for long vetoed British membership of the Exchange Rate Mechanism (ERM), a system whereby European currencies were kept in a stable relationship to each other. There was also little or no Cabinet discussion on economic policy in the first years of the Thatcher governments. Other indicators, according to Peter Hennessy, of the declining role of the Cabinet under Margaret Thatcher, were that fewer papers were circulated and fewer committee meetings convened compared with the 1950s and 1960s. Margaret Thatcher, therefore, has been cited as a classic case of a strong Prime Minister and as conclusive proof of the Prime Ministerial thesis.

Constraints

But we should note:

1. Dominant Prime Ministers are not new. Lloyd George, Churchill (1940-45) and Neville Chamberlain were probably each more dominant *vis-à-vis* their Cabinets than any post-war successor. This relationship was a product both of their personalities and skills and, in the case of the first two, of war crises.

2. The Prime Minister's shortage of time. Many broad departmental policies and most specific decisions are decided in the departments. The PM will usually be concerned with a few areas, usually the economy and foreign affairs (the major preoccupations, from Macmillan to Blair). But even here, attention will be distracted by other matters, and the PM's own initiatives, if not well informed in particular subjects, may be counter-productive. For support there is a small 'kitchen Cabinet' of political advisers, in the form of No. 10's Policy Unit (the 'Think Tank' was abolished in 1983), but on the whole the PM lacks the expertise and background to reverse, or even monitor, all but a few departmental policies.

And however energetic a Prime Minister might be (Margaret Thatcher was rumoured to work anything up to eighteen hours a day), there are limits to the extent that any individual can govern a large and complex country.

3. The Prime Minister needs the support of party. Leaders depend on the support of their followers, actually MPs. The latter have an incentive to get rid of an unpopular leader if they want to hold on to their seats. There are now ample precedents for MPs withdrawing that support.

Margaret Thatcher was a divisive leader by the time she was challenged in a leadership contest by Michael Heseltine in November 1990. Had Michael Heseltine succeeded her, he would have had difficulty in reconciling her supporters to his leadership. A great attraction of John Major was his lack of enemies and consequent (assumed) ability to unify the party.

4. Cabinet does restrain. Strong Prime Ministers may dominate Cabinets and bypass them when they can, but Cabinet government is still very much alive. According to *Guardian* columnist Hugo Young (6 June 1986), there is 'a collective mood of those who are in the Cabinet which acts, maybe often, as an inexplicit veto on what Prime Ministers want to do ... they may decide not to do things because they know they might not get approval'. Certainly the office of Prime Minister has become more presidential, especially during the Thatcher era. Because there are so few formal constraints upon the office, Prime Ministers can literally do what they can get away with. A dynamic and dominant personality can command immense power, especially when things are going well – but ultimately a Prime Minister must command party loyalty. In the end it was advice from Margaret Thatcher's Cabinet colleagues, that if she stood in the second ballot she would lose, that convinced her to resign.

Prerogatives

Most of these have been transferred over the years to the Prime Minister from the monarch. They are often called 'powers', yet they are also 'responsibilities' and, depending on how they are exercised, may undermine the PM's position. Possession of the prerogatives is important in distinguishing the Premier from colleagues. The power to appoint and dismiss them, after all, demonstrates that the PM is more than *primus inter pares* ('first among equals').

1. **Appointments.** A Prime Minister today disposes of over a hundred ministerial appointments. They include Cabinet ministers, non-Cabinet ministers, junior ministers and other MPs in paid posts. If the governing party has around 330 MPs and the Prime Minister eliminates some of them on the grounds of old age, inexperience or sheer incompetence, then some sort of office will be offered to about a third of the party's MPs. The criteria for appointment will usually include:

(a) *Personal and political loyalty.* Most leaders will want to reward some MPs who have shown personal loyalty.
(b) *Competence* is difficult to measure, for the criteria will vary with the office. Leadership of the House of Commons, for example, requires tact in dealing with people, mastery of procedure and a range of parliamentary skills, including firmness and the ability to help the House conduct its business. A Chancellor of the Exchequer obviously requires a mastery of economics (Kenneth Clarke's appointment in June 1993 was criticised because of his lack of economic experience but he was a successful Chancellor). Law officers will be drawn from among senior politicians who also have standing in the legal profession. More generally, certain politicians acquire a reputation as skilful debaters, effective communicators and efficient administrators over the years. Their 'political weight' and reputation ensure their consideration for appointment.

(c) *Representativeness*. The Prime Minister will also wish a Cabinet to be broadly representative of the main interests in the party. National politicians will be needed for the Scottish and Welsh offices, there must be at least one woman, and so on. Because the old Labour Party more obviously contained political factions, a Labour leader had to strike a balance between the political left and right. The Prime Minister will be aware that potential leaders of an opposition or 'troublemakers' may be restrained by the ties of collective responsibility and secrecy of the Cabinet. Let loose on the backbenches, a critic may become a focus of opposition. If Margaret Thatcher had to strike a balance between 'wets' and 'drys' in her early Cabinets, John Major also had to balance pro- and anti-European groups. But the PM also has to think of the cohesiveness of the Cabinet; after all, it has to arrive at collective decisions and then defend them.

2. Dissolution of Parliament. Claims that the PM can use this as a 'big stick' to overcome opposition in the House of Commons are wide of the mark. Of the thirteen dissolutions since 1945, the incumbent Premier has lost six subsequent elections. It is not credible to threaten rebellious backbenchers (as John Major did over the passage of the Maastricht Bill in 1993), for a divided government is hardly likely to inspire confidence among the voters.

Most PMs are now careful to consult colleagues before deciding on the election date. The fact that Edward Heath in February 1974 and James Callaghan in 1979 got their dates wrong certainly subsequently weakened their position in the party. Dissolution is a two-edged weapon, and nobody has more to lose from defeat than the PM. Because public opinion is so much more volatile and the economy enormously difficult to manage, it may now be less easy to manipulate an election-year 'boom' in the economy, as occurred in the 1950s and 1960s. Indeed, Major had to fight in 1992 in the depths of a deep recession.

3. Control of the Cabinet agenda. A skilful Prime Minister can certainly exploit the right to schedule items for Cabinet discussion, call ministers to speak, sum up the views of the meeting (which is then a decision), decide whether an issue should be referred to a Cabinet committee (usually yes, if the issue is divisive) and choose the members of that committee, to shape the outcome.

But much of the Cabinet agenda is fairly predictable, e.g. reports from the Foreign Secretary, statements about the following week's parliamentary business, reports on Ulster and EU matters, and recommendations from the committees. And it is difficult for a PM to keep important matters off the agenda: Wilson eventually gave way to pressure to discuss devaluation of the pound in 1967 and in 1981 Margaret Thatcher agreed to allow full Cabinet discussion of general economic strategy. Michael Heseltine's resignation in 1986 was on the grounds that Margaret Thatcher was trying to prevent Cabinet discussion of the full range of policy options for the rescue of the

Westland helicopter company. The episode harmed the Prime Minister's position and it was widely reported that she was later outvoted by a Cabinet which opposed the sale of Land Rover to a US firm. John Major made a point of involving the Cabinet fully in key policy discussions, notably over the ending of the poll tax, the Maastricht negotiations and plans for public spending.

The Prime Minister's role

1. Image. A PM has many opportunities for self-presentation as the government or, strictly speaking, as its spokesperson. On the mass media, on foreign tours and in the Commons, the Premier is seen as the authoritative spokesperson for Cabinet policy. At times Margaret Thatcher appeared to 'make policy' in this way, almost committing her Cabinet in advance. One has to remember that it is the PM's Cabinet; the Prime Minister appoints ministers and they hold office at the PM's pleasure. If the PM is overthrown or resigns, the resignation of the whole government follows. So the PM dominates public coverage of politics and we regularly talk of 'Margaret Thatcher's' or 'Tony Blair's' government.

2. Power. The difficulty here is: how do we measure the power? It is pointless to see it as something the PM gains and the Cabinet loses, or the reverse as a sign of the PM's weakness. A PM who frequently faces a divided Cabinet is heading for trouble, and no Premier can afford to be isolated in Cabinet discussions; he or she has to speak for a collective Cabinet viewpoint, and provide a lead for the party and the nation.

If getting one's way in Cabinet is an indicator of power, then to be successful, a PM need only ask what is sure to be granted or never give a lead for fear of being overruled.

Security of tenure is not a good indicator, either. Since 1945 Prime Ministers have lasted an average of nearly four years. No acting PM (apart from the unusual case of Margaret Thatcher) has been sacked; although there was pressure on Churchill (in 1955), Eden (to 1957) and Macmillan (to 1963) to go, each retired in his own time. It is difficult to organise a coup, simply because the obvious rival, if there is one, risks splitting the party and alienating influential ministers, thereby undermining his or her own position. In opposition, however, it is easier to remove a leader. The Conservatives now provide the opportunity to contest the leadership, and this is how Margaret Thatcher replaced Edward Heath in 1975 and was herself undone. Her fall was caused by lack of confidence within the governing Conservative Party.

A PM may sometimes prevail against strong Cabinet opposition. But to push for your own view all the time entails political 'costs'. The power of the PM is, effectively, the power he or she has in and with the Cabinet. British government is a collective enterprise, and a weak Cabinet weakens the PM. Many commentators believe Margaret Thatcher progressively lost support within her own Cabinet through her excessively authoritarian political style: dominating Cabinet discussions and not allowing others to speak; humiliating colleagues through public attacks upon them; and selected leaking to the press to undermine colleagues on particular issues. When Margaret Thatcher found herself in trouble in November 1990 there was insufficient support within the Cabinet to extract her from it without a leadership contest.

3. Political management. This occupies a good part of the PM's time. The PM does not want resignations, which reflect a failure of management and advertise disagreements to the opposition. Therefore it is important to anticipate the reactions of fellow ministers, the mood of backbenchers, the views of party activists and public opinion. A Prime Minister who is publicly committed before the Cabinet decides an issue risks loss of face if overruled. Ideally, outsiders should not be able to separate the PM's position on an issue from that of the Cabinet. Critics of John Major complained that his 'wait and see' policy towards membership of a single currency may have been forced by Cabinet divisions but it also showed a lack of leadership. They claimed that he should have decided one way or the other and risked resignations of displeased ministers.

The doctrine of collective responsibility binds the PM as well as ministers; it means that members have to make compromises and settle for a policy that is broadly acceptable in the group as a whole. After all, Cabinet ministers have publicly to defend the policy. Consideration of different points of view and different interests – which should be reflected in Cabinet discussions – should promote more coherent and acceptable policies. No PM wants to lose a Foreign Secretary or Chancellor through resignation (Margaret Thatcher strenuously tried to dissuade Lord Carrington from resigning in 1982, Leon Brittan in 1986 and Nigel Lawson in 1989). This is one reason why Margaret Thatcher at last gave in to John Major and accepted British entry into the Exchange Rate Mechanism in October 1990. Some ministers occupy a symbolic position and their resignation would weaken the government (e.g. Michael Foot, 1974–79, who was believed to represent the support of an otherwise hostile left wing or Michael Portillo, the hero of the right under John Major).

4. The art of leadership. Ideally the PM wants to let Cabinet decisions 'emerge'. But if the Cabinet is divided, the matter may be referred to a committee. There is no appeal against the committee's recommendation to Cabinet unless the chair agrees to re-open the matter. This is one factor invoked by those who claim the Cabinet has lost power. Margaret Thatcher referred many economic issues to a committee which was balanced in favour of her line of policy.

Another way is for the PM to try to agree a policy line with senior ministers (e.g. an inner Cabinet) or the appropriate departmental minister, or to make concessions to critical ministers beforehand. This process is sometimes called 'squaring' or 'fixing'.

Finally, the PM may mould a common Cabinet line, through force of argument (the Premier has the opportunity to take a broad view: many ministers are so preoccupied with their departmental duties that they may be only too willing to follow the PM) and strength of personality. Prime Ministers avoid votes on issues; they formalise divisions and make consensus more difficult to reach.

A Cabinet is a collection of colleagues – drawn from the same party – who want the government to 'succeed' in its policies and win the next election. It is also a collection of rivals – aspiring for the leadership now, five years or ten years hence – and advocates of different policies. It is also a collective political body which, when making decisions about policy, is arbitrating between different departments and reflecting differences in the parliamentary party, the party activists and public opinion.

The case of Margaret Thatcher

Margaret Thatcher was a remarkable Prime Minister. The key to how she operated lay both in her personality and in how she came to the party leadership. Her political beliefs – less State spending and personal taxation; support for the free market; and suspicion of the trade unions, of much of the public sector and of incomes policies – were not shared by many in the Conservative leadership in the 1970s. She was in a minority among the leadership on some economic questions, and promised a change of direction not only from previous Labour policies but from Conservative ones as well. She became party leader by accident in 1975 because she was the only major figure to stand against Edward Heath.

An examination of her record will provide some clues about how Prime Ministers manage to dominate the Cabinet. All Prime Ministers have certain fixed powers, including the right to recommend a dissolution, the right to sum up Cabinet meetings, and the right to appoint to, and dismiss from, Cabinet. Margaret Thatcher used these fixed powers to expand her influence. For example, she gradually dismissed many 'wet' critics of her early policies, including Gilmour, Soames and St John Stevas, 'exiled' Prior to Northern Ireland, and over time also managed to lose more independent-minded ministers such as Carrington (1982), Heseltine (1986) and Lawson (1989). In their places she gradually appointed ministers who owed their promotion to her. Gradually she acquired a Cabinet that until 1990 could be relied upon to support her. But Cabinet appointments have to represent the significant elements in the party also. The PM does not have a completely free hand.

Second, Thatcher used this power to set up Cabinet committees and 'fix' their composition. For example, the key economic policy-making Cabinet committees were always dominated by supporters of the Thatcherite approach. Although these decisions were reported to the full Cabinet, it was very difficult for individual ministers in Cabinet to overturn the recommendation of a Cabinet committee.

Third, Margaret Thatcher was successful in elections. Although she consulted over the timing of dissolutions, the final responsibility was hers. Elections are increasingly seen as personal mandates for successful party leaders and this increases their authority over their colleagues. Margaret Thatcher also made good use of her Policy Unit and other advisers to second-guess policies in departments. Her reliance on the advice of her economic adviser, Sir Alan Walters, who openly criticised Nigel Lawson, caused Lawson to resign in 1989. One way in which she made policy was to summon an individual Cabinet minister and his permanent secretary to No. 10 and, supported by her Policy Unit advisers, grill the departmental minister. She commissioned papers for herself, held seminars on subjects and in several ways helped to make policy free from the full Cabinet.

Yet it would be foolish to generalise from Margaret Thatcher's experience. Such a style of premiership requires extraordinary energy, personal commitment, and ideological zeal and luck. Very few other politicians have this. She was successful in many areas, e.g. reforming the unions, lowering inflation (until 1990), curbing strikes and increasing Britain's international standing. Success builds on success. It remains true to say that the relationship between a Prime Minister and Cabinet varies over time. Because Margaret Thatcher was more dominant than other Prime Ministers, it does not mean to say that others will follow her. British government has tilted more to being Prime Ministerial than Cabinet, but it is not presidential.

The case of John Major

John Major's style as Prime Minister was more consultative and collegial than Margaret Thatcher's. This reflected both his own style and a reaction to the Thatcher style. He listened to colleagues and sought genuinely collective decisions. Not surprisingly, this style gave rise to criticisms that he rarely gave a positive lead and that he hung on too long to discredited ministers, e.g. Norman Lamont and David Mellor. At first it appeared that the Conservative Party and the country wanted a more relaxed style after Margaret Thatcher. But over time Major attracted criticism, particularly after the exit from the ERM.

Major's position after the 1992 election was hardly a strong one. He was at times in a parliamentary minority, in contrast to the huge majorities that Margaret Thatcher enjoyed. Bitter divisions over Europe not only diminished his public standing but attracted press criticism and damaged his government. To move one way or the other on whether Britain should join the single currency risked splitting the party. As the party trailed badly in the opinion polls and did disastrously in local elections and by-elections, so John Major was seen as an election loser and his authority in the party weakened. The interesting question is whether he would have provided a more decisive style of leadership if he had had a larger majority and had membership of the ERM been a success.

The case of Tony Blair

As Labour leader Tony Blair proved a decisive leader; he reformed and centralised the party, and slapped down colleagues for speaking out of turn. He has promised to carry on with a similarly decisive style in government. New Labour's agenda of modernising Britain – the constitution, education and the Welfare State – is very much Blair's. His personal imprint was reflected in his decision to import his press secretary and many other of his personal staff into Downing Street. He also gave a key role to Peter Mandelson as a Minister Without Portfolio in the Cabinet Office to co-ordinate the government's communications. Mandelson and the press secretary, Alastair Campbell, imposed a tight grip over ministers' access to the media. As Prime Minister, Blair co-ordinates policy as one of a so-called 'big four' of John Prescott the Deputy Prime Minister, Gordon Brown the Chancellor of the Exchequer, and Robin Cook the Foreign Secretary. It is likely, however, that other ministers are too busy running their own departments and that effective power lies with Blair and the people around him in Downing Street. He has introduced some changes in style – e.g. a weekly Question Time for the Prime Minister rather than two sessions a week, asking colleagues to address each other by first names, and has a high media profile. He has also invited the Liberal Democrats to join a Cabinet committee on constitutional change. He has intervened personally on the big issues, e.g. the Irish peace treaty, constitutional reforms and 'welfare to work'. Polls showed that after a year in office he was the most popular Prime Minister ever recorded by opinion polls (see Box 15.1).

In keeping with the aim of providing strong leadership, Blair has substantially increased the staff in Downing Street. His policy unit (eleven staff) is the largest ever and he has virtually doubled the media personnel under his Press Secretary, Alastair Campbell. Cabinet's influence appears to have declined sharply in influence, as Blair relies on bilaterial meetings with ministers, and the Commons is less significant because of Labour's huge majority.

Box 15.1   Tony Blair and Cabinet government

Riding high on the wave of his massive election victory on 1 May 1997, Tony Blair, it was soon whispered, faced no opposition in Cabinet; it was similar to, or even more pronounced than, Margaret Thatcher at her most imperious and presidential. Soon the downside of this style of ruling expressed itself. In October 1997, it transpired that Labour's promised ban on tobacco advertising would exclude Formula One racing following representations made by Bernie Ecclestone, a major contributor to Labour Party funds. It also transpired that the Cabinet minister concerned, Frank Dobson, and the junior minister, Tessa Jowell, too, opposed this exclusion. Sir Alan Bailey, former Transport Permanent Secretary, wrote to the *Guardian* (19 November 1997) arguing that the episode 'shows the need to involve the relevant ministers in decision making, and to get back to proper cabinet government which has been in decline for the last two decades.'

The next day columnist Michael White in the same newspaper wrote: 'The word is around that too many decisions are being taken bilaterally on Mr Blair's sofa with the big players squared by phone, instead of the forum of full Cabinet.'

On 30 December Hugo Young, the doyen of the paper's commentators, magisterial as always, weighed in with: 'This is a government in thrall to its own disproportionate triumph on May 1st and to the leader who produced it. Its collective membership permits him to run it as a personal fiefdom, consulting here and there with selected colleagues, running the show through an inner cabinet, not all of whose members belong to the real thing or have any other base than a Blair familiar. The Cabinet has taken further giant strides into the desert of irrelevance towards which Mrs Thatcher propelled it. Nobody these days even talks about the Cabinet as a centre of power, or its meetings as occasions where difficult matters are thrashed out between people whose convictions matter to them.' Such a judgement would not have surprised Peter Riddell of *The Times*, who as early as the election campaign described 'Tony Blair and Gordon Brown and their small group of allies' as 'operating by coup and fait accompli rather than debate' (quoted by Gordon Prentice MP in the *Observer*, 11 January 1998).

Yet despite these criticisms Blair was still very popular in spring 1998. Young declared that overall this government was 'amazingly good so far' and a MORI poll in *The Times* (19 December 1997) revealed that most Conservative Party supporters preferred Blair even to their own leader, William Hague.

Dimensions of Prime Ministerial power

Prime Minister and government: the power of appointment

Sources

1 Appoints all ministers and subsequently promotes, demotes and dismisses.
2 Decides who does what in Cabinet.
3 Appoints chairs of Cabinet committees (now increasingly important).
4 Approves choice of ministers' parliamentary private secretaries.
5 Other patronage powers, e.g. appoints chairs of commissions, and recommends knighthoods, peerages and sundry other awards.

Constraints

1 Seniority of colleagues demands their inclusion, sometimes in particular posts.
2 Availability for office – experience, talent, willingness to serve.
3 Need for balance:
   (a) Ideological, left + right
   (b) Regional
   (c) Occupational
   (d) Lords.
4 Debts to loyal supporters.
5 Shadow Cabinet expectations.

Prime Minister and Cabinet: direction

Sources

1 Summons meetings.
2 Determines agenda.
3 Sums up 'mood' of meeting.
4 Approves minutes.
5 Spokesperson for Cabinet to outside world.
6 Existence of inner Cabinet (intimate advisers).

Constraints

1 Needs Cabinet approval for controversial measures.
2 Determination of groups of ministers to press a case or oppose a particular policy.
3 Power of vested departmental interests backed up by senior civil servants.

4   Convention dictates certain items will appear regularly on Cabinet
     agenda.

Prime Minister and Parliament

Sources

1   Commands a majority in the House (usually).
2   Spokesperson for government.
3   Question Time provides a platform upon which PM can usually excel.

Constraints

1   Activities of opposition.
2   Parliamentary party meetings.
3   Question Time: not always a happy experience.

Prime Minister and party

Sources

1   'Brand image' of party, especially at election time: PM's 'style' is that of
     the party.
2   Control over appointments.
3   Natural loyalty of party members to their leader and their government.
4   Threat of dissolution (but seldom a credible threat).
5   Fear of party members that opposition will exploit public disagreements.

Constraints

1   Danger of election defeat: can lead to loss of party leadership.
2   Existence of ambitious alternative leaders.
3   Need to command support of parliamentary party, particularly when
     majority is thin or non-existent.
4   For Labour Premiers, some constraints from party outside Parliament,
     e.g. National Executive Committee and party Conference.

Further reading

P. Hennessy, *Cabinet*, Blackwell, 1986.
B. Jones, *Is Democracy Working?*, Tyne Tees TV, 1986.
B. Jones, 'The Thatcher style', in B. Jones (ed.), *Political Issues in Britain Today*, Man-
    chester University Press, 1989; and 'Blair's political style', in 5th edn, 1999.

D. Kavanagh, 'Margaret Thatcher: a study in Prime Ministerial style', *Teaching Politics*, 1985.

A. King, *The British Prime Minister*, 2nd edn, Macmillan, 1985.

H. Young, *One of Us*, Macmillan, 1990.

Questions

1 'The power of the Prime Minister has increased, is increasing and ought to be diminished.' Discuss.
2 Would you say we have 'presidential', 'Prime Ministerial' or 'Cabinet' government in Britain today?
3 Using the chart on 'Dimensions of Prime Ministerial Power' (p. 167) compare any two post-war Prime Ministers.

16

The civil service

The British executive has two parts. There is the *political arm*, which consists of elected politicians who lead the departments and sit in Cabinet; and the *administrative arm*, staffed by permanent, expert civil servants. The linchpin of the relations between the two – and the key to understanding the constitution – is *ministerial* responsibility. According to this doctrine, ministers are answerable to Parliament for the conduct of officials in their departments. As long as it is assumed that the civil servants are acting as their agents, they can be questioned in Parliament on their activities and on policies. They are expected to protect the civil servants if the latter have acted on their instructions, to take the credit for the good and the blame for the bad.

According to the traditional view of relations between ministers and civil servants, ministers decide policies; and civil servants, though they do play an advisory role, are mainly concerned with carrying them out. In reality it is widely acknowledged that the civil servants' role in defining policy options and attaching recommendations to their reports is important in deciding policy itself. Even the way a programme is implemented may have an important policy component. A good example is immigration, where the officials have a good deal of discretion in applying the rules. Other factors which strengthen the position of the civil service include its permanence compared with the way ministers come and go, and the disparity in size between the eighty or so departmental ministers and almost 500,000 civil servants, or even the top 4,000 or so concerned with high policy matters. In recent years the conventions governing relations between ministers and civil servants and ideas about the role of the civil service in policy-making have both been questioned.

Principles of the civil service

Three interlinked principles which shape the role of the civil service are:

(a) *Impartiality*. Civil servants are servants of the Crown, and thus are responsible for some higher purpose than that reflected by the government of the day. As a corollary they are subject to limits on their political activity and freedom of expression. For example, they are required to resign once they have been adopted as parliamentary candidates. At senior levels a civil servant may not take part in national politics. The principle of impartiality means that promotion is on criteria of professional competence and not on political grounds.

(b) *Anonymity*. Civil servants are expected to remain publicly silent on political and other controversial matters. It is ministers, in line with the doctrine of ministerial responsibility, who answer questions in Parliament. In the wake of the Westland crisis in January 1986, the Thatcher government tried to argue that it is ministers and not civil servants who should answer policy questions raised by select committees.

(c) *Permanence* follows from the idea that members of the civil service are servants of the Crown and not of the government of the day. The civil service is much more of a closed corporation than is the case in the United States. There is little tradition of 'outsiders' coming in at top levels, except in wartime.

We can readily understand how these principles are interlocked. The principle of permanence depends upon impartiality, and this in turn is helped by anonymity. Because civil servants only advise, they remain anonymous: ministers are responsible to Parliament for policy.

In the last twenty years or so there have been demands for major reform. One aim has been to make the civil service more efficient, in particular to encourage more businesslike and economic methods of working. A second has been to make it more responsive to ministers. It is important to keep these two considerations separate.

The Fulton Inquiry

The first attempt was made by the Fulton Committee, established in 1965 to report on the management and structure of the service. To some extent the civil service of the day suffered from the general critique of British institutions. A 'What's wrong with Britain?' mood was in the air. The committee reported in 1968 and made five recommendations:

(a) the promotion of more specialists and the recruitment of graduates 'with relevant specialisms';

(b) the unification of grades and classes;

(c) the establishment of a civil service college which would provide training in management, data analysis, economics and other skills;

(d) the creation of a Civil Service Department;
(e) appointment of more outsiders.

Persisting problems

Since 1979 a number of developments have strained the traditional role of civil servants. Anonymity has been challenged as select committees have questioned them about matters of policy and the officials have become known to the public. In the Westland case (1986) civil servants were named and blamed for leaking information to the press. Some officials have acted in ways which have led people to doubt their impartiality. Moreover, critics ask, how can ministers be responsible for activities of which they may have little knowledge? James Prior refused to resign as Secretary of State for Northern Ireland over escapes from the Maze prison on the grounds that he was not personally responsible. Michael Howard, Home Secretary under John Major, was regularly found by the courts to have acted beyond his legal powers and hence overruled, but did not resign.

Clive Ponting leaked a document concerning the sinking of an Argentine warship during the Falklands War to an opposition MP because he believed the minister was misleading Parliament and hence the country. But in 1985 the head of the civil service, Sir Robert Armstrong, stated, 'The civil service as such has no constitutional personality or responsibility separate from the duly elected government of the day.' In other words, the government of the day represents the interests of the nation – a proposition which worries some critics.

The popular television series *Yes Minister* extracted much humour from the idea that Sir Humphrey Appleby, the permanent secretary in a ministry, was cleverer than his minister, Jim Hacker, and able to outwit him in order to achieve the civil service idea of what was good for the country rather than the elected politician's. There are ways in which politicians may feel that the civil service is not co-operating with them:

1. **Obstruction**, through delay, inadequate briefing, presentation of biased information or overloading the minister. Such complaints have more often come from Labour politicians (compare the diaries of Richard Crossman, Barbara Castle and Tony Benn). Another example was the eleventh report of the Expenditure Committee on the civil service (1976–77). It called for the appointment of more party political advisers, personal aides for each minister and greater political direction generally. But right-wing Conservatives have also complained, in particular about the centrist tendencies of the service. Sir John Hoskyns, a former head of Margaret Thatcher's No. 10 Policy Unit, has called for the appointment of more politically sympathetic civil servants by the government of the day.

2. Co-ordination. Departmental officials serve on committees which shadow the Cabinet committees. Their job is to reconcile different departmental views and to secure agreement about a policy before it goes to the Cabinet. Some ministers may feel that this practice tends to leave them exposed and vulnerable in Cabinet.

3. Overload. The sheer pressure of work (as general spokespersons for the government, in their constituency and in Cabinet, as well as running the department) means that ministers have to delegate and let civil servants exercise their discretion. It is also argued that the work of the civil service in sifting information, analysing options and making recommendations gives it too much influence on policy.

4. Permanence. On average ministers remain in their department for about two years. At any one time a number of ministers are likely to be new to their job and looking to their officials for guidance. In support of the claim that the civil service can obstruct politicians and/or play too great a role in policy formulation, critics point to the continuity of policies in many departments since the war. According to this view, radical governments are held back by consensus-inclined civil servants. On the whole, the idea that civil servants fail to obey their masters is far-fetched. Some of the criticisms smack of special pleading or of politicians seeking a scapegoat for their own failures. One has to remember, moreover, that civil servants cannot reply to this sort of criticism. It is worth bearing in mind that:

(a) Ministers and governments may not really want to effect radical changes in policy. Governments respond to electoral mood, or economic imperatives, or party pressures, as well as to civil service advice.

(b) The policies of a government may fail because they were inadequately prepared in the first place. Consider:

- The ineffectiveness of the 1971 Industrial Relations Act. The Heath government never expected that so few trade unions would register.
- The disastrous introduction of the community charge (or poll tax) as substitute for local rates in April 1990.

(c) The civil service should not be partisan but should point out the pros and cons of different policies in a reasonably detached way. The experience of Margaret Thatcher's government has raised particular difficulties for this line of analysis. After all, her administration brought radical change in many areas, e.g. trade union reform, privatisation, local government changes, and reforms in education and the health service.

The impact of Thatcher

During the Thatcher years the party normally associated with the Establishment challenged the civil service to a greater extent than Labour ever had.

l. **Reduction in the number of civil servants**, from 750,000 in 1979 to under 524,000 in 1995, a reduction of 28 per cent, and to 471,000 in January 1998. In part this reflected the government's dislike of the public sector (seen as a 'drag' on the rest of the economy) and its quest for greater efficiency.

2. **Abolition of the Civil Service Department in 1981**, following the civil servants' lengthy strike over pay. Responsibility for pay and recruitment was transferred to the Treasury (likely to be less generous) and the Management and Personnel Office of the Cabinet.

3. **The pursuit of financial savings.** Instead of leaving it to civil servants to find economies, Margaret Thatcher appointed a businessman, Lord Rayner, who had direct access to her. His unit conducted efficiency audits within departments. The scheme developed into the Financial Management Initiative, which provided departmental managers with more information on the use of resources.

4. **Margaret Thatcher's use of her Policy Unit** to question ministers and senior civil servants about policies.

5. **Her close interest in high-level promotions**, particularly at the level of Permanent Secretary and Deputy Secretary. It was alleged that she promoted 'Thatcherites', politicising the civil service. If true, this would put a question mark against the principles of impartiality, permanence and anonymity. Margaret Thatcher, however, seems to have been more concerned with overturning the tradition of seniority and promoting people who would get things done.

6. **The sheer number of policy changes** which broke the old consensus, e.g. in local government, privatisation, trade union reform, education and health. There are still critics on the right of the Conservative Party who criticise the civil service (and ministerial timidity), notably for failing to cut public spending or to privatise more (school vouchers, for example). But the extent of Margaret Thatcher's changes in policy hardly supports the claim that civil servants rule, and none would claim that she personally was in their thrall. Indeed, the opposite is a more persuasive argument. After several years of power in which she vigorously promulgated her relatively simple messages, civil servants were more effectively permeated by a Prime Minister's views than ever before.

Box 16.1   A mandarin's parting thoughts

Sir Robin Butler, as Cabinet Secretary and Head of the Civil Service, the most powerful official in Britain, retired in early January 1998 and made some valedictory comments on the state of government in Britain, as reported by Richard Norton Taylor in the *Guardian*.

'He believes the lack of trust in elected politicians and a fear of leaks have led to small groups of ministers taking decisions without adequate consultation or discussion, while being increasingly vulnerable to pressure from single issue campaigners.

Trust

"People are so distrustful of politicians that ministers pass decisions to someone even less accountable [e.g. privatised utility regulators, distributors of lottery cash]. It is a great paradox ... People have no redress against them. Things are moving too much away from democratic accountability."

Leaks

"It is very difficult to have discussions between consenting adults in Whitehall without all the time fearing they may leak." He points to Lady Thatcher's decision to ban unions at the GCHQ intelligence gathering centre. That, he says, was "one of the worst cock-ups he had witnessed".

He also points to Michael Heseltine's blunt announcement in 1992 that 30 coal pits would be closed with the loss of 30,000 jobs. The Major government was forced to backtrack, though it later closed even more pits. The original decision did not go to the full Cabinet because Heseltine was petrified of leaks ... The more secretive the decisionmaking process, the greater the likelihood of bad decisions by small groups of ministers or officials.

Single issue pressure groups

Public outcry over single, albeit traumatic issues and events tended to obscure "rational debate" ... pointing to the hasty decision to muzzle dogs after a spate of attacks on children and the ban of handguns following the Dunblane massacre.'

Source: Richard Norton Taylor, 'Plagued by leaks and lack of trust', *Guardian*, 5 January 1998.

Further reforms

Reforms are still being canvassed. They include:

1. Increasing the number of political aides, so that a minister has a Cabinet of political supporters who can put forward alternative views to those of civil servants. The number of special advisers in Downing Street and Whitehall has been increased under Blair.

2. Increasing the number of senior appointments from outside the service. A number of senior posts are filled as a result of advertisements and posts are open to competition from outsiders.

3. Making individuals directly responsible for particular policies. Indeed, the Thatcher government introduced Financial Management Initiatives in 1982 to give civil servants more discretion over their budgets. In this way they can be held accountable.

4. Greater accountability of ministers and civil servants to Parliament. The post-1979 system of select committees has regularly called ministers and civil servants to present papers and answer questions. The committees are often vigorous in their questioning. After the Defence Committee inquiry into Westland (1986) some ministers wanted the committees to be forbidden to interview senior civil servants. They claimed that since they were servants of the ministers it was the latter who were accountable to Parliament.

5. The introduction of agencies. The Ibbs Report, *Next Steps* (1988), envisages that the civil service will in future consist of a small, policy-making core of 20,000 to 30,000. Most departments would be converted to free-standing agencies delivering services directly to the public. The agencies are given performance targets, covering the reduction of costs, speedier delivery of services etc. The agencies are independent and no longer subject to ministerial direction or ministerial responsibility. They are led by powerful chief executives with wholly delegated powers over finance and staffing as well as goals to achieve. By the end of the decade, some three-quarters of all civil servants will be in such agencies. By April 1995 there were 108 Next Step Agencies, ranging from the Benefits Agency (65,500 staff) to the Wilton Park conference centre (30 staff). Some sixty-five activities, involving over 80,000 staff, are candidates for agency status in the future.

The first two suggestions would weaken the idea of a 'career' service and might raise a barrier between the political appointees and the rest. The third, fourth and fifth suggestions are likely to weaken the convention of ministerial responsibility. A major, though little discussed, problem is that the appointment of 'better' (i.e. more able or more expert) civil servants will perhaps create pressure for them to be allowed more influence over policy in relation to ministers who remain formally responsible for policy.

The old style of minister/civil servant relations has certainly come under strain. This came to a head in 1995. The Prisons Service was a newly created agency and its Chief Executive, recruited via outside competition, was Derek Lewis, who was subsequently made Director General. When the Home Secretary dismissed Mr Lewis in 1995, the issue of reconciling managerial independence with ministerial accountability to Parliament was posed. The

Home Secretary drew a distinction between policy, for which he was responsible, and operational matters, which belonged to the agency. Some observers thought that the distinction was hardly meaningful, given the many interventions which the Home Secretary had made in operational matters.

Strains

1. An increase in leaks, some of them very damaging to the government, of documents to the opposition. In the Westland affair, civil servants were instructed by Downing Street staff to 'leak' documents calculated to damage Michael Heseltine. Following this, new rules governing these matters were drawn up by the then head of the civil service, Lord Armstrong. Armstrong claimed that, as civil servants of the government of the day, it was not for them to decide to leak documents. Ministers effectively decided what was in the national interest and what was constitutional. If officials had doubts about a course of action they were recommended to raise it with their permanent secretary or the head of the civil service.

2. There has been a growing debate over politicisation, which is potentially damaging for the service. Some critics fear that civil servants may lose their detachment and become too eager to please their political masters. This may have happened with the poll tax and the Scott Report into the 'arms for Iraq' case, both of which provided evidence of senior civil servants colluding with ministers to mislead Parliament. Both cases raised a number of concerns about relations between ministers and civil servants. They were raised again when a number of government information officers left departments following clashes with new Labour ministers in 1997. Under John Major a new Civil Service Code was introduced which specified the duties and responsibilities of ministers and civil servants.

The ethos of the civil service probably changed under the Thatcher influence. There is more emphasis on good management, reducing costs, value for money and the emulation of practices of the private sector. A key measure for transforming the culture of the civil service is the Citizen's Charter (see p. 154. Another initiative has been market testing or subjecting the functions of government departments to competitive bids, including those from outside. Both the Major and Blair governments continued with these initiatives.

Further reading

M. Burch, 'Civil service reforms', *Talking Politics*, Autumn 1993.
J. Greenaway, 'The civil service: 20 years of reform', in B. Jones and L. Robins (eds),

Two Decades in British Politics, Manchester University Press, 1992.
J. Willman, 'The civil service', in D. Kavanagh and A. Seldon (eds), *The Major Effect*, Macmillan, 1994.

Questions

1 'The ability of ministers to control their civil servants is the acid test of democracy.' Discuss.
2 Do you think it is possible for civil servants to carry out the wishes of ministers, unaffected by personal political beliefs?
3 Criticise the notion of the 'generalist administrator'.

17

Government and the economy

Many important political issues are economic. This chapter examines the reasons for Britain's relative economic decline; the kind of instruments available to government for managing the economy; the two main economic philosophies in theory and practice over recent years; and the main aspects of public expenditure.

The political importance of economics begins with the high priority which most people attach to improving their standards of living. Popularly elected governments will naturally be bound by, and seek to meet, this demand. The result of this 'electoral bidding' has been a growing expectation – possibly unfounded – that governments are responsible for running the economy successfully and a corresponding disillusionment when they fail. Opinion polls suggest that the popularity of governments closely follows the ups and downs of the economy (though 1997 was an exception). The delivery of prosperity has become the most important expectation people have of their politicians.

Economic decline

In 1939 British Gross National Product (GNP) per head was second only to that of the USA. After the war the economy soon recovered, expanding at about 2.0 per cent a year. In 1951 the UK's position was still fourth. Production had more than doubled by 1970. At over £700 billion per annum in the early 1990s, the UK's GNP is the fifth largest in the world, and Britain still ranks among the richest 10 per cent of countries. This absolute improvement is seldom stressed; it is our relative performance that commands attention.

The growth rates of West Germany and Japan were, respectively, 7.9 and 7.7 per cent in the 1950s; and 4.6 and 10.5 per cent in the 1960s. Both countries now produce twice as much per head as Britain. During the 1970s all advanced countries suffered economic recession but Britain suffered more than most. Growth was negligible and, towards the end of the decade, contraction set in. Between 1975 and 1984 Japan's manufacturing output increased by 61 per cent, the USA's by 42 per cent and Italy's by 22 per cent – but Britain's declined by 4.3 per cent. Britain's manufacturers could no longer outsell foreign goods in their home market: industries in which Britain once excelled, particularly electrical goods and motor vehicles, became dominated by imports. However, in absolute terms, most Britons are better off. In September 1997 the Office of National Statistics published a report revealing that despite the fact that prices had risen by twenty times since 1947, the average male weekly wage was fifty times higher, rising from £6 to £300. Women have done even better; their wages have increased sixtyfold.

Awareness of this relative rather than absolute decline became a potent, almost obsessive, element in UK politics. Shorn of Empire and economic pre-eminence, the country indulged in gloomy introspection. Diagnoses of the 'British disease' were plentiful.

Historical explanations

1. The first country to industrialise, Britain became burdened with obsolete plant and attitudes which other competitors were spared.

2. Two world wars exhausted Britain economically. Overseas investments were sold to pay for the war effort.

3. The end of Empire, with the economic growth of former colonies, lost Britain many of the advantages it once enjoyed. Some emphasise the 'cushioning' effect of imperial preference and date the real decline from as early as the middle of the nineteenth century (see Weiner, 1981).

Geographical explanations

For an island with few natural resources except for coal and oil, dependence upon exports is greater than for any other developed country. This helps explain why world economic recessions hit Britain particularly hard.

Cultural explanations

1. Poor industrial relations reflect the deep class divisions in society. Trade unions have felt it necessary to defend their members' interests to the point where productivity suffers from insistence on unnecessary jobs (overstaffing) or work procedures (restrictive practices). Strikes were frequent. Between

1968 and 1977, 850 days were lost per 1,000 employees through strike action, compared with 241 in Japan and 53 in West Germany.

2. The education system reflects prejudice against business as a career. The ablest young people often turn to the media, the civil service, the law or banking rather than industry. Managers are frequently undertrained compared with their overseas competitors and lack flair in identifying new products and markets – e.g. missing out on TV games and pocket calculators – and exploiting them effectively; and our salesmen are rarely good at foreign languages. Moreover, top decision-makers have little experience or direct knowledge of business: senior civil servants have usually studied non-economic subjects and only one or two members of the Cabinet, as a rule (even Conservative ones), have had substantial business experience.

3. Immobility of labour. Over 60 per cent of houses are owner-occupied. Problems of moving house and the higher price of housing in the more prosperous parts of the country restrict the mobility of labour from areas of low to high employment and from declining to expanding industries. In 1990, the average cost of a semi-detached house in inner London was two to three times that of a similar house in the North. The fifth of houses which are council-owned, with their endless waiting lists, compound the problem, while the small privately rented sector (only 15 per cent in 1996) is often too expensive and unsuitable for families.

Political explanations

1. The social policies pursued by Labour, and to some extent Conservative, governments since the war have encouraged the growth of employment in the wealth-consuming public sector, e.g. central and local government, education and the health service.

2. Adversary politics. The tendency of successive governments in the last decade to reverse the measures of its predecessors has diminished the confidence of businesspeople in the future of their own country's industries. This has affected planning and investment.

Financial explanations

1. Industrial investment – crucial for competitiveness and growth – has regularly been lower in Britain. Between 1966 and 1976 it was 19.9 per cent of Gross Domestic Product (GDP) per annum, compared with 21.5 per cent in West Germany, 23.4 per cent in France and 30.9 per cent in Japan. Over

half Britain's investment is by private individuals and firms; in 1981 the
former Labour Cabinet Minister Harold Lever and the economist George
Edwards blamed British banks for denying the private sector the long-term
finance needed to develop imaginative or 'risky' projects. Unlike those in Germany and Japan, British banks favour short-term loans.

2. Relatively low investment in research and development (R&D) compounds
the problem. While Japanese spending on R&D increased by 90 per cent
between 1967 and 1980, and by 40 per cent in France and West Germany,
the British figure actually declined by 10 per cent during the same period.

Economic explanations

1. Low investment in new plant and equipment, combined with poor industrial relations, help to explain why productivity is low. Productivity (the ratio
of output to number of persons employed) inevitably suffers when investment
is low. In 1967–76 it increased by 3.1 per cent a year in Britain, compared
with 4.8 per cent in West Germany and 8.9 per cent in Japan. America's
rate, at 2.1 per cent, was actually lower, but that is scant comfort as in 1971
US productivity per head was already double the UK rate.

2. Inflation of prices and wages never used to be a serious economic problem
in the 1950s and 1960s, when it ran at 3 or 4 per cent, but in the 1970s
inflation took off. In 1974 prices rose by 19 per cent and wages by 29 per
cent. After a decline in the late 1970s it began to climb again and Margaret
Thatcher made its reduction her prime economic objective. Inflation is harm-
ful in that it:

(a) reduces competitiveness;
(b) reduces the value of savings;
(c) hits those – the poorest – who cannot keep up with it;
(d) creates uncertainty and ultimately chaos if it develops into hyper-infla-
    tion, as in Germany in the 1920s.

It should be stressed that none of these explanations stands independently.
They all interact to form a vicious circle: low investment causes low productivity, which causes traditional industries to decline and new industries
to remain stillborn, which causes falling living standards and social bitter-
ness, which exacerbates industrial strife, which helps promote rival political
antidotes, which a bewildered electorate vote in for alternating periods of
office, which saps business confidence, which causes low investment; and so
it goes on. Politicians, as we have seen, assure the electorate that their policies will work, but what can government do to control the economy?

Instruments of government control

1. Monetary policy. The supply of money and borrowed money (credit) in the economy will influence the level of economic activity. The more money available, the greater people's capacity to buy things (demand), hence the need for the production of goods, which in turn creates employment. Similarly, the lower the supply of money, the less demand, production and employment. The government can generally control the amount of cash available through the Bank of England and the Royal Mint; but credit, available from many sources – banks and finance houses – is harder to control. One important way is to regulate interest rates: the higher they are the more expensive repayments become and the less attractive the loan; the lower the rate the easier it is to borrow money. Government raises interest rates when it wishes to reduce the money supply and lowers them to increase it.

2. Fiscal policy. This aims to control demand and supply (the ability of the economy to meet demand) through taxation and government expenditure. The Chancellor of the Exchequer can reduce demand by increasing taxes or increase it by lowering them. This sort of exercise is often called 'fine tuning' the economy. Chancellors must be careful, for if they allow demand to rise too rapidly, industry may not be able to meet it and imports will rise. If they exceed exports by too much, too regularly, an adverse balance of payments may ensue. This can have several deleterious effects; the most obvious is that the rate at which other countries are prepared to exchange their own currency for pounds – the exchange rate – declines, making imports dearer and nudging inflation up.

Government revenue in the past has rarely been sufficient to meet expenditure, and in most years the deficit known as the public sector borrowing requirement had to be covered by borrowing from financial markets in the City of London. However, banks can use government 'bills' and 'bonds', issued in exchange for the loans, to finance other loans to several times their value. Government borrowing therefore has a disproportionate influence on money supply.

3. Direct control and intervention. Between 1939 and 1945 the government assumed control of almost every aspect of production and employment. In peacetime not all these controls were abandoned. For example, regular attempts have been made to keep prices in line with wages by means of prices and incomes policies, to achieve a more geographically balanced growth by subsidising depressed regions, and to regulate specific sectors of the economy by special institutions.

Economic philosophies

The combination of measures government chooses will depend upon its view of how the economy works. Two broad economic philosophies can be discerned.

1. Keynesianism. Unemployment was the most acute problem between the wars, and it is no coincidence that J. M. Keynes's *General Theory of Employment, Interest and Money* (1936) was, to a large extent, addressed to it. Keynes believed that in times of slump, when unemployment was high and investment low, government could reverse the downward spiral by spending money. Its expenditure might exceed income for a while, the deficit being made good by borrowing, but the injection of funds into the economy would increase demand and stimulate production and hence employment. Government spending, or 'demand management', would therefore transform a vicious circle into a virtuous one. Full employment and economic growth were simultaneously possible. Keynes was in favour of using the full range of economic controls to achieve this. His followers believed that keeping wages in line with prices would restrain any inflationary tendency. By 1944 Keynesian thinking had become so widely accepted that it was enshrined in a White Paper committing the post-war government to 'maintain the highest possible level of employment'.

2. Monetarism. This owes much to pre-Keynesian classical economists such as Adam Smith, but in its modern guise has emerged as an answer to the more recent economic bane: inflation. Its chief protagonist has been Professor Milton Friedman of Chicago University. He perceives deficit spending as Keynes advocated as at best only temporarily effective. As soon as businesspeople realise that people have more money to spend on consumer goods they will push prices up rather than increase production. Higher prices mean pressure for higher wages, and so the inflationary spiral begins. 'Inflation occurs when the quantity of money rises appreciably more rapidly than output, and the more rapid the rise in the quantity of money per unit of output the greater the rate of inflation' (Friedman, p. 299).

Government should therefore concentrate on strict control of the money supply. Apart from that, advises Friedman, it should leave the economy alone. If companies can produce goods at prices people can afford they will prosper; if not, they will give way to those who can. Give market forces free rein and, as the Japanese and American economies prove, everyone will grow rich. If money is kept tight, trade unions which insist upon inflationary pay rises will bankrupt their employers and lose their jobs; the threat of unemployment will consequently be a natural and effective substitute for an incomes policy.

To summarise: Keynes believed that by injecting money into the economy, the level of demand would be stimulated, production increased and more people employed. Friedman argues that, on the contrary, such injections 'merely stimulate price increases by business and wage demands by trade unions: in other words, inflation'.

Naturally, each approach has proved attractive politically. Keynes appealed powerfully to socialists as a justification for intervening in the economy to:

(a) reduce the power of privately owned business;
(b) encourage equality by channelling government money to the lower-paid;
(c) promote economic prosperity through planning and State investment.

He seemed to offer a route to economic prosperity which also led to social justice, the means to achieve a revolution without the fighting.

Friedman appeals to Conservatives, the party supporting business, because:

(a) he stresses more freedom for businesspeople from government controls;
(b) he places the logic of market forces before the need for full employment;
(c) he justifies the role of business in terms of the overall public good.

However, since the war Conservatives have been heavily influenced by Keynes, just as Labour in the 1970s absorbed, to a high degree, the teachings of Friedman.

The philosophies in practice

From 1945 to 1970 both Labour and Conservative governments put their faith in Keynesian 'demand management' and set up a variety of prices and incomes controls plus measures to stimulate investment and plan future growth. In 1970 Edward Heath's new government experimented briefly with a monetarist approach but, when major bankruptcies threatened, reverted to a Keynesian 'dash for growth', combining heavy investment with statutory controls over incomes. It foundered hopelessly when the miners challenged such legal controls, and Labour won the resultant general election in February 1974.

The runaway inflation of the next two years, combined with growing unemployment and stagnant growth, seemed to bear out Friedman's analysis rather than Keynes's. In 1976 the Labour Chancellor, Denis Healey, adopted policies of monetary control, urged on by the International Monetary Fund, which had advanced massive loans to support the collapsing pound. Healey's blend of monetary control – resulting in public expenditure cuts and increased unemployment – and Keynesian intervention through incomes restraint and government cash for ailing industries was not unsuccessful: in 1978 inflation was down, real incomes (helped by North Sea oil) were up, and there was a mood of some confidence.

However, Callaghan's attempt to win acceptance of a 5 per cent wages guideline resulted in the industrial chaos of the 'winter of discontent', 1978–79: his government stuttered to ignominious defeat in May 1979 and Margaret Thatcher was given the chance to apply her stricter brand of monetarism. She always claimed that she would need two terms in office for her policies to have full effect, and of course ended up serving for eleven and a half years in Downing Street.

Conservatives in charge, 1979–97

Margaret Thatcher set the tone for this eighteen-year period by insisting on a rigidly strict monetarist policy with high interest rates and no subsidies to ailing companies. Chancellors Geoffrey Howe and Nigel Lawson were her faithful instruments (until they fell out and both bitterly criticised her). Howe's monetarism, however, was short-lived; targets for money supply were overshot regularly and by Lawson's time the policy was pursued in name only. John Major continued with basically Thatcherite policies and his Chancellors, Lamont and Clarke, did his bidding, not always enthusiastically. The record of the Conservatives in office can be briefly summarised as follows:

1. GDP per capita. Economists disagree as to whether this is the best index of economic success but it is widely used. According to World Bank figures in 1994, the UK was ranked thirteenth in the world in 1979, above Japan and Germany. By the end of the period the UK had slumped to eighteenth, overtaken by Italy (17), Japan (7) and Germany (13), as well as the 'Asian Tigers' of Hong Kong (5) and Singapore (4), but ahead of Sweden (20) and the Netherlands (19). The most significant aspect of these figures is that the UK's relative rate of decline, once plummeting, was slowed down by the Conservatives (see Figure 17.1).

2. Productivity. Over the period productivity per worker in the UK increased substantially, reducing the gap which once gaped between the UK and Japan and the USA; more recent figures suggest a UK improvement running ahead of our main rivals. Partly this is because of 'flexible' labour-market policies which made it easier for employers to hire, fire and employ part-time (antiunion legislation, tighter rules on unemployment, etc.). It was also because of the billions of pounds of investment which the UK attracted from overseas; e.g. 40 per cent of Japanese and American direct investment into the EU came to Britain.

Figure 17.1   *GDP per person, 1994*

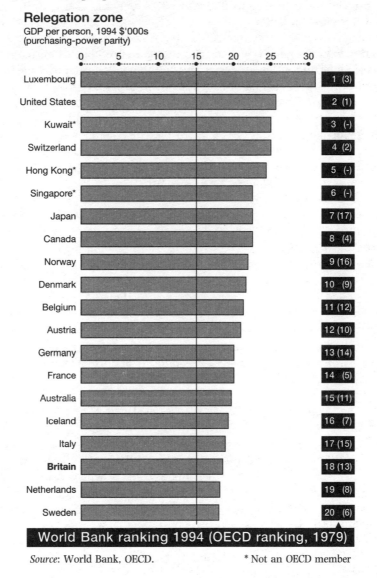

Relegation zone
GDP per person, 1994 $'000s
(purchasing-power parity)

	World Bank ranking 1994 (OECD ranking, 1979)
Luxembourg	1 (3)
United States	2 (1)
Kuwait*	3 (-)
Switzerland	4 (2)
Hong Kong*	5 (-)
Singapore*	6 (-)
Japan	7 (17)
Canada	8 (4)
Norway	9 (16)
Denmark	10 (9)
Belgium	11 (12)
Austria	12 (10)
Germany	13 (14)
France	14 (5)
Australia	15 (11)
Iceland	16 (7)
Italy	17 (15)
Britain	18 (13)
Netherlands	19 (8)
Sweden	20 (6)

Source: World Bank, OECD.   * Not an OECD member

3. Balance of trade. In 1985 the UK registered a balance of trade surplus but after that ran a deficit – 4 per cent of GDP in 1989 – although Lawson argued it was not serious, despite a devaluation of the pound of 15 per cent over the period. Manufacturing has slumped as an engine of export earnings, providing only 22 percent of GDP in 1995, compared with services' 54 per cent (financial services alone were 21 per cent of total output).

4. Public expenditure. Despite Conservative rhetoric about 'rolling back the State', the level of public expenditure in 1997 was still 41 per cent compared with 44 per cent in 1979.

5. Real incomes. There is debate about the figures but, according to the *Economist* (Election Briefing, March 1997), the gap between average incomes in the North and South diminished during the period and in every region increased by at least one-fifth.

6. Unemployment. In May 1979 there were 1.3 million unemployed and Thatcherite policies soon pushed the figure to 3.4 million (and in reality many more) by 1986. However, allowing for a renewed rise in the early 1990s, the figure gradually declined to 1.9 million in May 1997.

7. Investment. Investment is crucial to economic growth and to productivity, as it enables obsolete factories and methods of production to be replaced by more efficient means. In this area the UK has long lagged behind competitors. Between 1980 and 1994, investment averaged only 17.2 per cent of GDP compared with figures of 20.4, 20.9 and 29.6 per cent in France, Germany and Japan, respectively, and 18.1 in the USA. Why investment is so low in Britain has long concerned economists; some say it is the 'short-termism' of the City, obsessed with a quick profit rather than long-term projects which might create bigger returns. One possibility offered by some, including Tony Blair, is the history of economic booms followed by disastrous recessions which may deter long-term investment.

8. Inflation. Labour's record in 1973–79 averaged 15.6 per cent, and the Conservative's 6 per cent in 1979–96 was much improved though higher than in Japan, the USA, France and Germany. Lawson's attempts to control inflation via interest rates came unstuck in 1987 when he believed the way to stimulate growth after the stock market crash was through rate cuts. Instead, he merely fuelled a wild consumer boom which had to be reined in by interest rates so high a deep recession resulted, with unemployment soaring again and house repossessions multiplying. Major believed that joining the European Exchange Rate Mechanism (ERM) would ensure low inflation, but the rate at entry was unsustainably high and speculators forced Britain out in 1992 (see Box 17.1).

Labour and the economy

The recovery in the economy which characterised the period following ejection from the ERM was not attributed to the Conservatives and voters preferred to believe in their incompetence. This helped Labour storm to its

---

Box 17.1 Black Wednesday and the ERM

Having won an unexpected and narrow victory in the 1992 election, with the country in the depths of recession, John Major decided to pin his hopes on remaining within the European ERM — a system whereby the leading governments of Europe agreed to maintain their currencies within a certain relationship to each other. Britain had entered at a rate in relation to the Deutschmark thought by many to be too high to be genuinely competitive. However, Thatcher and then Major refused to agree any lowering of the rate: a fatal decision. In the autumn of 1992 speculators, especially the financier George Soros, decided to seek a profit by forcing down the value of sterling. Chancellor Lamont tried to bully the head of the German national bank to lower its rate of interest but succeeded only in alienating the powerful Germans. Speculators sold sterling in massive waves and confidence in the currency wilted. The Bank of England tried to stem the tide with over a billion pounds of reserves but this was burnt away in hours. Traders in the City speak in awestruck terms of how the realisation hit home that the Bank was no longer defending the pound and that it was in 'free-fall'. Meanwhile Major, Hurd, Heseltine and Clarke were sitting in the Admiralty Building as No. 10 was being refurbished. Lamont's attempts to raise interest rates to 12 (and later to 15) per cent to defend the pound proved futile and the hurricane of the assault against the pound continued. Clarke recalls a bizarre aspect of the crisis when the four senior Cabinet ministers suddenly realised that, stranded in their temporary home, they were among the worst informed people in the country and a search was instigated for a transistor radio. Clarke later heard the interest-rate ploy had failed from his driver, who had heard it on the car radio. Finally, Lamont had to face the cameras and declare Britain was leaving the ERM, the so-called 'bedrock' of government policy to rein in inflation and maintain growth. At a stroke the pound was devalued effectively by 10 per cent, but perversely the economy responded well and a period of growth resulted.

Britain's ejection from the ERM was the biggest single reason why the Conservatives lost the election in 1997. Their reputation for economic competence, which had survived the deep depression of the early 1990s, was finally shattered; it never recovered and even the reviving economy won it few votes as it was not attributed by a sceptical electorate to government policies.

---

famous 1997 victory. Following the victory Labour moved swiftly to strip the Bank of England of some of its regulatory powers while giving it power to fix interest rates on the basis of economic and not political criteria. Economists applauded the measure but left-wing critics deplored the surrender of key economic power to a supremely capitalist institution. In the summer and autumn of 1997 the economy performed more or less as under the Tories, although inflation evinced an upward blip to 3.5 per cent.

The key, indeed momentous, economic decision facing the Labour government in 1997 was the decision of whether to enter the single currency

Figure 17.2   *Government income, 1998–99 (£bn)*

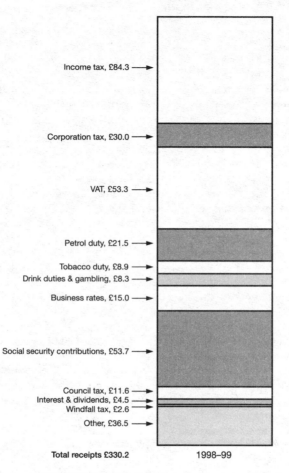

Income tax, £84.3 ⟶

Corporation tax, £30.0 ⟶

VAT, £53.3 ⟶

Petrol duty, £21.5 ⟶

Tobacco duty, £8.9 ⟶

Drink duties & gambling, £8.3 ⟶

Business rates, £15.0 ⟶

Social security contributions, £53.7 ⟶

Council tax, £11.6 ⟶

Interest & dividends, £4.5 ⟶

Windfall tax, £2.6 ⟶

Other, £36.5 ⟶

Total receipts £330.2   1998–99

Source: *Guardian,* 17 March 1998.

Figure 17.3   *Government expenditure, 1998–99 (£bn)*

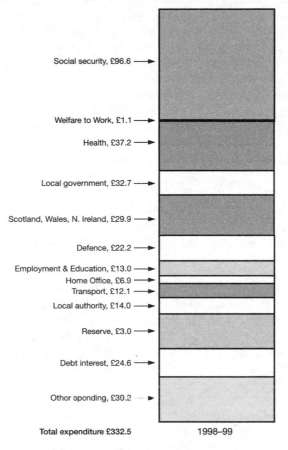

Social security, £96.6 ➝

Welfare to Work, £1.1 ➝
Health, £37.2 ➝

Local government, £32.7 ➝

Scotland, Wales, N. Ireland, £29.9 ➝

Defence, £22.2 ➝

Employment & Education, £13.0 ➝
Home Office, £6.9 ➝
Transport, £12.1 ➝

Local authority, £14.0 ➝

Reserve, £3.0 ➝

Debt interest, £24.6 ➝

Other spending, £30.2 ➝

Total expenditure £332.5   1998–99

Source: *Guardian,* 17 March 1998.

due to take off in 1999. Brown decided to express support in principle but to defer entry until five criteria of 'convergence' had been established between Britain and the single currency countries; and until experience of the currency in practice revealed whether it would be to the UK's advantage to join. One of the key problems related to interest rates and the economic cycle. The UK was well out of its recession and expanding by 1997, and required rates of interest which would dampen down demand and hence inflation; the major European economies, on the other hand, were emerging from recession and needed low rates to stimulate growth (see Chapter 20). The Conservative opposition were determined to be sceptical and Hague declared his party would oppose entry for ten years at least – a policy which Kenneth Clarke and Michael Heseltine condemned as likely to be overtaken by events.

Public expenditure

The money government spends has to be raised by taxes and, as Figure 17.2 shows, the major part derives naturally from income tax. However, in addition surprisingly large slices come from VAT receipts and social insurance payments. Spending is shown in Figure 17.3 and reveals the major spending departments to be social security, health, defence and education, with a surprisingly large slice going to payment of debt interest every year. In the run-up to the 1997 election, Labour was paranoid about appearing to advocate the 'tax and spend' policies associated with Old Labour and which had stymied its 1992 election effort. Consequently, it entered power committed to accept, for two years, the income tax and spending levels inherited from the previous government. With education and health services desperate for cash, and Labour committed to help them, the government soon ran into criticism that its commitments to revive welfare services after the depredations of the Conservative years were merely warm words.

Further reading

Economist Election Briefing, March 1997.
M. Friedman, *Free to Choose*, Penguin, 1980.
A. Gamble, *Britain in Decline*, Macmillan, 1985.
M. Moran, 'Economic policy', in B. Jones *et al.*, *Politics UK*, 3rd edn, Prentice Hall, 1997, Chapter 27.
A. Weiner, *Britain's English Culture and the Decline of the Industrial Spirit*, Cambridge University Press, 1981.

Questions

1 Is central government planning essential for, or inimical to, economic prosperity?
2 What additional requirements has 'globalisation' imposed upon governments regarding their economies?
3 How can governments regulate: (a) demand in the economy; and (b) unemployment?

18

Pressure groups

The theory which underpins Britain's government is that of representative democracy. At least once every five years voters elect their representatives to the House of Commons. The majority party forms the government and proceeds to carry out its programme with the help of the civil service and the regular parliamentary endorsement which its majority provides. At the next election voters can decide whether or not the ruling party deserves another term of office. Figure 18.1 illustrates the theory.

This is a very simplified view, of course. In reality voters never express a genuine collective wish, and even those who have voted for the party in

Figure 18.1   *How pressure groups fit into the theory of democracy*

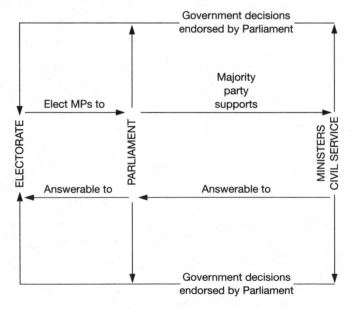

power will disagree with aspects of government policy. Many will seek to use their membership of pressure groups – over half the population belong to one kind of pressure group or another – to influence, counteract or reverse government policy. Similarly, governments do not faithfully carry out their programmes in a vacuum. At every stage they consult and negotiate with these organised groups, amending, transforming or even abandoning their policies where necessary or unavoidable.

What happens at elections sets the general context for policy decisions – by selecting the party which forms the government. Remember, too, that policies are usually formed in opposition only in outline. The determination of specific policies in government emerges from a complex process involving, at its heart, consultation between a triumvirate of ministers, civil servants and representatives of those interests likely to be affected. The latter are often pressure-group leaders, who seek to strengthen their hand in dealing with ministers and civil servants by influencing Parliament, other pressure groups, the media and public opinion.

A classic study of pressure groups concludes that 'Their day-to-day activities pervade every sphere of domestic policy, every day, every way, in every nook and cranny of government' (Finer, p. 17). Figure 18.2 shows how the theory is affected in practice by the permeation of pressure-group influence.

Figure 18.2   *The reality of pressure-group relationships to the democratic system*

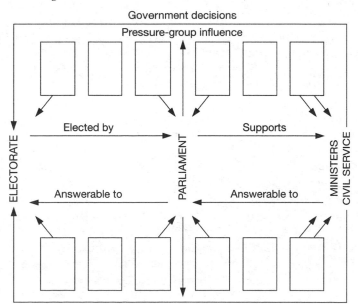

Representative democracy, which under the present voting system is based upon geographical areas, is therefore supplemented in practice by what can be seen as 'functional' democracy or 'group representation'.

Some scholars, S. E. Finer, S. H. Beer and the Norwegian Sven Rokkan included, have argued that such 'informal' representation is now more important than the 'formal' parliamentary system. Certainly people are more prepared to join and be active in groups which defend or advance their particular interests, such as the Salvation Army, than in political parties which organise electoral representation across a very broad and impersonal spectrum.

Some see the two systems as complementary, but others fear that pressure groups 'short-circuit' the democratic chain of representation and accountability. This question is returned to in the final section.

Development of pressure groups

Government has always had to deal with groups in society, but in the last two centuries they have organised themselves more effectively as society has become more complex and government intervenes in more areas of life. The anti-slavery movement and the Anti-Corn Law League were two early examples. Many philanthropic societies grew up in the nineteenth century, and government came to support, subsidise or even take over their roles altogether.

The nineteenth century also saw the formation of the major groups concerned with industrial production. Trade unions increased in membership and coalesced to form bigger units, while business groups too formed federations in order to negotiate more effectively with the unions and the government, itself an increasingly important economic interest. This process was catalysed by two world wars and Labour's 1945–50 nationalisation measures.

Types of pressure group

Pressure groups can be described as organised groups which seek to influence government policies. This definition is a useful catch-all for all the extra-governmental influences upon policy, but it puts a youth club that writes to its local MP on the same level as the Trades Union Congress (TUC) or Confederation of British Industry (CBI) seeking to influence economic policy. When over half the population belong to groups which at some time or other try to influence government policy, it is hardly surprising that most definitions are unsatisfactory. However, useful distinctions can be made between:

1. Economic (or interest) groups

(a) *Trade unions*, representing workers, seek to improve their members' pay and conditions of employment, and to influence public and government thinking on a whole range of social and economic issues. Their central or 'peak' organisation is the TUC.

(b) *Business organisations* are interested in maintaining the social and political conditions that favour their activities. Their peak organisation is the CBI. Increasingly important are the multinational companies. These are large international businesses with varied interests which use enormous investment power and the ability to switch operations to other countries (where conditions might be more favourable) to influence government decisions.

(c) *Professional associations* that represent and defend the interests of people with advanced training and qualifications, e.g. the British Medical Association, the National Union of Teachers. Increasingly these organisations are affiliating to the TUC.

2. Cause groups

(a) *Sectional groups* defend and promote the interests of specific social groups, e.g. Age Concern (old people), Shelter (the homeless or badly housed), the Child Poverty Action Group, the Automobile Association (motorists), and the typically British local voluntary associations which exist in great numbers at both national and local level.

(b) *Attitude groups* share common beliefs and objectives on a particular issue and seek change in the interests of society as a whole, e.g. the Howard League for Penal Reform, the Electoral Reform Society, the National Council for Civil Liberties (now renamed 'Liberty').

Such classifications can be misleading in that some pressure groups have more than one of the above characteristics: for example, inasmuch as they represent the interests of working-class people, trade unions are also sectional groups; and the Politics Association – closely connected with this book – is both a professional organisation representing the interests of politics teachers and an attitude group seeking to alert government and society to the need for political education.

3. Values and pressure groups are closely related and provide an interesting alternative form of classification. The more acceptable its objectives, the more likely a pressure group is to achieve them. Richard Rose (pp. 234–5) identifies six possible relationships between group aims and cultural norms, briefly summarised and adapted as:

(a) *harmony*, e.g. the RSPCA;

(b) *increasingly acceptable values*, e.g. the women's rights movement, gay rights;

(c) *fluctuating acceptability*, e.g. trade unions;
(d) *indifference*, e.g. the anti-smoking movement before it was backed by medical evidence;
(e) *fading support*, e.g. the Lord's Day Observance Society; and
(f) *conflict with cultural values* (e.g. those groups advocating racist ideas).

Having no need to win acceptability, a group in harmony with cultural norms may seek to identify its aims with the interests of the country as a whole or, more typically, to concentrate upon influencing administrative decisions; other groups will need to spend time and resources fighting for acceptability.

Insider and outsider groups

Wyn Grant (1989 and 1990) uses a somewhat similar typology based upon the degree of intimacy pressure groups have with the policy-making process. He identifies three kinds of insider group, all of which are constrained to some extent by the 'rules of the game': *prisoner* groups dependent upon government support (e.g. those Third World charities financed mainly by government); and *low-profile* (e.g. the Chamber of Shipping, which works closely with the Ministry of Defence) or *high-profile* groups (e.g. the CBI used to be a discreet, behind-the-scenes group, but then chose to court the media and acquire a higher profile). Outsider groups are less constrained; once again there are three. *Potential insider* groups will strive to establish credibility through media campaigns, meetings with ministers and civil servants. *Outsider* groups by necessity lack the political skills to become insiders; for example, they will tend to couch demands in extravagant or strident language, instead of the sophisticated, esoteric codes of the Whitehall bureaucracy. *Ideological outsider* groups deliberately place themselves beyond the pale of Whitehall because they wish to challenge its values and authority. Grant illustrates his typology with the example of animal welfare groups, which range from the respectable, 'insider' RSPCA to the 'ideological outsider' Animal Liberation groups, using threats and violence to pursue their ends.

Pressure-group personnel

Cause groups usually have only a small permanent staff and rely upon voluntary help which is often middle or upper class in origin. Government sometimes channels funds into cause groups which it regards as particularly important – e.g. MIND at one time received one-fifth of its income from central government – or helps establish them where they are thought to be necessary, e.g. in the field of race relations. Trade unions and professional and business associations have large staffs, and the TUC and CBI employ several hundred people who shadow the work of government departments. Over the years the large pressure groups and government bureaucracies have become increasingly similar in recruitment and mode of operation, and pressure-group personnel are often drawn into government employ. Nowadays they are often career professionals rather than activists, but this is not so true of pressure-group leaders, who tend to be committed people who often move over into mainstream politics, e.g. in the 1970s John Davies from the CBI to the Conservative Cabinet, David Ennals from MIND to the Labour Cabinet, and Frank Field from the Child Poverty Action Group to Labour MP and then social security minister.

Relations with government

These are usually cordial and co-operative: each can give what the other wants.

Pressure groups want to protect and advance the interests of their members through access to the decision-making process; the recognised right to be consulted; contacts with ministers and civil servants; and real influence on policy formulation.

Governments rely heavily upon pressure groups for information and advice; civil servants, after all, are not trained, professionally qualified experts in all the matters they must advise ministers upon. They also hope that, in exchange for a say in policy-making (i.e. becoming 'insider' groups), pressure groups will support measures passed; co-operate in their implementation; accept the authority of government; respect the confidentiality of discussions; and, unless they want to risk favoured status, behave in a 'responsible' fashion.

Hidden from public view, these transactions take place all the time. Indeed, without them government would be impossible. With government controlling nearly half of all economic activity it is inevitable that it should work closely with the economic pressure groups: they are virtually interdependent. Occasionally, however, they cannot agree and conflict ensues. It may be because government policy has changed radically, as in 1945 when the British Medical Association challenged Labour's plans to nationalise the health service, or as in 1971, when Edward Heath tried to bring trade unions within the framework of his Industrial Relations Act. On such occasions both government and pressure groups are forced back upon the power they can command.

Government naturally has the greater power. It controls the vast economic resources of the State and the decision-making process; can freeze out a group from the process if it chooses; and has the authority of law and, in the last resort, commands the forces of law and order, brought into play when the Thatcher government clashed with striking miners in 1984/5.

Pressure groups do not have such monolithic power but they can bargain, threaten or retaliate in a variety of ways, as follows.

Methods

1. Violence and illegality. Hijackers and terrorists have shown how effective these techniques can be, albeit at high risk to themselves. Few groups would consider such extreme measures, but some do occasionally break the law to draw attention to their cases. Particularly active from the mid-1980s onwards have been various Animal Liberation groups, which have frequently broken the law to direct attention to the use of live animals in scientific experiments, the killing of animals for furs, and so forth. In June 1990 a bomb under the car of a scientific researcher exploded, badly injuring a one-year-old in Bristol.

In the 1990s direct action became very high profile as environmental campaigning occupied sites of motorway bypasses in the West Country and the site of the second runway at Manchester Airport. The soil-smudged face of Swampy (Daniel Hooper), one of the key occupiers, became a national icon for young campaigners for the environment in 1996–97.

2. Denial of function. As most cause groups seek to publicise ideas or serve the interests of social groups, this is not a technique they can use: it is the preserve of economic groups. Business concerns can lock out their workers or direct investment elsewhere; multinationals can, and often do, threaten to move their activities to other, more agreeable countries. Trade unions, of course, can withdraw their labour through strike action.

3. Publicity-seeking techniques are used by all pressure groups and include demonstrations, marches, advertising, articles, books, specialist reports, broadcasts and so forth: a glance at a newspaper any day will reveal how successful their efforts have been. The more unusual the technique, the more likely the media are to be interested: women camping outside the cruise missile site at Greenham Common in the 1980s attracted considerable media coverage.

4. Political parties. Most cause groups try to pitch their message above the party political debate, but some seek to influence one party in particular. The Campaign for Nuclear Disarmament, for example, was able to command substantial support in the Labour Party, and this was a key factor in the party's adoption of a non-nuclear defence policy for a time in the 1980s.

5. Parliament. Many MPs automatically represent economic interests by virtue of being businesspeople, trade unionists, doctors, lawyers or whatever, and can be relied upon to articulate and defend the interests of such groups (see Box 18.1).

Box 18.1 MPs and lobbyists

It became obvious in the early 1990s that some MPs were using their position in the legislature to influence ministers and ask questions on behalf of outside business interests; instead of representing their constituents they were paid instruments of vested interests. Foremost among lobbyists was Ian Greer, who used his connections to recruit MPs to assist his business clients. In 1994 the *Sunday Times* approached two Conservative MPs, Graham Riddick and David Tredinick, and offered them money to table parliamentary questions. When they agreed and the paper exposed them there was a huge furore and John Major set up a Commission on Standards in Public Life under Lord Nolan. In the autumn of 1995 Nolan recommended that MPs disclose their earnings; be forbidden from tabling questions on behalf of outside interests; be restricted in what they can say on behalf of such interests on the floor of the House; and be obliged to register all interests with a Parliamentary Commissioner (since March 1996 Sir Gordon Downey). For more on this, see Box 13.2 and Box 18.2.

---

6. Ministers and civil servants substantially control the taking of executive decisions and the initiation of major legislation. Consultations with pressure groups take place mostly away from public view, most typically in the hundreds of joint advisory committees. This is the inner sanctum of influence to which most groups seek access.

Governability

As the economy has become more complex since the war, its elements have become more interdependent. Small groups of key workers are consequently able to wield great power by threatening to disrupt the working of the economy. To be successful, government economic policy has to win general acceptance, but this is not easy. In the 1970s many urged the TUC and CBI to reach annual agreements on such subjects as wage levels – as in Sweden or West Germany – but these bodies are only loose coalitions: they cannot enter into agreements and be sure that their members will keep to them.

Some commentators, such as Professor Anthony King, have argued that the difficulties of reaching consensus between such wide ranges of antithetical autonomous groups have made Britain harder to govern. Margaret Thatcher's answer was to disavow the consensus approach and assert the executive power of government.

Thatcher's style, and to an extent the style of her government, was to squeeze pressure groups towards the periphery of decision-making, to be less interested in listening and more concerned to act in accordance with what had already been decided as necessary.

Economic groups and political parties

The support of important economic groups has proved vital to political parties as a source of finance and membership.

1. Business and the Conservative Party. While there is no formal link, businesspeople are to be found at every level of Conservative Party organisation. Constituency associations provide only a quarter of party finance; some 60 per cent is derived from company donations – 80 per cent in election years. 'Front' organisations such as British United Industrialists or Aims of Industry exist to channel donations from companies to the party coffers. However, in 1981 three-fifths of the top fifty industrial and commercial bodies did not give money for political purposes, and the amount from those that do is subject to the vicissitudes of the economy. The close congruence of values which obviates the need for formal connections does not prevent business from falling out with Conservative governments. The Director-General of the CBI once called for a 'bare knuckle' fight to make Margaret Thatcher change her deflationary policies, but the CBI normally takes a markedly pro-Conservative line on economic issues.

2. Trade unions and the Labour Party. This connection was once very important as the party emerged out of collaboration between unions and socialist societies in 1900. Unions provided the money and personnel to run the party and make it a credible electoral force. However, the resource became a liability after the 'winter of discontent' in 1979 when, after a Labour decade of industrial disputes and high inflation when trade union leaders were held to be more powerful than Cabinet ministers, low-paid workers went on strike for more money and the country was brought to its knees. Margaret Thatcher won the resultant election and set about weakening the unions. She squeezed them out of economic decision-making and, unlike her predecessors, refused to see their leaders. Her three Employment Acts of 1980, 1982 and 1984 made unions legally responsible for the actions of their members; a majority vote of members necessary before a strike could take place; 'secondary picketing' illegal; and an 80 per cent vote by employees necessary before a closed shop could be established. The bitter miners' strike in 1984 proved the efficacy of the new legislation and it collapsed when union assets were seized. But Thatcher succeeded in destroying the power of the unions and their ability to hold business to ransom for better pay and conditions. The fact that they were weakened by massive unemployment and had lost 3 million members inevitably assisted the efficacy of the Thatcher victory.

Neil Kinnock worked hard as Labour leader to remedy Labour's electorally damaging association with the still unpopular unions. John Smith, his successor, continued this work but the real reduction of union influence occurred after 1994 when Tony Blair became leader. He owed no allegiance to the union influence and campaigned successfully to abolish Clause 4 of the party's constitution – much beloved of union leaders – which committed the party to common ownership of the economy. Under Blair the union link has been gradually weakened. Blair is on good terms with many business leaders and has involved them in his various task forces.

The Labour–union connection

(a) *Affiliation*: about half of all union members are affiliated to the party and provide a large slice of its membership.
(b) *Finance*: in 1995 over half of Labour's income was derived from union sources (down from 77 per cent ten years earlier).
(c) *Membership*: in 1995 there were 4.1 million political levy payers and 365,000 individual members. Union members who pay the levy can join the party via a reduced fee.
(d) *Representation*: union leaders used to be able to cast all their members' votes in votes on policy at conference – the so-called 'block vote' – but this was gradually reduced to 50 per cent. Blair's aim is to remove the block vote completely and replace it with one member, one vote. Unions were given 40 per cent of Electoral College votes in 1981 for the election of the party leader and deputy leader, but this was changed in 1995 to one-third only.

In the 1997 election campaign Blair was at pains to point out that a Labour government would treat unions with 'fairness but no favours', something he insisted on to disabuse middle-class voters that Labour was still, according to the Conservative jibe, 'in the pockets of the union barons'. He insisted that under Labour Britain would still have one of the 'strictest' set of labour laws in Europe; some said he was in reality glad that Mrs Thatcher had slain the union dragon for him. At the 1997 TUC conference Blair lectured union leaders on the same theme and exhorted them to 'modernise' their organisations and attitudes.

Pressure groups and democracy

It can be argued that pressure groups complement the process of government by providing:

Box 18.2 Blair and tobacco advertising

One of Labour's election promises as part of its commitment to improve the nation's health, was to ban tobacco advertising. However, on 6 November 1997 health minister Tessa Jowell announced that the ban would exclude Formula 1 motor racing. Questioned on Radio 4's *Today* programme, she defended her decision somewhat desperately as 'practical politics' but the *Observer* on 9 November argued that she had favoured a complete ban but had been overruled by Tony Blair. Martin Jacques wrote that the decision to exclude F1 was the 'result of assiduous lobbying by two key figures in motorsport, Max Mosley, president of the FIA [F1's peak organisation] and promoter Bernie Ecclestone'. F1 argued that because its sport was heavily dependent on tobacco advertising they would suffer disproportionately; in response to the ban F1 could easily shift its operations out of EU countries; such a move would end the UK's dominant position in the industry, losing thousands of jobs; and that such advertising does not affect consumption. Jacques ridiculed these arguments pointing out that:

● the tobacco companies would not pay millions to gain access to F1's young audience if it did not pay a sales dividend;
● F1 could easily adapt with economies and new sponsorship;
● moving out of the EU does not make economic sense; and F1 in the UK would survive any ban.

As Jackie Stewart said, 'I don't think it would be the end of the motor racing industry in the UK, as there are so many different formulae dependent on British technology.' The *Observer* expressed its dismay at the ease with which powerful lobbyists could sway Blair and suggested that this failure of nerve was comparable to Clinton's failure to reform health in his first term: an event which signalled his loss of decisive left of centre support. The row accelerated vigorously during the following week as more damning information emerged from a reluctant government. To rumours that Ecclestone had contributed a large amount to Labour funds the party agreed it was more than £5,000 but looked foolish and indubitably 'sleazy' when the sum proved to be £1 million. On the advice of the standards watchdog, Sir Patrick Neil, Labour handed the money back to a bemused Ecclestone. On 16 November Tony Blair publicly apologised for the mishandling of the issue and promised reform of party funding. The issue signalled the end of the nation's innocent honeymoon with Blair's new administration.

(a) Detailed information on specific areas of economic and social activity without which good government would be impossible.
(b) Continuity of communication and consultation between government and public between elections.
(c) Defence for minority interests, particularly those connected with parties not in government.

(d) Increased participation in the political process by people not necessarily active in political parties.

(e) A counter to the monopoly of the political process in Parliament by political parties. Cause groups raise items for discussion which fall outside party manifestos, and economic groups bypass much potential party conflict by dealing directly with ministers and civil servants.

(f) Dispersal of power downwards from the centralised legislative and executive institutions and in the process providing checks upon their power.

Against this can be argued:

(a) Pressure groups are often unrepresentative and only rarely reflect the broad mass of their membership. Union leaders are often elected by small activist minorities, though we should note that business organisations and other pressure groups often have appointed officers. Neither kind of officer is accountable to the public as a whole, despite the fact that their influence on policy is considerable.

(b) A corporate State? Pressure groups have reduced the power of Parliament by working so closely with ministers and civil servants. By the time Parliament sees legislation it is all but decided, and only a small minority of bills are substantially amended on the way to the Queen's signature. Some commentators have discerned the rise of a 'corporate State' in which decisions are shaped, and even made, by ministers and officials who are not elected by the public (see Moran, pp. 144–9).

(c) Pressure groups do not represent society equally. For example, they favour the strong groups in society – key industrial workers, educated professionals, the business elite – and they favour producer groups rather than consumer interests. Weaker groups such as immigrants, old-age pensioners, children or the unemployed have low bargaining strength and are often poorly organised.

(d) They often work in secret. Their consultations with top decision-makers take place behind closed doors, hidden from public scrutiny. S. E. Finer rather dramatically ends his classic study of pressure groups with a plea for 'More light!'

Conclusion

The nature of pressure-group politics has demonstrated considerable change over the last twenty years; business interests are concentrated into fewer and fewer hands; and the traditionally powerful pressure groups – especially the unions – have found their access to decision-making less easy and less effective. On the other hand, there has been a startling increase in nationwide popular movements, many of them using opinion-influencing techniques to good effect. If a pressure group can demonstrate a high level of public support for its campaign, this can prove decisive in turning the tide.

This has been particularly true of environmental groups (see Table 3.1). Band Aid, Live Aid and, in 1990, the Mandela Concert have shown the power of the media and popular music to change people's minds and win their support. The anti-apartheid movement, moreover, has chalked up many successes since the 1980s, notably the withdrawal of Barclays Bank from South Africa in 1986.

The professional campaigner Des Wilson has been a potent influence in the development of citizen power. Despite Margaret Thatcher's assertion of executive initiative and the decline of trade union power, pressure-group politics at the national and local level seems to be as vigorous as ever. Certainly, Blair was influenced by the Countryside Alliance's march in London in autumn 1997.

But has the influence of pressure groups declined over the past decade? Many commentators argue that it has. Certainly, this is true of a major block of interest groups, the trade unions; but business groups, because of their compatibility with government values, have been able to sustain their influence at all levels. Pressure groups have also shifted their mode of activity, concentrating more on the House of Lords and Conservative backbenchers than of yore. Margaret Thatcher's assertion of executive power has probably led to the decline of consultative influence 'behind the scenes', but this is very difficult to discern and generalise upon. As Baggott argues, 'pressure-group politics has definitely changed over the last decade', but this change has been more of a shift than an absolute decline – something which some commentators possibly exaggerate.

Further reading

R. Baggott, 'Pressure groups', *Talking Politics*, Autumn 1988.

R. Baggott, *Pressure Groups Today*, Manchester University Press, 1995 (the best single study).

S. H. Beer, *Britain Against Itself*, Faber, 1982.

A. Cawson, *Corporation and Welfare: Social Policy and State Intervention in Britain*, Heinemann, 1982.

S. E. Finer, *Anonymous Empire*, Pall Mall Press, 1966.

W. Grant, *Pressure Group Politics and Democracy in Britain*, Phillip Allan, 1989.

A. King, *Why is Britain Becoming Harder to Govern?*, BBC Books, 1976.

M. Moran, *Politics and Society in Britain: An Introduction*, Macmillan, 1989.

R. Rose, *Politics in England*, 2nd edn, Faber, 1985.

Questions

1 Are pressure groups both necessary and evil in democratic politics?
2 How do you organise the campaign to stop your historic local town hall being demolished?
3 Should professional lobbyists be allowed to operate in the corridors of Westminster and Whitehall?

19

Is local government necessary?

Writing in the *Guardian* on 3 September 1997, Tony Blair declared that 'Local government is the lifeblood of our democracy' but it is easy to gather the impression from frequently voiced criticisms that local government is virtually unnecessary. The cases for and against are considered below, followed by examination of recent changes in local government finance and other aspects of how local services are delivered.

The theoretical justification

This is similar to the case for any representative government. Elected councillors ensure that government is carried out in the interests of those who ultimately control it: the community as a whole. If representatives are judged to have failed, then they can be replaced by the electorate at local elections. Within the broad guidelines set by central government, local government provides the opportunities for:

(a) participation by local people in the making of decisions which affect them and for their civic education;
(b) representation of local opinion and the accountability of local government officers to it;
(c) greater efficiency through popular control and the adaptation of national policies to local conditions;
(d) the autonomy of local councils from central control.

Reform of local government

In 1974 an ancient patchwork system of 1,400 local authorities, varying enormously in size and function, was replaced in England and Wales by a two-tier system: forty-seven county councils and 333 constituent district councils. Six new metropolitan counties were created in heavily built-up areas in the North and the West Midlands. In addition, Greater London was changed into an area-wide metropolitan county and thirty-three constituent districts. In 1986 the metropolitan councils were abolished by Margaret Thatcher, who considered them wasteful as well as Labour 'enemy' strongholds, their functions being distributed downwards to other authorities. In 1992 John Major initiated a rethink of the much-changed system via the Local Government Commission (LGC) under its chair, Sir John Banham. Meanwhile, Welsh and Scottish Office reviews resulted in the former's eight counties and thirty-seven districts giving way to twenty-one new unitary authorities in charge of all functions, and the latter's sixty-eight districts replaced by twenty-eight unitary authorities. The LGC shied away from the blanket unitary approach which the government favoured and recommended variations according to the county concerned. The government did not like its sensitivity to local pressures and in 1995 Banham was sacked and replaced by Sir David Cooksey, who proved more pliable, but the numbers of unitary newcomers were not significantly increased in the event. In 1994 the Isle of Wight became unitary, followed by Cleveland, Avon, Humberside and North Yorkshire, with more due at the end of the decade. When this occurs, as Gray wearily points out, 'The new structure of English local government will be a patchwork of two-tier and unitary authorities representing the old 1974 structure, an amended 1974 structure and the new unitaries' (Gray, 1997, p. 373).

Has it all been worth it? Below arguments for and against local government are considered in an attempt to answer the question posed in the title of this chapter. Some of the critical arguments, of course, could equally be used, and frequently are, to urge a strengthening of local government rather than its abolition.

Participation

Against

(a) By reducing the number of authorities, and hence councillors, the new system has reduced participation and accessibility.
(b) Electoral turnout in local elections averages about 30–40 per cent – compared with about 75 per cent at general elections – and a large slice of local government seats are uncontested. Surveys show that only about 15 per cent of voters ever contact their local councillors; slightly more people contact local government officials direct in their town halls.
(c) Ignorance of local government is widespread. A survey by one of the authors way back in 1974 revealed that out of 100 people interviewed

in an inner-city ward of Manchester, only one person knew the names of all three councillors, and he was himself an ex-councillor! In July 1981 Michael Heseltine asked an unemployed Liverpool youth whether he had consulted his local councillor; the youth replied, 'What's a councillor?'

(d) Reorganisation has confused what understanding of the system already existed, and the larger areas have made town halls even more remote and anonymously bureaucratic. Neighbourhood councils, the bodies which the government hoped would involve people at grassroots level, have, despite some successes, generally failed to gain support and acceptance.

(e) As councils have become increasingly dominated by central government, people have accorded local government less attention.

(f) Despite the recommendations of the Skeffington (1968) and Dobry (1975) Reports on increasing public participation in planning, many local authorities prefer secrecy in decision-making and regard public participation as merely a public relations exercise (see Minogue, pp. 184–202).

(g) Pressure groups in Britain are not well developed at the local level, at least by comparison with the USA, often preferring to work through headquarters rather than liaise directly with councils.

For

(a) The new system is more logical and easier to understand than its original 1974 predecessor: local government units are now roughly similar in size and the distribution of functions more uniform countrywide.

(b) It may be a lower figure than that for general elections, but a large number of people do vote in local elections and a substantial number are very active; after all, it is the local party activists who essentially select parliamentary candidates and organise general election campaigns. Councillors themselves become passionately involved in local issues, which also offer a valuable training ground for those who may go on to make their mark at the national level, e.g. David Blunkett, Margaret Hodge, Ken Livingstone and Graham Stringer.

(c) Pressure groups may not be as powerful as in the USA but thousands, particularly voluntary organisations with a social purpose, constantly engage in lobbying locally to win resources and advance their causes.

(d) A new emphasis on local participation is discernible; the Liberals and Social Democrats made decentralisation and local democracy a major plank of their political programmes in the 1980s. They argued that low levels of knowledge and participation are arguments for reinvigoration rather than further contraction or abolition.

Representation

Against

(a) Councillors are unrepresentative of the public, being dominated by middle-class, middle-aged men: only a minority of local councillors are female (see Stanyer, pp. 95–116).

(b) Councillors are of poor quality, it is often maintained, too often inflated by self-importance and awareness of their status. Moreover, too many seek office for their own private interests rather than those of the community, e.g. the business contacts that can be made or the planning and financial power that can be wielded. Evidence of corruption at the local level, e.g. the extensive network of councillors and officials built up by the corrupt contractor John Poulson in the early 1970s suggests that desire for personal gain all too frequently tempts councillors into illegal activities.

(c) The increasing domination of local politics by political parties, it is argued, has diminished representation in that:

    (i) Local councillors can no longer exercise their independent judgement on issues that have to follow the party line.

    (ii) 'Non-party' people of good will in local communities have been deterred from involvement.

    (iii) National political issues such as education or social policy tend to squeeze out the truly local ones.

    (iv) Splits in national parties tend to be mirrored at the local level, e.g. after 1979 Manchester councillors split into bitterly opposed moderate and leftist factions.

    (v) Local elections have become mere occasions for registering dissatisfaction with the governing majority party. When their party wins a general election, party activists must allow themselves an inward groan as they contemplate their virtually inevitable losses in mid-term local elections. In June 1986 the Widdecombe Report judged this permeation of politics to be a 'malign influence' on local government and urged party balance on committees, a register of interests for councillors and no political affiliations for senior officers.

(d) The establishment of local Ombudsmen in 1974 to receive complaints about maladministration suggests that councillors are not properly doing their job of redressing public dissatisfactions and grievances.

For

(a) No council can be a truly representative sample of the public: mature, educated people are bound to be overrepresented and maybe this is no bad thing from the standpoint of efficiency. Moreover, local councils are generally less unrepresentative than the House of Commons: with 25 per cent women councillors, for example, they exceed the House's 20 per cent.

(b) Everyone must make up their own minds on the motivations of councillors, but many are genuinely public-spirited people who devote much of their time and energy to the benefit of the community. A 1973 Maud Committee Report and the 1976 Salmon Report on Standards of Conduct in Public Life both revealed the incidence of fraud and corruption in local government to be very low. There seems little doubt that the majority of councillors are honest, and safeguards such as open committees, opposition parties, the press and the Ombudsmen ensure that this will remain so.

(c) The development of parties in democratic systems is almost inevitable and is indeed necessary for consistency of policy and stability of government. It is natural that local parties should be influenced by national policies, as many of them – education, housing, social services – are concerned with how local government should operate. On the other hand, studies reveal a wealth of essentially local issues which engage councillors from day to day and in election campaigns. Not all councils are dominated by parties, though some studies suggest, interestingly, that these councils are less democratic in their operation than those that are (Minogue, p. 106).

(d) On the Ombudsmen, some councillors argue that their 'failure' to deal adequately with local grievances was never established and that the utility of the new officers has yet to be proved.

Efficiency

Against

(a) Since the war local government has lost a wide range of functions to central government, e.g. hospitals, social security (or 'poor relief' as it used to be called), gas, electricity and water. Why, then, should this centralising logic not be applied to education, housing or social services? Such a development – it can be argued – would avoid duplication of effort and ensure uniform standards throughout the country.

(b) Reorganisation of local government into bigger units has not led to staff savings; quite the opposite. In 1959 there were 1.6 million local government employees; in 1990 there were some 2 million. Few would argue that the country is now substantially better served by its local government.

(c) Elected councillors are part-time amateurs in the complicated business of government. When their influence is not being skilfully bypassed by professional officers they can just as easily harm the public interest as advance it.

(d) Certain local government functions could be performed more efficiently by private companies, e.g. Southend Council was the first of many to contract out its refuse collection to a private company which (in Southend's case) increased efficiency, cut costs, and raised workers' wages and (allegedly) their morale.

For

(a) Efficiency is not, and should not be, the sole yardstick of local government: it is also important that, even when they conflict with efficiency, people's needs should be met and their rights protected. For example, a decision to build a multi-storey car park for council employees in the middle of a park near the town hall might promote efficiency, but is it right to spoil a park and deny its use? Pushing the decision through without consultation will avoid delay, but is it right that objections are not heard and considered? Moreover, such 'efficient' procedures may be counter-productive in that they may generate a groundswell of opposition later, alienate public opinion and harm the co-operative relationship with the public upon which local government is, to an important degree, based.

(b) In certain cases accountability to local councillors might be salutary. Some argue that if social security officers were responsible to local councils the fear of councillors intervening on behalf of constituents would improve the quality of service provided.

(c) Larger units can provide more and better services than the previous small, uneconomic councils.

(d) Councillors are not impediments to good government. On the contrary, as the Redcliffe-Maud Report pointed out, 'The control of the expert by the amateur representing his fellow citizens is the key to the whole of our system of government . . . The best professionals readily agree that they do their best work when they can rely on the informed criticism, stimulation, counsel and support of good councillors. Good professionals and good councillors need one another. Neither is likely to remain good for long without the other' (1969, para. 235).

(e) The changes recommended by the Bains Report in the early 1970s, and widely implemented since, have served to streamline committee structure. Previously councillors had sought direct control of services through a large number of committees which frequently concerned themselves with the minutiae of day-to-day matters. Bains urged the gathering of functions together under a reduced number of committees and subcommittees with a powerful 'Cabinet'-like committee – commonly called 'Policy and Resources' – to co-ordinate the work of the council and concentrate on policy. Bains also urged the 'corporate planning approach', which has been widely accepted; it emphasises clarity of purpose, co-ordination of departments and future policy.

(f) Privatisation may improve efficiency in certain areas but it is inappropriate in others, e.g. could private companies provide cheaper and more efficient social workers (if indeed one could measure their efficiency)? Moreover, the introduction of the profit motive conflicts with the whole spirit and purpose of local government as it has developed in the UK.

Autonomy

Against

(a) Strict legal control is exerted by Parliament. The 1972 Local Government Act established a framework of legal powers and other Acts impose similar constraints, some very specific. Local councils, therefore, have no real autonomy in that they are legally subject to Westminster. They can do only what Parliament says, and have no right to initiate action not so sanctioned, however sensible.

(b) Extensive judicial control is exerted by the courts. If councils do anything which exceeds the authority granted by parliamentary Act, or its equivalent (e.g. provisional order or delegated legislation), they can be judged to be acting *ultra vires*, 'beyond the law'. If expenditure has been incurred, then the government accountant who annually inspects local government spending, the District Auditor, can 'surcharge' the people responsible. The Redcliffe-Maud Commission felt that this form of central control deterred enterprise and initiative. Similarly, if a council fails to perform its legal duties a court can order it to do so with an order of mandamus.

(c) Substantial administrative control is exercised by central departments via detailed directions and regulations. Close supervision and inspection are exercised over certain services such as the police, the fire service, education and children's services. Further influence and informal control are exerted by regular circulars from central government which advise and urge desired courses of action. Personal contacts with senior civil servants and exhortatory statements by ministers complete this dense network of formal and informal administrative controls.

(d) Financial control by central government is the most important form of control, as it underpins the three mentioned above. Central government provides over half the funds required by local authorities and uses them to ensure compliance, some say subservience.

(e) Quangos. The Conservative government took its dislike of local government to the extent whereby several functions were hived off from it and given to unelected bodies appointed by the government charged with running services such as further education, grant-maintained schools, and training and enterprise councils which formerly were run by elected councils (see Jones, 1994). In the early 1990s quangos accounted for one-fifth of all government spending. Labour attacked the 'quangocracy' bitterly and claimed that in Wales, for example, the Conservatives had lost the local democratic fight but had won anyway as they had simply reallocated local government functions to quangos which they appointed. Whether labour dismantles the undemocratic structure it condemned before the election will be one of the benchmarks by which its democratic credentials will be tested, but one year after the election the signs were not auspicious.

For

Supporting arguments accept that some measure of central control is necessary to maintain uniform standards and for the management of the economy as a whole (local government spending, after all, is some 15 per cent of GNP), while stressing the freedom of action which councils enjoy.

(a) Legal control is not rigidly applied. Section 110 of the Local Government Act, 1972, gives some latitude in that councils can do anything 'which is calculated to facilitate or is conducive or incidental to the discharge of any of their functions', even if no statutory power authorises it. Moreover, legislation distinguishes between duties – functions which authorities must perform to a given standard, such as school education – and discretionary powers, such as adult education, which leave wide scope for initiative to individual councils. In 1979, 300 central controls over local government were abolished.

(b) Once minimum standards are achieved, central government is happy to allow local authorities to set a standard of service which they think appropriate for local conditions.

(c) There is a wide and important area occupied by local councils between forming policy in Whitehall and applying it in particular local circumstances. The application of national policies poses all kinds of questions and options upon which councils can take decisions. Further, central departments vary considerably in the degree of control they apply even over the services which councils have a duty to perform. Ministers of Education, moreover, have been known to complain that they have no real executive power; that their role is essentially one of persuading local authorities to accept and apply central policy.

(d) The ability of councils to set local tax rates (subject to some central control) gives them an independent source of finance (see below).

(e) Local authorities can exert substantial influence on party organisations and central government via the three powerful local authority associations, of Metropolitan, County and District Authorities. These bodies liaise closely with Whitehall departments and act as permanent pressure groups for local government interests. Government needs the co-operation and advice of local government and does not lightly ignore its representations.

Assessment

Considered together, the complex network of legal, judicial, administrative and financial controls seems to offer a formidable constraint on local freedom of action and initiative. Local government cannot be said properly to exist if it is merely doing the bidding of Westminster and Whitehall. Those who argue thus have a powerful case, particularly when it is considered that local government has lost many functions since the war, had a less than ideal two-tier structure imposed upon it by way of reform, and was disappointed at least in the late 1970s over the saga of devolution. If local government is merely the agent, the servant of central government, then why not dispense with the fiction altogether?

The answer is that local government is a vital democratic element in British government. In practice it enjoys considerable latitude. Central government for the most part has no wish to dominate local councils, merely to ensure their efficiency; control is often, if not usually, applied with understanding and sensitivity. In a large number of areas the relationship is one of genuine partnership and mutual assistance. People should be involved in decisions which affect them and have the power to influence and alter, and perhaps reverse, them.

Joseph Chamberlain, the great nineteenth-century prophet of local government (and later a Conservative Cabinet member), put it neatly as long ago as 1874: 'I have an abiding faith in municipal institutions, an abiding sense of the value and importance of local government . . . our corporation [Birmingham] represents the full authority of the people. Through them, you obtain the full and direct expression of the popular will.'

Central control may seem seductively efficient but in the long run it would more than likely prove counter-productive. Government cannot work without the consent and co-operation of the governed. If the balance has been shifting towards the centre since the war, then – as Redcliffe-Maud (1969), Layfield (1976) and a wide body of councillors and officers argue – it should be corrected. The problem is that, in the view of her critics, Margaret Thatcher transformed a shift into a veritable stampede.

Margaret Thatcher and local government

Margaret Thatcher was unwilling to grant local government greater freedom of action if the result was more latitude for Labour councillors. She maintained that certain socialist-led councils tended to be profligate, inefficient and not especially popular. A number of measures resulted.

1. Abolition of the metropolitan county councils and the GLC. By 1981 Labour had won control of all six metropolitan counties and the Greater London Council (GLC). In 1983 a Cabinet committee recommended abolition of this tier of government and a commitment to this effect appeared in the Conservatives' election manifesto. A bitter three-year fight ensued to turn the undertaking into reality.

Despite the opposition of influential Tories and one major reverse in the Lords, the GLC and other counties disappeared in April 1986. The Inner London Education Authority survived the process as a new, separately elected body, but it too bit the dust four years later. Despite all the apocalyptic warnings, the abolitions, especially outside London, had remarkably few repercussions.

2. City technology colleges. The Education Secretary's announcement of twenty new city technology colleges (CTCs) at the Conservative Party Conference in 1986 nevertheless came as a surprise. The colleges are controlled centrally, not locally, and have selective rather than general entry, with an emphasis on science and technology to aid the national economy. Private finance for CTCs, however, proved hard to come by and the initiative met with very limited success.

3. Local government finance: changes in the rates, 1979–87. While at Environment, Michael Heseltine changed the system of funding local government in an attempt to achieve expenditure cuts and exert stricter financial control. Under the old system, revenue account income (for day-to-day running expenses) was derived from rates on local property, income from certain services and grants from government amounting to about 60 per cent of total spending. The largest of these was the Rate Support Grant (RSG), calculated on the basis of a subsidy to domestic ratepayers, a resource element to compensate areas of the country with low rateable values, and a needs element based upon social need, using past spending patterns as criteria. In theory there was no limit to how much a local authority could spend, and this open-ended remit conflicted with government determination to rein in public expenditure and curb inflation.

The Local Government Planning and Land Act, 1980, replaced the RSG with a block-grant formula – Grant Related Expenditure – based not upon past spending but upon a Whitehall estimate of how much local authorities needed to provide services at a uniform national level. Civil servants calculated average spending on particular services and allocated each authority a sum which it 'should' spend. The idea was to enable ministers to control the overall level of grant and distribute it in a way that hit the 'overspenders'. Heseltine believed they were politically motivated, i.e. Labour-controlled.

Naturally, councils denied that the grant which they had formerly received could raise extra finance by levying higher rates, but the new system allowed only a 10 per cent excess over the 'correct' figure; if they exceeded it they would be penalised by a corresponding reduction in grant.

The Rates Act, moreover, in 1983 enabled the government to control the expenditure of 'extravagant' authorities and provided a reserve power to control all local authority expenditure. Of the eighteen councils selected for rate-capping in 1984, the sixteen Labour-controlled councils agreed not to comply. Several refused to reduce expenditure and ran a deficit, but by the end of 1985 only the Militant-led Liverpool Council had refused to accept the new system. In 1984 a deal with Patrick Jenkin enabled the city to survive, but in 1985 its leaders were forced to borrow from Swiss banks to make ends meet. By this time Derek Hatton and his colleagues had exhausted their credibility in the Labour Party, and its NEC moved in 1986 to expel them.

The poll tax

By 1988/89 the percentage of local government finance provided by central government had fallen to 48 per cent, compared with 60 per cent in 1979. Local government spending, however, had continued to rise through creative accounting of many and ingenious kinds – some councils sold off property and then leased it back – and sustained increases in the rates. The 1985 revaluation of rates in Scotland had already provoked protests from badly hit Conservative property-owners, which helped reinforce Margaret Thatcher's resolve to replace the rates with root and branch reform.

Conservative critics of the system focused upon its low degree of popular accountability. Only half of the electorate paid rates and one-third of those received rebates. That meant that in most places a majority of people did not bear the full burden of the rates and were not too worried if their elected representatives levied high rates to pay for services. As Nicholas Ridley, the Environment Secretary, noted: three out of four people in local elections vote to 'spend other people's money'. As business rates provided more than half of locally raised revenue, Conservatives also argued that councils which set a high rate unfairly penalised the business community, thereby deterring the creation of wealth and employment. In their favour, however, rates were widely understood, cheap to collect, difficult to evade and were levied roughly in accordance with ability to pay (people in large properties paid more, but usually earned more, and the lower-paid were either exempt or qualified for rebates).

The 1981 White Paper *Alternatives to Domestic Rates* found against the rates, but also opposed the introduction of local income, sales or payroll taxes and specifically opposed a per capita charge, or 'poll tax'. By 1986, however, the atmosphere had changed. The 'poll tax' concept was exhumed, dusted down and presented anew. The Conservatives' 1987 manifesto declared that the rates would go.

The extended debates over the resultant Local Government Finance Bill resembled the trench warfare of the First World War. At times it seemed as if no one in the Conservative Party, from backbenchers to senior Cabinet ministers, really supported the measure except for Margaret Thatcher herself. Rebellions were frequent, both in the Commons and the Lords, but the Bill finally became law in July 1988. Subsequent events proved that Conservative reluctance to support the measure was justified.

The Act simplified the block grant system into a centrally determined revenue support grant which could be adjusted during a transitional period (1990–94) to mitigate the effects upon the new business rate and community charge, as the poll tax was officially named.

This comprised three elements:

(a) The personal flat rate charge upon all adults over eighteen, excluding the homeless, mental patients, prisoners and certain other categories. Rebates of up to 80 per cent were available for those on low incomes.
(b) The standard charge was levied upon second homes or empty properties.
(c) The collective charge was paid by hoteliers, hostel managers and landlords on numbers of guests resident.

Criticism of the poll tax concentrated on: its *unfairness* (a roadsweeper paid as much as a lord; *cost* (reckoned to be nearly three times the cost of collecting rates); *ease of evasion* (it was possible to avoid registration or keep on moving); *lack of accountability* (by imposing its own calculations upon local authorities the government contradicted the whole spirit of the reform); *centralising tendencies* (it resulted in greater power for the centre over the localities); and *complexity* (theoretically simple, the tax was very complicated in practice).

By March 1990 the tax was perceived as the most important local issue and riots took place in big cities, including London in April 1990.

From a simple, well-intentioned idea, Margaret Thatcher's third administration managed through lack of foresight and political mismanagement, aided and abetted by Tory MPs who suppressed their doubts, to create a monster which devoured the government's credibility in 1989–90 and became the biggest single factor in the fall of Margaret Thatcher on 22 November of that year.

The council tax

Following Margaret Thatcher's political demise, Michael Heseltine was put in charge of creating a substitute or replacement for the poll tax. After much deliberation and debate, the government presented the new council tax. This is a system rather like the old rating system but with bands introduced to reflect the value of houses and the incomes of those who live within them. Houses are allocated by the Local Valuation Officer to one of eight bands from A to H. The top band is for houses worth £360,000 or more and such householders pay the highest possible rate of council tax.

Councillors and officers

The Commission for Local Democracy revealed in 1995 that nearly 80 per cent of councillors were over forty-five and a third were in retirement. Because of high membership turnover, a quarter had less than three years' experience. Some critics claim that local government has been so stripped of its powers and is so dominated by party machines, it no longer attracts quality candidates. Gray raises the possibility that 'in a world dominated by unitary authorities and compulsory competitive tendering ... a new type of representation (might) be required' (Gray, p. 376). Senior local government officers resemble civil servants in that they concentrate on giving policy advice to elected representatives and are politically neutral. However, they tend to be more specialist than their Whitehall equivalents and often have professional qualifications. The work of councils is essentially through committees served by officers, beginning with Policy and Resources and downward to the functional committees of Education, Social Services, Leisure and Recreation, Planning and Transport, Public Protection and the Police. These are often controlled by co-ordinating committees of Finance, Personnel, Land and Performance Review. Some local authorities have sought to modernise their structures and have introduced management 'boards' to replace committees. Some commentators have observed that with the fragmentation of so much local government through the introduction of new agencies and CCT (see Box 19.1), the traditional role of councils, whereby they exerted strategic control, has given way to a new relationship in which the council is an 'enabling authority', paying for and regulating services which are provided by agencies which were traditionally internal but are often contracted out. However, the Commission for Local Democracy in 1995 concluded that structures were insufficient to meet present needs: 'the present system of

---

Box 19.1 Compulsory competitive tendering (CCT)

This idea first appeared in the 1980 Local Government Planning and Land Act, which obliged local authorities to put out to tender their functions of highway repair, building construction and maintenance work. 'In house' provision had to compete for the 'business' with outside bidders, the work going usually to the lowest offer. In 1988 a whole raft of new functions was added, including school meals, refuse collection and street cleaning. A White Paper in 1991 proposed even further extensions, even into the citadel of local administration: finance, personnel, central administration and legal work. These developments caused great controversy as they separated functions within local government and severely affected employment and promotion prospects for thousands of staff. Verdicts on the success of CCT, however, are mixed. Some claim savings and innovative systems have resulted, while critics claim quality has plummeted as 'work on the cheap' has become a matter of course (see Gray and Jenkins, 1997). Labour did not abolish the much-hated system but replaced it with the Best Value programme aimed at 'providing efficient quality service at a price people are willing to pay ... handing back responsibilities to local government and making councillors more accountable to their electorate'. Blair announced that 150 councils had applied to participate in Best Value projects by November 1997.

---

local government in Britain is seriously inadequate to meet the requirements of a mature democracy. It obscures and distorts what should be open and lively political activity for the majority of citizens and it fails to supply clear lines of local accountability' (pp. 16–17).

Reform proposals

The last Conservative government, as we have seen, sought with some success to impose its 'unitary' preference on local government, but the incoming Labour government (1 May 1997) had many ideas of its own.

1. Local mayors. The idea of an elected mayor on American lines appealed strongly to Heseltine, who wished there to be 'someone in command in order to bring local spending under control'. Mayors in British practice are usually no more than ceremonial figures elected by their fellow councillors and put in charge of opening functions and such like. In America, on the other hand, the mayor is the most powerful local politician and runs local government, hiring, firing and facing re-election on his/her record. Surveys suggest that this idea is popular with the public in Britain though not with councillors. The mayor of New York, Rudy Giuliani, has established a track record for

efficient leadership, especially in the area of crime control (crime has plummeted by 43 per cent under his leadership) and city finances, which are now
solvent. All this has strengthened calls for such a system to be introduced in
London and other cities. In the *Observer* (2 November 1997) Andrew Adonis
argues that Labour proposals for an elected London mayor – a 2–1 referendum in May 1998 approved the idea and a 'capital-wide authority' – with a
small 'cabinet' of professional councillors, would leave such an officer feeble
compared with the New York equivalent, with no power to intervene even
in areas where he/she has direct responsibility (see Box 19.2). Candidates for
the new office were already lining up in 1998, with entrepreneur Richard
Branson leading the early polls as the favourite should he wish to stand, followed, at some distance, by Ken Livingstone and (Lord) Jeffrey Archer. However, both these candidates are unpopular with their parties as 'loose
cannons' and may be prevented from representing a party banner.

Box 19.2 London mayor's limited powers

Writing in the *Observer* (3 May 1998), Will Hutton wondered if the position of
the new mayor carried enough clout to be effective:

> The more open question is whether Labour's plans for a mayor, drawn up when
> Conservatism was in its pomp, will actually deliver good city government. New
> Labour was so anxious to counter Tory claims it was introducing an expensive
> layer of unnecessary government that it is offering London nothing but a mayor,
> a small assembly and a 250-strong secretariat with no tax raising powers, no bor-
> rowing powers to initiate anything. London Weekend Television is more gener-
> ously staffed. The susceptibilities of London's jealous boroughs have been
> zealously protected so that in key policy areas like housing and education the
> mayor has no power at all.
>
> It may be true that he or she will be the agent through which £3.4 billion of
> central government spending is channelled to Londoners but the capacity to
> tamper with what, for example, London Transport or individual education
> authorities will regard as theirs by right will be negligible. The mayor will have
> planning and economic development powers, and could win the right to retain
> any car levies to limit traffic congestion as a limited source of revenue, but the
> idea that somehow the mayor will be one of the most powerful political positions
> in the country is wide of the mark.

---

2. Devolution. The overcentralisation of political decision-making in Britain
has long concerned reformers: a decentralisation of such activity away from
London their answer. In the early 1970s plans for regional councils were
elaborated and discussed, but even regional assemblies for Scotland and
Wales failed to materialise and the idea died for a generation. Labour
breathed life into it again, with referendums on assemblies in the Celtic coun-

tries being passed in September 1997. English regional assemblies, however, received scant attention, the commitment was not emphasised and many thought the idea 'shelved' through lack of both enthusiasm and legislative time. In mid-November 1997, eleven Labour MPs called for a directly elected northern assembly by the year 2002. A full page advertisement, also signed by 400 figures from politics, arts and sport, claimed their region was hindered by 'neglect and isolation from over-centralised government in London'. The Campaign for a Northern Assembly did not criticise Scottish devolution but it was fuelled to a degree by the widely known fact that the funding formula for Scotland and Wales served to give them proportionately more than the regions of England.

3. Local 'sleaze'. While sleaze, so much the characteristic of Conservative central government in the 1990s, was tackled by a number of initiatives such as the Nolan/Neil Committee, local government scandal was relatively rare. However, revelations about politics in Glasgow, Paisley, South Tyneside, Hull, Doncaster and elsewhere proved that Labour had a problem at a level which they dominated with 10,000 councillors and 470 local authorities. Problems are most acute in councils dominated by a single (usually Labour) party. Writing in the *Guardian* (3 September 1997), Tony Blair anticipated a 'new framework which enshrines the need for councils to modernise [that key Blairite buzzword], deliver best-value services, and uphold the highest standards of conduct in public life.' On 7 April 1998, *Modernising Local Government: A New Ethical Framework* was published. This consultation paper – the final of six outlining reforms – proposed locally tailored codes of behaviour covering declaration of interests, the relationship between councillors and officers, rules on expenses and the use of council facilities. In addition, an independent Standards Board would investigate allegations of corruption through a system of regional panels. Subsequently, Labour has called for rigorous overview of local spending by the Audit Commission and more involvement by business and voluntary groups in decision-making. The *Guardian* (8 April 1998) commented that eighteen years of Conservative rule had 'removed local council powers, capped their taxing capabilities, and transferred £30 billion of services to unelected quango control.' The editorial welcomed the proposed elected mayors idea as something which would help boost participation in local government. However, Labour seems intent on retaining capping and the council tax and control of setting the business rates. This is a consequence of determination to control public spending. 'A local government system that is dependent for 80 per cent of its finance from the centre is neither free nor independent' (*Guardian*).

Further reading

M. A. Bains, *The New Local Authorities. Management and Structure*, HMSO, 1972.
J. A. Chandler, *Local Government Today*, Manchester University Press, 1991.
Commission for Local Democracy, *Taking Charge. The Rebirth of Local Democracy*, Municipal Journal Books, 1995.
H. Elcock, *Local Government*, Methuen, 1982.
A. Gray and B. Jenkins, 'Local Government', in B. Jones *et al.*, *Politics UK*, 3rd edn, Prentice Hall, 1997, Chapter 22.
S. Horton, 'The Local Government Finance Act, 1988. The end of the rates', *Talking Politics*, Summer 1989.
B. Jones, 'Unknown government: the Conservative quangocracy', in B. Jones (ed.), *Political Issues in Britain Today*, Manchester University Press, 1994.
F. Layfield, *Local Government Finance*, HMSO, 1976.
G. Lee, 'Town hall versus Whitehall', in B. Jones (ed.), *Political Issues in Britain Today*, 3rd edn, Manchester University Press, 1989.
Redcliffe-Maud Report, HMSO, 1969.
J. Stanyer, *Understanding Local Government*, Martin Robertson, 1980.
G. Stoker, *The Politics of Local Government*, Macmillan, 1989.

Questions

1 Do you think that most government should be local?
2 'For the most part, elected councillors are merely puppets of full-time local government officers.' Is this fair comment?
3 Consider the arguments for and against the abolition of metropolitan county councils.

20

Britain and the European Union

This chapter looks at the consequences for British politics of membership of the European Economic Community, now the EU or European Union, as a result of the Maastricht Treaty. (The background to relations between Britain and the European Community has already been discussed in Chapter 1 and the constitutional implications in Chapter 6.)

Whether or not Britain should join was a major issue on and off during the period 1961–75. We might observe how, in the course of events, the issue has raised:

(a) constitutional questions, such as the sovereignty of Parliament, the convention of collective Cabinet responsibility and the use of the referendum (1975); and
(b) doubts about the role of Parliament as the exclusive 'consenting' body.

This connects with:

(c) bitter divisions in the two main parties;
(d) the relative decline of Britain's economic strength and international standing. From being eagerly courted and offered the leadership of Western Europe in the immediate post-war years, Britain's applications for entry were rebuffed in 1963 and 1967.

The idea of a united Europe – 'the European idea' – can be traced back over the centuries. However, in the post-1945 context of an integration of Western European States it derives from:

(a) Desire for peace and security. Europe has been the cockpit of two great wars this century, as a result of which 90 million lives were lost and whole countries laid waste. A union offered a new answer to the search for peace and to traditional Franco-German rivalry.
(b) Awareness of growing social and economic interdependence, and that approaches to problems of trade, inflation, energy, foreign policy, etc.,

225

might be better handled by co-operation between governments. Some economists also became convinced of the economic advantages of large-scale markets. If Europe was to compete with the United States in high-technology industries such as aviation, then individual States would have to pool their research and development costs. The EC promised access to a market of some 250 million.

(c) Expectations that a unified Western Europe would have greater international influence than separate medium-sized States.

For a number of years the questions of whether Britain should enter the Community and then whether it should remain a member were live political issues. The second was apparently settled in 1975 when, in a referendum, the British electorate voted 2 to 1 in favour of Britain staying in the EC and after the 1983 general election when the Labour Party abandoned its advocacy of British withdrawal. Since then withdrawal has not been an option. In one sense Europe is no longer an issue in British politics; all three major political parties are for membership, although some Conservatives favour withdrawal or a looser relationship. But the European issue remains significant.

Party conflict

Britain had become so deeply entrenched in Europe anyway that withdrawal was hardly practical politics. The UK's trade with Europe has always been substantial: it was 10 per cent of GDP in 1688; 27 in 1850 and 51 in 1875. Since joining the EC, the patterns have been transformed: exports were £22 million in 1958 and £55.5 billion in 1992. Now 60 per cent of trade is with Europe and we have more trade with Germany than with the USA, and more with Holland than with China and the six 'Asian Tigers' combined (Table 20.1).

Table 20.1   *British trade patterns with the world, 1996 (%)*

Asia	19
Australasia	2
Europe	55
USA	20
Africa	3

Conservative splits

At the same time Conservatives have become increasingly divided over British relations with Europe.

Divisions on the issue went to the heart of the Thatcher Cabinet. Margaret Thatcher favoured the idea of Europe as a group of independent States co-operating largely on economic issues. Others, including Sir Geoffrey Howe, favoured closer integration on political and foreign matters. Margaret Thatcher experienced the spectacular resignation of a number of heavy-weight ministers over Europe-related issues. These include the resignations of Michael Heseltine in 1986, her Chancellor of the Exchequer, Nigel Lawson in 1989 (because of the anti-ERM views of her economic adviser), and Sir Geoffrey Howe in November 1990 following her anti-European speech in the House of Commons. In his resignation speech Howe attacked Mrs Thatcher's negative stance on Europe.

In October 1990 Margaret Thatcher at last agreed to British member-ship of the ERM of the European Monetary System. This meant that Britain was pledged to maintain the value of the pound against other European countries and would use interest rates to do this, regardless of domestic con-siderations.

The Single European Act, which Margaret Thatcher signed in 1986, com-mitted the country to an 'ever developing process of economic and political integration'; the Maastricht Treaty in 1992 refers to an 'even closer union among the peoples of Europe in which decisions are taken as closely as pos-sible to the citizen'. At Maastricht also the EC would become the EU, or the European Union. The Commission proposed steps to achieve a greater eco-nomic union, a common defence policy, a Social Charter and more powers for the European Parliament. Britain signed the Treaty only at the last moment when it was agreed that Britain would be exempted from the pro-visions of the Social Charter and that a future Parliament could decide on the terms and timing of a monetary union. Crucially, the Treaty extended the areas where European law prevailed and for qualified majority voting (as opposed to unanimity).

The ERM disaster

There were remorseless pressures on sterling and the government was forced to pull out of the ERM on 16 September 1992. This was a humiliation for the Major government and its electoral support tumbled, never to recover. The recession and the losses in jobs and bankruptcies appeared to have been in vain. The whole episode only encouraged sceptics in the party, usually on the right, and the Conservative press. The ERM and Europe were blamed for the economic recession. Critics said that Britain's economic policy was effec-tively being decided by the German Bundesbank and that Britain had lost control of much of its macroeconomic policy. The Euro-sceptics (largely found in the Conservative Party) were joined by pragmatic critics who say that Britain joined the ERM at too high an exchange rate. The critics were vindicated when Britain pulled out of the ERM, dropped interest rates and made a steady economic recovery.

The ERM disaster provided an unfortunate background for the government's attempt to pass the Maastricht Bill (EC (Amendment) Bill) through the House of Commons. For the first six months of 1993, the government was regularly humiliated in the Commons as between twenty and twenty-five Conservatives voted regularly against the party and a similar number abstained. As the whips were defied, so John Major's authority was undermined. Conservative divisions were graphically reported and prevented any chance of electoral recovery.

In 1995 a beleaguered John Major resigned the party leadership and faced the challenge of the Euro-sceptic John Redwood. Although Major saw off the challenge his leadership was not fundamentally strengthened. Moreover, disputes over fishing rights and the BSE beef scare caused further troubles with other European States. The EU was portrayed as a scapegoat by the Conservative press, and Conservative opinion in the constituencies and among MPs, and even the Cabinet, became increasingly sceptical. Another problem was what to do about the *single currency*, due to be launched in 1999. John Major was caught between two groups:

(a) *supporters*, who wished to keep open the option of membership, the position which John Major had negotiated at Maastricht. The group included Cabinet heavyweights such as Douglas Hurd, Michael Heseltine and Kenneth Clarke.
(b) *sceptics*, who wanted to rule out membership for the next Parliament or for ever.

John Major refused to rule out membership because Britain would be affected if a currency was created. He did not welcome the creation of a single currency but wanted to be present at negotiations so that he could influence its form. Hence the 'wait and see' or 'negotiate and decide' policy. In 1996 he agreed to hold a referendum before entering, if the government favoured membership, a position which the Labour Party subsequently adopted. Unfortunately for the Conservative Party, during the 1997 general election more than half of the candidates declared against entry and the 'wait and see' line. The Conservative disunity over Europe was a prominent theme of the campaign. William Hague, the new Conservative leader, has abandoned 'wait and see' and ruled out British membership for at least ten years.

The *main institutions* of the EU include:

1. The Council of Ministers, which is the main decision-making body and co-ordinates policies. It consists of Foreign Ministers of the member States and, when appropriate, other ministers. The Council meets some 100 times a year, ministers varying according to the topic concerned, i.e. The Council of

Agricultural Ministers meets with its fellow agricultural ministers, etc. It takes most decisions on the basis of unanimity, so a government may use a veto to protect what it regards as its national interest. But the Council has agreed to majority voting for matters relating to the single market, although members are keen to extend the use of majority voting.

2. The Commission. This is the 'civil service' of the EU but does not have to await ministerial initiatives; it can suggest policies itself. Members of the Commission are appointed by governments but their primary loyalty is to the Commission and its European perspective. It formulates proposals for the Council to consider which, where approved, are then implemented by the Commission. Where measures are not implemented it may bring the matter to the attention of the European Court of Justice. The body also has important powers of delegated legislation. It has 14,000 officials headed by twenty commissioners, two each from Italy, Spain, Germany, France and the UK, serving for five years each. One of the Commissioners acts as President: Jacques Santer succeeded Jacques Delors in 1995.

3. The European Parliament. Originally MPs from the member States were nominated by their national government. Direct elections of Euro-MPs were first held in June 1979. But the body does not have much power, apart from approving the budget. It can dismiss the Commission but has little control over the powerful Council of Ministers. Britain, as a larger member State, elects eighty-seven Euro-MPs to the Parliament. The Parliament has 626 members drawn from its fifteen member States. MEPs sit in transnational groups according to their beliefs: socialist, liberals, Christian Democrat, Green and so forth.

4. The European Court of Justice. This body consists of judges who interpret binding arbitrations on legal questions falling within the scope of the Rome Treaty. It is superior to national courts and Parliaments.

Consequences

1. Parliament and other British authorities now have to accept the rules and regulations embodied in the original Treaty, commitments flowing therefrom and future decisions taken by EU institutions. In 1972, on entry, Parliament had to accept forty-three volumes of existing EU legislation. The major incursion on Parliament's sovereignty derives from the direct application of EU legislation in Britain. The moment EU law is passed by the Community, it has a binding effect in the UK under the provisions of the 1972 Act. Simply put, European law is 'superior' to that passed by the British Parliament. Lord Denning has said that the effect of EU legislation has been like 'an incoming tide. It flows up the estuaries and cannot be held back'. The full extent of the tide was made manifest in 1990 when Spanish fishermen were able successfully to overrule Britain's own Merchant Shipping Act. Another prominent jurist, Sir Thomas Bingham, commented on that occasion: 'a United Kingdom statute is no longer inviolable as it once was' (see below).

The House of Commons has the traditional devices for making the executive accountable to it: Question Time, Supply Days, Adjournment Debates. It has also established a Scrutiny Committee to select EU documents for debate, and the government usually allows debate on these before the Council of Ministers makes decisions. But there is no denying that membership has further overloaded the work of the House of Commons and increased centralisation in the hands of the government.

2. The courts. EU institutions have also acquired rights against the British executive, as have groups and individuals in the United Kingdom. This increases the likelihood that British courts will have to adjudicate on the validity (in relation to EU law) of Acts of Parliament, a task they have studiously avoided in the past. Moreover, given the primacy of EU law, the decisions of British courts may be overruled by the European Court in cases where they appear to conflict with EU laws.

3. Pressure groups. Most pressure groups still lobby their national governments, but in some areas, notably agriculture, environmental policy, regional and, above all, economic policy, the EU is important. Groups can go direct to Brussels or operate via national government.

4. Whitehall. Some departments are heavily involved, e.g. Agriculture, Trade and Industry, and the Foreign Office, and a good deal of co-ordination is done by the latter. Where much co-ordination of policies is required, civil servants have to harmonise legislation with other States. For civil servants in Whitehall, shuttle flights to Brussels are virtually commuting journeys.

5. The parties. The European issue has been troublesome for the parties, and at times brought John Major's government to a virtual standstill. Over time, surveys have shown that Labour MPs have become more pro-EU, while the Conservative Party has become more sceptical. This change in mood enabled William Hague to rule out British membership of the single currency for at least the next decade, something Margaret Thatcher dared not have done in 1990.

6. Sovereignty. The sovereignty of Parliament has been reduced in that it is no longer the sole law-making body for the country (see above). The government's formal independence has also been reduced by membership: it now takes some decisions in agreement with the other member States. Some

Box 20.1   Arguments for and against EU membership

A few diehard politicians (Referendum Party in 1997, right-wing Conservatives) argue that Britain should pull out of the EU and seek its destiny unfettered by ties which strangle national identity. Some of the points for and against are rehearsed below.

1. Trade
For: Europe is the UK's biggest market.
Against: Since 1973 we have sold them £87 billion less than they have sold us. If we left we are too important to them for them to start a trade war.

2. Tariffs
For: We benefit from low tariffs in EU trading.
Against: Such tariffs have fallen all over the world. If we left, the maximum tariff the EU could levy would be 6 per cent; the equivalent of only £6 billion extra costs to British industry.

3. Investment
For: Our membership attracts inward investment from countries which see the UK as a 'Trojan horse' for the EU market, for example Japan.
Against: Inward investment arguably is attracted as much, if not more so, courtesy of the UK's flexible labour markets, enabling management to hire and fire as necessary and keep costs down.

4. The UK could join another economic grouping
For: These countries are obliged to implement all single market legislation without having any say in its formulation.
Against: The UK could join the European Economic Area along with Iceland and Norway, whose members can have tariff-free access to EU markets.

5. Europe is a declining economic area
For: Europe is a dying market and the developing world is the future, where growth rates have run at 8–10 per cent per annum over the past decade.
Against: Europe will be a major market for the foreseeable future and the Asian Tigers took a major downwards dip in late 1997.

6. The single currency (EMU): arguments for and against
For: A single currency would reduce business and travel costs and help keep inflation down and interest rates low.
Against: (a) some countries are in different parts of their economic cycles, and the interest rates suitable for an expanding economy are not so for one in recession.
(b) the need to meet low borrowing criteria to stay in EMU would push unemployment upwards; in 1991 it was 14 million in the EU and efforts by countries trying to meet borrowing criteria forced it up to 19 million.
(c) by abandoning exchange rate changes, EU countries will have only budget cuts available as a tactic for adjusting their economies.
(d) EMU will mean that all EU economies will arguably become subordinate to Germany's.

argue that the claims about loss of sovereignty are irrelevant, because Parliament and the government have already lost effective power in many areas: for example, on defence, to NATO; on trade, to GATT (an international agreement on import/export tariffs); and on economic policy to the International Monetary Fund. Moreover, Britain's room for manoeuvre is already limited by the decisions of other governments, e.g. the fourfold increase in oil prices in the 1970s. Limits on sovereignty were clearly demonstrated in the government's failure to get its own way over fishing rights in our coastal waters and over exports of British beef after the BSE row. If Britain joined a single currency then the limits on our economic independence would be greater still. Membership of the currency, say supporters, at least gives Britain a say in drawing up the policies.

Conclusion

Europe has not greatly interested the public. In spite of its growing importance, it was hardly mentioned in the 1992 election. But its impact is seen in:

1. Political and constitutional disturbance, e.g. the referendum; the relaxation of collective Cabinet responsibility (in the 1975 referendum and in 1977 regarding the electoral system for the direct elections); and the introduction of a large element of a written constitution, with a consequently greater role for the courts and a limit to parliamentary sovereignty. The parties, particularly Labour in the 1970s and the Conservatives today, have been bitterly divided.

2. The debate, and Britain's decision to enter, reflect an acknowledgement of Britain's reduced standing in the world, and the failure of a 'special relationship' with the USA or the Commonwealth to provide a useful role.

3. The biggest division in the Conservative Party possibly since free trade at the turn of the century. The schism between 'European' and 'Euro-sceptics' has led to many close votes over the ratification of the Maastricht Treaty in 1993 and a split over membership of a single currency in the 1997 general election. Many Conservatives have doubts about the future direction of the EU, on the grounds that its policies of excessive employment regulation and high labour costs will cost jobs. They are more impressed with what they see as an Anglo-American model, based on flexible labour markets and low levels of tax and public spending, which is more successful in creating jobs. But many are also unhappy about the prospect of the EU having a common foreign and defence policy and emerging more and more as a so-called 'super-State', which will gradually erode the sovereignty of Parliament and national independence.

4. The Labour and Conservative positions on Europe have been reversed. If the latter has ceased to be a pro-Europe party, Labour has abandoned its stance as anti-European. It was converted in the late 1980s by the social dimension of EC policies. It still retains a 'wait and see' position on the single currency, but this is more positive than the Conservative position. It is faced, however, by a hostile public and a highly critical press.

Further reading

D. Baker *et al.*, 'The parliamentary siege of Maastricht', *Parliamentary Affairs*, Spring 1994.

S. George (ed.), *Britain and the European Community*, Oxford University Press, 1992.

N. Nugent, *The Government and Politics of the European Community*, 3rd edn, Macmillan, 1994.

P. Riddell, *Parliament under Pressure*, Gollancz, 1998.

Questions

1 Why has Labour changed its attitude to Europe over the past two decades?
2 Is it inevitable that a strengthening of European integration would lead inexorably to increased centralisation within the EU?
3 Consider the arguments for and against British membership of the single currency.

21

Political concepts

This chapter asks what is meant by a 'concept', and by the term 'politics', and examines a number of key political concepts.

What is politics?

'Politics' is one of those words which describes an activity as well as the study of that activity, so it is important to be clear about the sense which is being employed. What activity does 'politics' describe? Let's begin with what 'politicians' do. A number of functions immediately spring to mind:

(a) They direct or help direct our system of government.
(b) They help formulate laws.
(c) They are responsible for the defence of the country and for law and order.
(d) They try to resolve disputes between different groups in society.
(e) They take decisions upon how resources should be distributed.

The list could be much longer, of course, but the message seems to come through that politics is concerned with government, institutions and processes. But is this all that politics means? Consider the following news items:

American President is criticised by Congress
'Shelter' demands more financial aid for homeless
Car workers threaten strike action for more pay
Soap-opera star sacked after dispute with producer

Which are political? Clearly the first is highly political: the American government's chief decision-maker is being criticised by that nation's legislature. The second is not so obviously political but relates to a call by a pressure group – a body seeking to influence government policy – to increase the resources society makes available to the homeless. The third is even more remote from government but is surely political to some extent. All strikes in major industries have implications for employment, inflation and exports – and isn't there a broader sense in which we talk of 'the politics of the car industry' or the 'politics of the shop floor'? The fourth item appears to have nothing to do with politics at all – yet think about it. Do we not talk of the 'politics of the staff room', 'the politics of small groups', even the 'politics of the family'?

There would appear to be a sense of the word 'political' in topics as diverse as congressional attacks upon the US President and disagreements within the cast of *EastEnders*! What is this sense?

The common thread is conflict. In its most general sense – politics with a small p, if you like – politics is about conflicts and their resolution. That is to say, politics is concerned with the conflict of interest between individuals and groups, and with the processes whereby such conflicts are resolved. 'Interests', the object of the conflict, are the things people care about and are prepared to struggle over, e.g. money, power, status, privilege, dignity, honour. At the personal or 'micro' level, the means of resolving conflict can take the form of tact, diplomacy or compromise.

Politics also has a specific sense – politics with a capital P – relating to the national, or 'macro', level. This sense is more complicated but at heart still relates to the way society manages conflicts of interest. The devices it uses are elections, laws, government, regulations or organisations, public debate, demonstrations, and so forth. Typical conflicts at the national level revolve around:

(a) The distribution of wealth, status and power.
(b) Debates about the most desirable forms of social and economic organisation.
(c) Discussions about the values or moral rules which should govern public decision-making.

Harold Lasswell summed up politics as being about 'who gets what, when and how'. This is a neat summary. Less pithily one might say that politics in its broad sense relates to conflicts and their resolution, and in its specific sense to the national dimension of such conflicts and to the governmental processes designed to manage or resolve them.

What is a concept?

Let us stop for a moment and ask precisely what we have been doing. We have been discussing what it is people generally mean when they use the word 'politics'. Consideration of the various ways in which the word could be used revealed that it pertained to more than mere government and had both a general and a specific meaning. Eventually an essential core of meaning was isolated and offered as a general definition. Most words have this central core of meaning. For example, take the concept of an object nearby – a chair. What are the essential characteristics of a chair?

Answering the question is not as easy as it might at first appear. We can all recognise a chair but can we define its features in advance, so that someone who had never seen a chair before could recognise one? Clearly, the idea or *concept* of a chair embodies a horizontal platform designed for seating one person. Should it have a backrest? Yes, otherwise it would be a stool. Should it have legs? Well, usually it will have four, but some designs dispense with legs: maybe it is better to talk of a chair as being raised above floor level by some form of support. So we end up with three basic elements which go to make up a chair. If an object lacks any of them – a backrest, a horizontal platform for one person and some degree of support from the floor – it is unlikely we would call it a chair. But we must always be aware that inventive designers are constantly challenging our ideas; maybe the concept of a chair in future will be less specific and allow for more variation.

This kind of argument is not always merely semantic. An ecclesiastical dispute arose in 1986 over an altar carved by Henry Moore for a church in London. The 'altar' was a circular marble block some 3 ft high, weighing 8.5 tons. Unfortunately, the official definition of an altar, dating back to 1845, was that it should be 'a raised surface incorporating legs or a central pillar at which people might sit'. As a result permission for the installation of the carving was withheld, but the decision was hotly contested by those with a different concept of what an altar could or should be.

The conclusions to be drawn by this brief foray into the philosophy of language should be fairly obvious. Words provide frameworks for interpreting the world. Everyday concepts such as 'chair', 'table' and 'cup' enable us to recognise and use such objects to our advantage. More abstract concepts help us to organise the world, again to our own advantage; the concept of 'number', for example, enables us to count, record and assess quantity. In academic disciplines special concepts have been developed which help us to understand the subject matter. Some (e.g. 'power' and 'authority' in the case of political science) are in general currency but are often used carelessly or wrongly outside the discipline. Sometimes new concepts have been developed within a discipline to help understand its more refined areas (e.g. 'partisan dealignment', 'government overload').

As we have seen from our discussion of the concept of politics itself, part of the debate within a discipline will focus on the precise meaning of its central terms or concepts: what elements precisely do they or should they comprise? To become familiar with politics, therefore – or any academic discipline – we need to be aware of the concepts we employ and alive to their strengths and weaknesses. We must regard them rather like a camera lens which has to be focused so that the picture of the world we receive is sharp and accurate. What follows is an attempt to explain some of the most familiar and much-used concepts in political science and in so doing enhance their own explanatory value for embryonic political scientists.

Power and authority

These two key concepts are perhaps best explained by comparing their meanings. Consider the two following events.

(a) A man with a gun orders you to accompany him. You comply.
(b) A policeman orders you to accompany him. You comply.

The outcome is the same but the nature of your *relationship with* the person giving the orders is vastly different. In event (a) the gunman was able to get his way through your fear of what would happen if you did not comply. In event (b) you obeyed the policeman, almost certainly, because you accepted his right to order you. *Power* is the ability to command: to get others to obey, even if they are reluctant. *Authority* is achieved when other people accept your *right* to tell them what to do.

The similarities and differences between the two concepts are illustrated by the responses to these three questions:

1. How do people exercise power over others? Most commonly by the threat of unpleasant consequences, e.g. physical or economic, but also through the offer of rewards. It is a crude relationship, which is frequently found in everyday life and in everyday politics. One point needs to be stressed: in event (a) you would obey the gunman only if you thought the gun was real and he seemed likely to use it. His power is a function of the credibility of his threat. The same goes for the power which government can exercise, e.g. if the credibility of its law enforcement agencies is low its ability to maintain law and order may be reduced.

2. How do people come to have authority over others? There are a number of ways. They include:

(a) Special expertise, e.g. doctors.
(b) Natural leadership or 'charisma', difficult to define but not to recognise.
(c) Democratic decisions, e.g. those reached by elected representatives.
(d) Appointment by acknowledged authorities, e.g. police officers are appointed ultimately by the State, which is controlled by elected representatives in Parliament.

Political 'authority' in a democratic country is not consciously granted by its people to a government at a particular time (as some of the early 'social contract' theories seemed to imply) but develops gradually over the years; it is partly inherited by the national culture and partly reinforced through regular events such as elections.

3. Are political power and authority necessarily related? No, it is possible to have political power without authority and authority without political power. But in practice the two are often closely associated. Democratic government, for example, combines the authority with which popular support invests it together with the power of the police and, ultimately, the armed forces. To return to event (b): if you refused to accept the policeman's authority he could ultimately – if you had broken the law – force you to, even if his colleagues had to assist him. Similarly, if a particular group of people refuse to accept the authority of government, the force at the disposal of government can be used to make them. However, even though its strength may in the last resort rest upon organised force, no democratic government wishes to exercise it more than it has to. Government by popular consent is easier and more stable.

This short discussion has revealed that:

(a) Political concepts are the tools of the political scientist's trade.
(b) Such concepts are often used carelessly and inaccurately by others. It is better to be absolutely clear about the terms you use and the way in which you use them.
(c) By thinking about these key concepts we gain important insight into the subject itself.

Conceptual analysis of this kind almost provides an alternative way into the subject matter of the discipline. This chapter is too short to compare and contrast other key concepts, so short definitions will have to suffice. But to make the exercise more useful they are organised into four categories.

The political process

A number of concepts help us to understand the way in which the political process takes place. Central are the concepts of power and authority already considered. But also important are:

1. Influence. This concept is much used but is quite hard to pin down. It describes a weak form of power and authority: it is the ability to dispose people favourably – normally without the use of threats – towards behaving in a particular way.

2. Force. As already mentioned, governments rely upon popular acceptance to conduct political business on a day-to-day basis, but they can fall back on force should their authority prove insufficient. In Britain the State rarely uses force but in times of civil strife, for example the 1984–85 miners' strike, its existence and extent are revealed.

3. Pressure. The means by which people seek to influence government across the whole spectrum of political activity. It could entail strike action, demonstrations, use of the media, private meetings and so forth.

4. Consent. The general acceptance of a government's right to command obedience provides its authority, or 'legitimacy', to use a closely related term. But be aware of the distinction between *explicit* and *tacit* consent. Explicit consent is thought to be provided by electoral victories: parties claim a mandate to implement their programme based upon their success. However, can Margaret Thatcher's 42.5 per cent of votes cast in 1987 have been said to represent such a form of consent – and what about the *majority* who did not vote for her? Opinion poll findings are cited as evidence of consent but they are often unreliable and in any case reflect rapidly changing views. Tacit consent is often claimed by governments when no significant opposition is voiced to a particular policy. If such 'consent' is based not upon understanding but upon ignorance or indifference, can it be said to be genuine?

Another body of concepts is associated with forms of:

Political organisation

1. The State. What constitutes a State has long been the subject of profound philosophical and legal debate. What seems reasonably clear is that a State is a geographic and institutional entity widely recognised as such. Its other characteristics are less certain, but according to one popular view its government must have sovereign power: it must have monopoly control over the legitimate use of force within its borders.

2. Constitution. Politically, constitutions comprise the rules by which government is conducted. Most countries have a written constitution and special legislative procedures are necessary if it is to be changed. Britain is unusual in having no formal written constitution but a collection of laws and conventions (traditional ways of doing things). No special procedures exist for changing our constitutional arrangements: a majority vote in the House of Commons is basically all that is required, allowing, of course, for the Lords' delaying powers and the need for the Royal Assent (see Chapters 6 and 13).

3. Bureaucracy. This term is often used to describe the civil servants who carry out the commands of government. Weber maintained that as governments try to control increasingly complex societies, the power of bureaucracies inevitably grows, whatever the colour or system of government. He lieved, possibly with justice, that the expertise of bureaucracies would create a new kind of distant and increasingly centralised authority.

4. Representation is the idea that the interests of the many can and should be taken care of by people chosen – usually by election – to act on their behalf. An MP's relationship with the constituency on the one hand and Parliament on the other is the focus of a great deal of debate and attention from political scientists. Burke, for example, drew a classic distinction between a representative and a delegate: 'a delegate merely mirrors and records the views of his or her constituents, whereas a representative is elected to judge according to his own conscience'. Members of Parliament, asserted Burke, should be representatives rather than delegates. This view is maintained by most MPs.

Values

Another set of concepts is associated with values: things which are believed to be desirable and ought to characterise the means and the ends of political activity.

1. Justice is what people feel to be fair and reasonable. This judgement will vary enormously according to individual values, but in practice there is substantial agreement when justice has not been done. Aristotle made the important distinction that justice is not necessarily what is in the interests of the powerful; might does not make right, so it is conceivable that laws may not accord with commonly shared views of what is right. If this dichotomy is too wide and too frequent, and if the legal system is not seen to be equally fair towards all groups, society may judge the government itself to be unjust, and instability will result.

2. Natural rights are usually defined as the basic requirements of a tolerable way of life – 'life, liberty and the pursuit of happiness', said Jefferson, but others have their own formulations. These rights are held to be fundamental and superior to purely legal rights, which can be influenced by governments.

3. Individualism is the emphasis upon each person's uniqueness and the idea that the purpose of political activity is to constrain the individual as little as possible and provide the conditions in which he or she can achieve personal fulfilment and happiness.

4. Liberty, or freedom, has two senses: freedom from oppressive controls, and freedom to pursue one's choices. It has long been a principle of English law that citizens can do as they please provided no law says they cannot. But J. S. Mill's idea, that individual freedom should not encroach unjustifiably upon the freedom of others, is widely accepted. Precisely when such encroachment becomes unjustifiable, of course, is a constant source of debate.

5. Collectivism is the antithesis of individualism in that it asserts the rights of a group of people above those of the individual, and the obligations of individuals towards them.

6. Equality is a complex concept and the word is frequently misused. It has at least three main senses:

(a) Equality of treatment before the law.
(b) Equality of opportunity, especially career opportunity.
(c) Equality of result, i.e. people have a right to a more equal – or a less unequal – share of economic, social and political resources.

Politicians argue about the extent to which people are born with equal capacities and the extent to which the potential for personal development can be influenced by social and economic background.

Analytical concepts

Political scientists have created hundreds of conceptual frameworks which, to a greater or lesser extent, help us understand political reality. Some are very specialised and, depending upon the degree to which they have become accepted, occasionally obscure. Here only three of the main analytical concepts can be mentioned.

1. The political spectrum: left, right and centre. Terms such as 'left', 'right' and 'centre' are regularly used to distinguish and analyse political arguments, policies and so forth. The idea originated from the Estates General in France after 1789, in which the nobility sat on the king's right and the representatives of the popular political movements on his left. The right of the spectrum is usually associated with tradition, individualism, liberty and free enterprise, while the left asserts change, equality, collectivism and the common ownership of resources. *Conservatism* is associated with ideas towards the right of the spectrum and socialism with those on the left. There are a variety of positions in between these two poles, most importantly liberalism and social democracy.

The dichotomy between left and right can be seen as a gross over-simplification. Many people subscribe to right-wing ideas on some issues and left-wing ones on others; to place them on the left–right continuum is to offer a crude synthesis indeed. H. J. Eysenck suggests that a 'tough' and 'tender' spectrum should be added to the inadequate but widely accepted left–right axis (see p. 43). It would enable political means or methods to be separated from ends or objectives, as Figure 21.1 illustrates. According to this two-dimensional approach, 'tough' authoritarian right-wingers would occupy positions in the top right-hand quarter; tough left-wingers in the top left; 'tender' or democratic right-wingers the bottom right and tender lefties the bottom left.

2. Class. This term is used to distinguish between groups of people who differ in wealth, power, status and privilege – hence upper, middle and lower classes are commonly distinguished. Marx argued that social classes were created and changed in accordance with the economic means of production at any particular time. He argued that classes are constantly engaged in bitter conflict, that morally superior social orders result from such conflict and that ultimately a classless society will emerge when the conflict between the property-owning middle classes and the exploited, wage-earning working classes reaches its climax. Class is therefore a concept which is used in a neutral analytical sense but can also have strong political and value-laden overtones.

3. Elite. In its general sense an elite consists of those in charge of a particular activity, but in its more specific political sense it refers to those who control the institutions and processes of government. W. L. Guttsman calculated that the people who controlled the United Kingdom's system of government numbered just over 11,000 (Members of Parliament, civil servants, industrial leaders, etc.) and were in effect a 'self-perpetuating' ruling class irre-

Figure 21.1   *Two dimensions of political ideas*

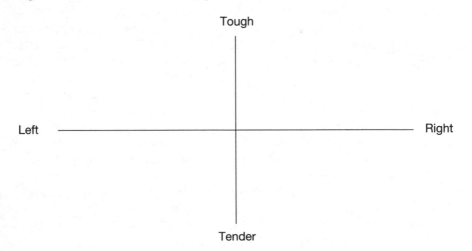

spective of which party was in power.

Conclusion

This chapter has been able to identify only some of the most important concepts used by political scientists. There are many more which students will encounter and assimilate. Concepts are the means whereby we learn more efficiently and are able to explore new aspects of the subject. To be aware of concepts and the way we use them guards against misuse and sharpens our ability to make greater sense of the many-faceted world of politicians and political activity.

Further reading

B. Crick, *In Defence of Politics*, Penguin, 1982. See also his 'Basic concepts of political education', in B. Crick and A. Porter, *Political Education and Political Literacy*, Longman, 1978.
M. Laver, *Invitation to Politics*, Martin Robertson, 1983.
A. Leftwich, *What is Politics?*, Blackwell, 1984.
A. Renwick and I. Swinburn, *Basic Political Concepts*, Hutchinson, 1980.
D. Robertson, *The Penguin Dictionary of Politics*, Penguin, 1985.
R. Scruton, *A Dictionary of Political Thought*, Pan, 1983.

Question

Describe and explain the concepts of: (1) pluralism, (2) hegemony, (3) feminism, (4) alienation, (5) charisma, (6) false consciousness, (7) privatisation, and (8) separation of powers.

Index